Usability Engineering

*U*sability Engineering

JAKOB NIELSEN

SunSoft
2550 Garcia Avenue
Mountain View, California

Morgan Kaufmann

AN IMPRINT OF ACADEMIC PRESS
A Harcourt Science and Technology Company

San Diego San Francisco New York Boston
London Sydney Tokyo

ACADEMIC PRESS
A Harcourt Science and Technology Company
525 B Street, Suite 1900, San Diego, CA 92101-4495 USA
http://www.academicpress.com

Academic Press
Harcourt Place, 32 Jamestown Road, London, NW1 7BY, UK

Morgan Kaufmann
340 Pine Street, Sixth Floor, San Francisco, CA 94104-3205
http://www.mkp.com

Library of Congress Catalog Number: 93000488
International Standard Book Number: 0-12-518406-9

Printed in the United States of America
01 02 03 SB 12 11 10

Table of Contents

Preface

Software developed in recent years has been devoting an average of 48% of the code to the user interface [Myers and Rosson 1992]. It would thus seem justified to allocate a reasonable proportion of the effort in software development projects to ensuring the usability of these user interfaces. This book tells you what to do if you decide to improve usability.

The main goal of the book is to provide concrete advice and methods that can be systematically employed to ensure a high degree of usability in the final user interface. To arrive at the perfect user interface, one also needs genius, a stroke of inspiration, and plain old luck. Even the most gifted designers, however, would be pressing their luck *too* far if they were to ignore systematic usability engineering methods.

Audience

The book has a very wide intended audience. First of all, it is naturally intended for the people who actually design and develop computer systems and user interfaces since these individuals have the ultimate power to improve usability. The book is crammed with practical advice for including usability considerations in the software engineering process, and developers and project managers should read through the entire book. The book is also intended for people who design documentation, help systems, and training courses, since these are elements of the "total user interface" just as much as the screen designs. This book is not intended to teach technical writing as such, but it can help writers produce support materials that users will find easier to use.

Furthermore, large parts of the book should be helpful to the users themselves and to computer support managers who need to determine which computer systems and software to recommend to their users. Even though it is fairly rare for customer organizations to perform their own usability testing, there is no reason why a large organization should not use some of the techniques in Chapter 6, Usability Testing, to compare software packages and whole systems before deciding on what to buy. Smaller organizations and individual users can use the definitions in Chapter 2, What Is Usability?, and the usability principles in Chapter 5, Usability Heuristics, as a checklist to consider whether an interface seems usable before buying it. Multinational corporations and other international organizations should benefit from Chapter 9, International User Interfaces, when planning the requirements for their information systems. Finally, user organizations that contract out for software development can use Chapter 4, The Usability Engineering Lifecycle, and Chapter 8, Interface Standards, to help set requirements that will ensure the usability of the product they will eventually receive from their vendor.

The executive summary in Chapter 1 is intended to help those readers who may not have time to read the entire book. It is especially intended for managers who are considering whether their companies are devoting sufficient effort to usability and what concrete steps they can request to ensure improved usability of their systems. It should be read by all readers, however, as it is not just a summary; it also addresses several topics that are not covered in the rest of the book, such as the cost/benefit trade-offs of taking human factors seriously.

Most of the examples in the book come from user interfaces to computer systems. The methods can be used for the development of interfaces to any kind of interactive system, including most consumer electronics products, and they are even useful for the development of certain information-intensive types of noninteractive products such as computer printouts, time tables, and driving directions. For example, van Nes and van Itegem [1990] describe the use of a logging method (see also page 216 ff.) in a usability study of an advanced car radio with 37 functions. For half a year, four drivers had every use of practically all of these functions from their new car radio automatically recorded. The results showed that some of the novel features went unused and that others were used differently than the designers had intended. A follow-up user interview revealed that the users still had not understood some features after half a year of use. One user complained that the auto-search tuning mechanism skipped some radio stations, whereas in fact it operated at three successive sensitivity levels and would pick up the missing stations at the second or third scan.

Any object, product, system, or service that will be used by humans has the potential for usability problems and should be subjected to some form of usability engineering. Human–computer interaction serves as the main focus of this book because it is the author's special area of expertise and because the potential for usability problems seems to be especially severe in computers, due to their ability to implement complex features and intricate interactions. For other kinds of interfaces, slight modifications may have to be made, but the main principles in this book should still hold. For example, questionnaires and user testing have been applied to improve the usability of railroad cars [McCrobie 1989].

Teaching Usability Engineering

Several universities have developed both traditional courses and continuing education efforts in various aspects of human–computer interaction [Baecker 1989; Carey 1989; John *et al.* 1992; Mantei 1989; Mantei *et al.* 1991; Preece and Keller 1990, 1991; Strong

1989; van der Veer and White 1990]. The Association for Computing Machinery's Special Interest Group on Computer–Human Interaction (ACM SIGCHI) has even developed a recommended curriculum for the teaching of human–computer interaction [ACM SIGCHI 1992]. Typical topics covered in such courses include theoretical approaches to human–computer interaction, the implementation of user interfaces, and the actual design of user interfaces. The latter is often taught through exercises [Nielsen *et al.* 1992; Winograd 1990]. In a survey of skills needed by usability practitioners [Dayton *et al.* 1993], the four skills rated as having an importance of more than 9.0 on a 1–10 scale were oral presentation, dialogue design, task analysis, and usability evaluation. The presence of presentation skills at the top of the list indicates that no usability project is conducted in isolation: to be successful, it needs to impact a larger development team.

Usability engineering as such also seems to be taught more these days, either as part of a general HCI (human–computer interaction) course or as a course in its own right [Nielsen and Molich 1989; Perlman 1988, 1990]. This is especially true of courses taught by corporate training departments or offered as continuing education for software engineers.

My main advice for the teaching of usability engineering would be to base the course firmly in the laboratory. Even though there is a substantial amount of theory and principles that can be taught in the auditorium, the most important aspects of design and evaluation require a hands-on approach. Certainly, a required part of any usability engineering course should be to have the students conduct a user test with a small number of real users. Not only is this a good way to teach proper evaluation methodology, but more important, it is the only way to achieve the required revolutionary change in student attitudes. Most professional programmers and computer science students gain profound insights the first time they actually sit down with test users and observe them struggle with supposedly "easy" software. This is especially true if the software was designed by the programmers or students themselves!

Appendix A lists several practical exercises touching upon important aspects of usability engineering. The way these exercises are described is mostly intended for self-study readers, but they can easily be expanded into more elaborate assignments for class use.

Acknowledgments

Many colleagues graciously answered questions about specific issues, provided comments on the treatment of their special interests, or even read through the entire manuscript. For this help, I would like to thank Jeff Abbott (Tivoli Systems), David Ackley (Bellcore), Alfred V. Aho (Bellcore), Gregory H. Anderson (Anderson Financial Systems), Mary M. Anthony (Tivoli Systems), Sonia D. Bot (Bell-Northern Research, Canada), Andreas Buja (Bellcore), Mike Coble (TRIPOS Associates), Bill Curtis (Software Engineering Institute), Tom Dayton (Bellcore), Susan T. Dumais (Bellcore), Lawson J. Dumbeck (Western Washington University), Tom Emerson (Symantec Corporation), Peter W. Foltz (University of Colorado), Ellen Francik (Pacific Bell), George Furnas (Bellcore), Marc Fusco (Bellcore), Thom Gillespie (University of California, Berkeley), Michael Good (Digital Equipment Corporation), Peter Henriksen (Microsoft), Hiroshi Ishii (NTT Human Interface Laboratories, Japan), Robert E. Jackson (Space Telescope Science Institute), Janice James (American Airlines), Jeff Johnson (Hewlett-Packard Laboratories), Peter R. Jones (Symantec Corporation), Anker Helms Jørgensen (Copenhagen University, Denmark), Hannah Kain (Citibag), Alistair Kilgour (Heriot-Watt University, U.K.), Thomas K. Landauer (Bellcore), Jonathan Levy (Bellcore), Robert L. Mack (IBM T. J. Watson Research Center), Miles Macleod (Hatfield Polytechnic, U.K.), Deborah J. Mayhew (Deborah J. Mayhew & Associates), Rolf Molich (Baltica Insurance, Denmark), Michael Muller (U S WEST), Robert M. Mulligan (AT&T Bell Laboratories), Gerhard Nielsen (Denmark's Radio), Randy Pausch (University of Virginia), Gary Perlman (Ohio State University), Steven Poltrock (Boeing Computer Services), Dan Rosenberg (Borland International), Kjeld Schmidt (Risø National Laboratory, Denmark), David Schnepper (Borland International), Tom Semple

(Symantec Corporation), Brian Shackel (Loughborough University of Technology, U.K.), Ben Shneiderman (University of Maryland), Scott Stornetta (Bellcore), Kurt Sussman (Symantec Corporation), Desirée Sy (Information Design Solutions), Michael Tauber (University of Paderborn, Germany), Bruce Tognazzini (SunSoft), Hirotada Ueda (Hitachi Central Research Laboratory and FRIEND21 Research Center, Japan), Gerrit van der Veer (Free University of Amsterdam, The Netherlands), Floris L. van Nes (Institute for Perception Research/Philips Research Laboratories, The Netherlands), Robert Virzi (GTE Laboratories), Christopher A. White (GTech Corporation), Richard Wolf (Lotus Development Corporation), and Peter Wright (University of York, U.K.).

The resulting book is solely the responsibility of the author, and the people mentioned above should not be held responsible for the way I have interpreted their comments and advice. Most of this book was written while I was on the applied research staff of Bellcore but it should not be taken as necessarily representing any official views or policies of Bellcore.

This printing of the book has been updated with a number of literature references and comments on developments since the book was first published. Among other things, I added the new synergy review method, which I invented just a few weeks after sending in the final copy for the first printing. Mostly, the book is unchanged, though, since the basics of usability engineering remain fairly constant and do not vary from year to year.

Jakob Nielsen
Mountain View, California
April 1994

Chapter 1   *Executive Summary*

Have you ever seen one of the people who will be users of your current project?[1] Have you talked to such a user? Have you visited the users' work environment and observed what their tasks are, how they approach these tasks, and what pragmatic circumstances they have to cope with? Such simple user-centered activities form the basis of usability engineering. More advanced methods exist and are covered later in this book, but just a simple field trip to observe users in their own environment working on real-world tasks can often provide a wealth of usability insights.

In one example, three one-day visits to branch offices of a medium-sized insurance company produced a list of 130 usability problems [Nielsen 1990b]. The system design was sound, and most of the problems were simple enough to fix once they were known (but, of course, they would not have been known if it had not been for the field study). Many of the 130 items were serious problems only for novice users. However, even very experienced users were estimated to waste at least 10 minutes every day because of usability

---

1. Note that you have to talk to the individuals who will be using the system. Talking to the users' manager or vice president for data processing does not count since these people are likely to have a completely different understanding of the job than the actual users.

problems, costing the company large amounts of money in both labor costs and lost sales opportunities.

The staff was often interrupted by telephone calls or walk-in clients. Unfortunately, several subsystems were not designed for interruptions—users lost all of their work if a transaction was not carried to completion. At one small branch, an agent stated that she never used the damage-claims subsystem during periods where she was the only person in the office and had to answer all calls. In some cases, agents were observed using other agents' terminals (and "borrowing" their passwords) to deal with interruptions rather than quit one of the unforgiving subsystems in the middle of a transaction.

In another case, the system allowed only one line for error messages, so it had to give an obscure, truncated version of a long message. The full message was available by pressing the help key, PF1, an action the developers in the central data-processing office felt was very natural. But users in the branch office had not made the conceptual leap that told them the help key was doubling as an extended-error-message key. Instead, they wasted a lot of time trying to understand the truncated message. A better design would have used the one line on the screen for a brief indication of the error, followed by "`PF1 for more information`" or a similar instruction.

1.1   Cost Savings

There are several well-documented examples of cost savings from the use of usability engineering methods.[2] For example:

- When a certain rotary dial telephone was first tested, users were found to dial fairly slowly. A human factors expert spent one

---

2. There are more examples of cost savings that are less well documented. As noted by Chapanis [1991], most case studies fail to meet the rigorous method-ological requirements that are necessary to be absolutely sure what cost savings can be attributed to user interface improvements since there are often several other changes made simultaneously (e.g., [Thompson *et al.* 1986]).

hour to come up with a simple graphical interface element which speeded up users' dialing behavior by about 0.15 seconds per digit, for a total annual saving of about $1,000,000 in reduced demands on the central switches [Karlin and Klemmer 1989].

- An Australian insurance company had annual savings of A$536,023 from redesigning its application forms to make customer errors less likely [Fisher and Sless 1990]. The cost of the usability project was less than A$100,000. The old forms were so difficult to fill in that they contained an average of 7.8 errors per form, making it necessary for company staff to spend more than one hour per form repairing the errors.

- A major computer company saved $41,700 the first day the system was in use by making sign-on attempts faster for a security application. This increased usability was achieved through iterative design at a cost of only $20,700 [Karat 1990].

- The 25 "human factors success stories" discussed by Harris [1984] include the improvement of the Boeing 757 flight deck interface to allow operation by two instead of three pilots, the 35% increase in alignment speed in a production line for integrated circuits, the reduction from 3,000 words to 150 words of instructions needed to operate a paging device, and even an improvement in a drunk-driver detection system that increased the arrest rate per police officer patrol-hour by 12%.

Unfortunately, the cost savings from increased usability are not always directly visible to the development organization since they may not show up until after the release of the product. As an extreme example, Fisher and Sless [1990] report that the Australian government can process a tax return for A$2.25 on the average. At the same time, the average Australian resident spends 11 hours filling in the form, and 62% of Australians have to use agents to help do the job. If the complexity of the tax forms were reduced, these "customers" might therefore realize huge savings in time and advisor fees, but the government might only save a few cents in processing costs. In the same way, making a spreadsheet easier to learn might only save the vendor a small amount in reduced hotline staffing levels, even though each customer might save several hours of unnecessary work.

Distributed benefits of a few hours per user are hard to measure and do not immediately add up to hard cash [Sassone 1987]. For example, redesigning the interface to an oscilloscope increased user productivity by 77% during the time they were using the scope [Bailey *et al.* 1988], but the productivity impact on the total workday of an engineer was much less dramatic and therefore had less impact. The customers *do* save with better interfaces, though, and these savings presumably translate into a better reputation for the product and therefore eventually increase sales. Unfortunately, the effect of having increased usability lead to increased sales has mostly been documented only anecdotally.[3] In several cases, the relative usability of competing products is well known in the industry, and computer salespersons often recommend certain software packages on the basis of their usability.

Because much of the financial payoff from usability methods shows up after the release of the product, some usability specialists [Grudin *et al.* 1987] have advocated shifting parts of the responsibility for usability engineering toward middle and upper management levels instead of the development managers. Even the development manager may see some immediate benefits from usability engineering, however, in the frequent case when early usability studies reveal that there is no need for certain contemplated features. If users' needs are not known, considerable development efforts may be wasted on such features in the mistaken belief that some users may want them. Users rarely complain that a system can do too *much* (they just don't use the superfluous features), so such over-design normally does not become sufficiently visible to make the potential development savings explicitly known. They are there nevertheless.

---

3. In one of the few documented cases, a usability study of the first version of a fourth-generation database system revealed 75 usability problems. Twenty of the most serious problems were fixed in the second release, which generated 80% higher product revenues than the first release [Wixon and Jones 1994]. This revenue increase was 66% higher than sales projections and so is probably due to the improvements in usability since field test customers were reported to point to the user interface as the most significant improvement in the product.

Usability studies can often be conducted very quickly and with small budgets. For example, Bailey [1991] gives an example of a study that required no more than five and a half hours to find out that the addition of color did not help users in a certain menu selection task. A development group could easily have spent many more staff hours arguing over this design issue in meetings than it took to resolve it by testing.

A study of software engineering cost estimates showed that 63% of large software projects significantly overran their estimates [Lederer and Prasad 1992]. When asked to explain their inaccurate cost estimates, software managers cited 24 different reasons and, interestingly, the four reasons that were rated as having the highest responsibility were all related to usability engineering: frequent requests for changes by users, overlooked tasks, users' lack of understanding of their own requirements, and insufficient user–analyst communication and understanding. Proper usability engineering methodology will prevent most such problems and thus substantially reduce cost overruns in software projects.

Even though the use of usability methods definitely involves some benefits, some managers might hesitate to use them because of their perceived high cost and complexity. For example, a paper in the widely read and respected journal *Communications of the ACM* estimated that the "costs required to add human factors elements to the development of software" was $128,330 [Mantei and Teorey 1988]. This sum is several times the total budget for usability in most smaller companies, and one interface evangelist has actually found it necessary to warn such small companies against believing this estimate [Tognazzini 1990]. Otherwise, the result could easily be that a project manager would discard any attempt at usability engineering in the belief that the project's budget could not bear the cost. Luckily, usability projects can easily be completed at substantially lower budgets as discussed in the section on Discount Usability Engineering (page 16). This entire book is aimed at presenting usability methods that can be used no matter what budget is available.

5

	Bottom Quartile (Q_1)	Median (Q_2)	Top Quartile (Q_3)
Project size in person-year	11	23	58
Actual usability budget relative to total	4%	6%	15%
Ideal usability budget relative to total	6%	10%	21%
Actual usability effort in person-years	1.0	1.5	2.0
Ideal usability effort in person-years	1.7	2.3	3.8

Table 1 *Results from a survey of the usability budgets of 31 development projects that had usability engineering activities.*

In January 1993, I surveyed 31 development projects that had usability engineering activities to find how much of their budget was devoted to usability. Respondents were also asked to estimate how large the usability budget ideally should be for their project. The results are shown in Table 1 and indicate that usability accounted for about 6% of the budgets for these projects and that the respondents felt that the ideal usability budget would have been 10%. The ideal desired usability effort in person-years is essentially independent of project size ($r = .12$) when three very large outlier projects of 250–350 person-years are excluded from the analysis. This result makes some sense in that many usability activities take about the same time to perform, no matter how difficult the program is to implement. Very large systems may have more elements in their user interfaces (screens, dialogue boxes, menus, etc.), meaning that they may need somewhat more time for usability activities, though definitely not proportionally more. The main conclusion to be derived from Table 1 is thus that two person-years of usability engineering is the median effort to aim for in a project and that four person-years would be sufficient for most projects. Of course, the actual amount of usability work needed in a project will depend on the characteristics of the project.

In a study of several corporations, Wasserman [1989] found that many leading companies allocated about 4–6% of their research and development staff to interface design and usability work. He believes that 2% is the critical lower limit for designing competitively effective products but acknowledges that many companies are significantly below that level. There is not necessarily a conflict between Wasserman's findings and Table 1. First, the survey in Table 1 is more recent, and usability has increased in importance in recent years.[4] Second, my survey only involved those projects in the various companies that have active usability engineering efforts, and many companies still have some projects without any usability engineering activities, which would contribute to making their overall usability budgets smaller than the usability budgets for those projects that had usability activities.

The final budget recommendation for any given product or company would of course depend on the specific nature of the projects. If a product is aimed at the population at large, then a substantial usability effort is probably necessary to ensure broad acceptance of the product. Similarly, a product that is going to see substantial daily use in a business can also cost-justify a large usability investment from the expected savings. And finally, one would normally recommend a rather limited[5] usability effort for systems that are only going to be used by a small number of highly skilled and trained users.[6]

When considering usability budgets, remember that your system *will* be tested for usability even if you don't do so yourself. Your customers will do it for you, as they struggle to use the system. Any usability problems found by users in the field will undermine

---

4. A 1971 paper estimated that a reasonable level for usability budgets for non-military systems was about 3% [Shackel 1971], providing some additional evidence that usability has increased in budget share over the years.

5. "Limited" does not mean "nonexistent," however. There is *always* a payoff to be gained from applying a few, cheap usability methods.

6. For certain applications such as a tactical support system for a fighter pilot or the control room for an expensive or dangerous plant, small differences in user performance can be a matter of life or death, and major usability efforts may be called for even though the users are few and highly trained. Two thirds of aircraft accidents can be attributed to the cockpit crew rather than to equipment malfunction and thus could potentially have been avoided with better human factors [Nagel 1988].

your reputation for quality products and the resulting change requests will be about 100 times more expensive to implement than changes discovered by yourself in the early phases of the project.

1.2   Usability Now![7]

User interfaces are now a much more important part of computers than they used to be. The revolution in personal computers and falling hardware prices are making computers available to ever broader groups of users, and these users are using computers for a larger variety of tasks. When computers were only used by a small number of people who mostly performed very specialized tasks, it made sense to require a high degree of learning and expertise of the users. Also, computers were once so expensive that it was reasonable to let users suffer a little if the computer could be utilized more efficiently. Now it pays to dedicate a large proportion of the computational resources (CPU cycles, memory use, communication bandwidth, screen space, development effort) to "nothing else" than making life easier for the user.

Furthermore, video games and some of the better personal computer software have shown users that it is possible to produce pleasant and approachable interfaces, so they are becoming much less willing to suffer from low usability. *Business Week* had a cover story in 1991 entitled *"I Can't Work This ?#!!@ Thing!"* [Nussbaum and Neff 1991], reporting on consumer dissatisfaction with over-complex interfaces on video recorders and other gadgets and that several major companies were redesigning their products to make them easier to use.

Time itself is on the side of increasing the perceived need for usability since the software market seems to be shifting away from the "features war" of earlier years [Telles 1990]. User interface design and customer service will probably generate more added

---

7. After writing my first draft of this section, I learned that the U.K. Department of Trade and Industry (DTI) has a research and development program that also is called *Usability Now!* [Wiggins 1991]. So much the better.

value for computer companies than hardware manufacturing [Rappaport and Halevi 1991], and user interfaces are a major way to differentiate products in a market dominated by an otherwise homogenizing trend toward open systems. Now most software products have more features than users will ever need or learn, and Telles [1990] states that the "interface has become an important element in garnering good reviews" of software in the trade press.[8] In an unpublished study from 1990, Tim Frank Andersen from the Technical University of Denmark read 70 reviews of software products in various personal computer magazines and counted 784 comments on the usability of the reviewed software. This is an average of 11.2 usability comments per software review. Now, many of these comments were fairly superficial, but their sheer number indicates the importance of usability in today's marketplace. If anything, usability has increased in importance in software reviews since the 1990 study to the extent that some personal computer magazines now have usability laboratories for use in comparative testing of software products and include usability statistics like average task times in their reviews [Reed 1992].

Recently, we have even seen political demands for regulations with respect to usability. Currently, most such political initiatives seem to be directed toward hardware ergonomics, but some also include software usability. As further discussed in Chapter 8, several international user interface standards are currently being developed. These standards may well gain the force of law in certain countries and will certainly have great impact in many other countries [Stewart 1990]. The European Union has passed a directive[9] on work with display screens stating that since December 31, 1992,

---

8. The trade magazine *InfoWorld* assigns explicit weights in its software reviews: Ease of learning is weighed at 4–10%, ease of use at 8–13%, and quality of documentation at 5–8%, with the exact weights determined by the type of application being reviewed. These three review criteria account for between 18% (spreadsheets) and 30% (word processors) of the final review scores. Error handling is assigned a further 5–8% of the review weight as a combined category including both user errors (a usability issue), software bugs, and recovery from hardware crashes. Notice, by the way, how favorably these percentages compare with the allocation of 6–10% of a development project's budget to usability mentioned on page 6; usability is a comparatively cheap way to improve product quality.

9

- Software must be suitable for the task
- Software must be easy to use
- The principles of software ergonomics must be applied

for all display screen workstations (computers and such) put into service in the E.U. Even though the requirements are very general in nature, they still indicate the direction of the political pressure for increased usability.

1.3   Usability Slogans

Major parts of the usability approach in this book can be summarized in the short slogans given here. You will find that some of the slogans contradict each other. Unfortunately, usability is filled with apparent contradictions that are only resolved after more detailed analysis. Some contradictions and trade-offs will always remain, and it is the job of the usability engineer to arrive at the best solution for the individual project's needs. There are very few hard and firm rules in usability that do not have some exceptions. For the full story, read on.

Your Best Guess Is Not Good Enough

A basic reason for the existence of usability engineering is that it is impossible to design an optimal user interface just by giving it your best try. Users have infinite potential for making unexpected misinterpretations of interface elements and for performing their job in a different way than you imagine.

Your design will be much better if you work on the basis of an understanding of the users and their tasks. Then, by all means design the best interface you can, but make sure to validate it with user tests and the other methods recommended in this book. It is no shame to have to revise a user interface design as a result of user

---

9. Council Directive of May 29, 1990, on the minimum safety and health requirements for work with display screen equipment (90/270/EEC), *Official Journal of the European Communities* No. **L 156**, 21.6.1990, 14–18.

testing. This happens to the best of usability experts, and it might indeed be a true measure of usability maturity that one is willing to acknowledge the need to modify initial design choices to accommodate the users. Julius Caesar is widely acknowledged as one of the greatest generals of antiquity. Even so, his true talent was not perfect campaign planning but his ability to adjust to the situation as it evolved. He often placed his legions in highly problematic situations which they only survived because he changed his plans to accommodate the facts. If Caesar could conquer France by admitting his mistakes [Caesar 51 B.C.], then maybe you can win some market share by admitting yours.

The User Is Always Right

As mentioned, all experience shows that any initial attempt at a user interface design will include some usability problems. Therefore, the user interface developer needs to acquire a certain design humility and acknowledge the need to modify the original design to accommodate the user's problems. The designer's attitude should be that if users have problems with an aspect of the interface, then this is not because they are stupid or just should have tried a little harder. Somebody once tested the usability of a user manual and found that users almost always made a mistake in a certain step of a particular procedure. Their solution was to frame the difficult step in a box and add a note saying *"Read these instructions carefully!"* Of course, the correct conclusion would have been that the description was too difficult and should be rewritten.

The User Is Not Always Right

Unfortunately, it does not follow that user interface designs can be derived just by asking users what they would like. Users often do not know what is good for them. One example is a study of the weight of telephone handsets conducted in the 1950s when people were used to fairly heavy handsets. The result of asking users whether they would like lighter handsets was no, they were happy with the handsets they had [Karlin and Klemmer 1989]. Even so, a test of handsets that looked identical but had different weights showed that people preferred handsets with about half the then-normal weight.

Users have a very hard time predicting how they will interact with potential future systems with which they have no experience. As another example, 73% of the respondents in a survey of 9,652 commuters said that they would not use a proposed information service with continual up-to-the-minute traffic information. But after they were shown sample screens from a prototype of the service, 84% of the respondents said that they would in fact use it [Gray *et al.* 1990].

Furthermore, users will often have divergent opinions when asked about details of user interface design. For example, studies of how people name things [Furnas *et al.* 1987] have shown that the probability of having two people apply the same name to an object is between 7% and 18%, depending on the object, clearly making it infeasible to design command names just by asking some user.

Users Are Not Designers

The ideal solution to the usability question might be to leave the design of the interface up to the individual users. Just provide sufficient customization flexibility, and all users can have exactly the interface they like. Studies have shown, however, that novice users do not customize their interfaces even when such facilities are available [Jørgensen and Sauer 1990]. One novice user exclaimed, "I didn't dare touch them [the customization features] in case something went wrong." Therefore, a good initial interface is needed to support novice users. Expert users (especially programmers) do use customization features, but there are still compelling reasons not to rely on user customization as the main element of user interface design.

First, customization is easy only if it builds on a coherent design with good previously designed options from which to choose. Second, the customization feature itself will need a user interface and will thus add to the complexity of the system and to the users' learning load. Third, too much customization leads each user to have a wildly different interface from the interfaces used by other users. Such interface variety makes it difficult to get help from colleagues, even though that is the help method rated highest by both novice and expert users [Mack and Nielsen 1987]. And fourth, users may not always make the most appropriate design decisions.

For example, Grudin and Barnard [1985] compared command abbreviations they defined with abbreviations defined by individual users, and found that users made about twice as many errors when using their own abbreviations. Even when given the chance to redefine their abbreviations after the experiment, six of seven test users kept their poor abbreviation sets virtually intact, typically explaining that while yes, they had some problems with it, it seemed as good as any other set they could think of. Of course, users have other jobs and do not work as user interface professionals.

Designers Are Not Users

System designers are human and they certainly use computers: both characteristics of users. Therefore, it can be tempting for designers to trust their own intuition about user interface issues, since they do share these two important characteristics of the real users. Unfortunately, system designers are different from users in several respects, including their general computer experience (and enthusiasm) and their knowledge of the conceptual foundation of the design of the system. When you have a deep understanding of the structure of a system, it is normally easy to fit a small extra piece of information into the picture and interpret it correctly. Consequently, a system designer may look at any given screen design or error message and believe that it makes perfect sense, even though the same screen or message would be completely incomprehensible to a user who did not have the same understanding of the system.

Knowing about a system is a one-way street. One cannot go back to knowing nothing. It is almost impossible to disregard the information one already knows when trying to assess whether another piece of information would be easy to understand for a novice user. Landauer [1988b] uses a hidden animal picture as an analogy for developers' understanding of their own system. Hidden animal games, as well as popular children's books of the type, "*Where is so-and-so?*" show images with various levels of details, among which is the animal or character one is supposed to find. Initially, it is very difficult to pick the animal out of the background, but once you have seen where the animal is, it is very easy to see it again. In fact, it is impossible to ignore one's knowledge of where the animal is and regain a perspective on the picture where one would have to search to find the animal.

A survey of 2,000 adults in Oregon showed that only 18% could use a bus schedule to find the time of departure [Egan 1991]. This finding does not indicate that the remaining 82% of Oregonians are less intelligent and should never be allowed on a bus.[10] Instead, the likely explanation is that the bus schedule was designed by people with extensive knowledge of buses and local transportation who just *knew* the meaning of every element on the schedule, and therefore never considered that parts of it might be difficult to understand for people who rarely take a bus.

Vice Presidents Are Not Users

Many CEOs and other top corporate executives have started to realize that usability is becoming one of their main competitive parameters, as user interfaces account for a steadily higher proportion of the value added in their products and services [Sculley 1992]. The downside of this higher visibility for user interfaces is that these executives may start meddling in user interface design.

Vice presidents and other corporate executives should realize that they are no more representative of the end users than the developers are. With the possible exception of management information systems and other software *intended* for vice presidents, corporate executives in a high-tech company are very different from the average user, and their intuitions about what would make a great design may not be accurate.

Boies *et al.* [1985] report that they sometimes had "a powerful person" in their company propose changes to their interface. They avoided making these changes by pointing out that this person

---

10. The same test showed that 97% of Oregonians could read a newspaper article and that 96% could tabulate two entries on a bank deposit slip.

probably had very different characteristics than the intended users and that their design had been tested on such real users. Of course, all design suggestions should be welcomed in order to serve as inspiration, but one should never be unduly swayed by a comment from a single person. People get promoted to vice president because of their managerial and decision-making skills, not because of their design skills.

Less Is More

One tempting solution to the user interface design problem might be to throw in any imaginable option or feature. If everything is there, then everybody should be satisfied, right? Wrong. Every single element in a user interface places some additional burden on the user in terms of having to consider whether to use that element. Having fewer options will often mean better usability because the users can then concentrate on understanding those fewer options [Brooks 1975]. Software reviewers are becoming aware that more features are not always better, and a major popular computer magazine ran a cover story lamenting the tendency of some programs to double in size every two years, coining the term "fatware" to describe bloated software [Perratore et al. 1993]. See also the discussion of the "less-is-more" principle on page 120.

Details Matter

Unfortunately, usability often depends on minor interface details, which is why systematic usability engineering work is necessary to ferret out those details. For example, Simonelli [1989] reports on the development of instructions for a frozen-dinner microwave indicator that would gradually change from being white to being blue. User testing showed that the phrase "turns blue" was much poorer than "white disappears" for describing this change, even though the two phrases are logically equivalent relative to this process. The blue color was not uniform—it was dark blue in some places and light blue in others— so users were uncertain "how blue is blue?" when the first wording was used.

Help Doesn't

Sometimes, online help and documentation doesn't really help the users [Mack *et al.* 1983]. That is to say, users often do not find the information they want in the mass of possible help and documentation and, even if they do find it, they may misinterpret the help. Also, help adds an extra set of features to a system, thus complicating the interface just by virtue of existing. In any case, the possibility for providing help should not been seen as an excuse to design a needlessly complex interface. It is always better if users can operate the system without having to refer to a help system. Usability is not a quality that can be spread out to cover a poor design like a thick layer of peanut butter,[11] so a user-hostile interface does not get user-friendly even by the addition of a brilliant help system. See also the section on Help and Documentation (page 148).

Usability Engineering Is Process

Most of this book consists of advice for activities to perform as part of the system development process. Readers may sometimes lose patience and wish that I had just told them about the *result* rather than the process: What makes an interface good? Unfortunately, so many things sometimes make an interface good and sometimes make it bad that any detailed advice regarding the end product has to be embellished with caveats, to an extent that makes it close to useless, not least because there will often be several conflicting guidelines. In contrast, the usability engineering *process* is well established and applies equally to all user interface designs. Each project is different, and each final user interface will look different, but the activities needed to arrive at a good result are fairly constant.

---

11. The peanut butter metaphor for misapplied usability engineering has been attributed to Clayton Lewis.

1.4 Discount Usability Engineering

Usability specialists will often propose using the best possible methodology. Indeed, this is what they have been trained to do in most universities. Unfortunately, it seems that *"Le mieux est l'ennemi du bien"* (the best is the enemy of the good) [Voltaire 1764] to the extent that insisting on using only the best methods may result in using no methods at all. Developers and software managers are sometimes intimidated by the strange terminology and elaborate laboratory setups employed by some usability specialists and may choose to abandon usability altogether in the mistaken belief that impenetrable theory is a necessary requirement for usability engineering [Bellotti 1988]. Therefore, I focus on achieving "the good" with respect to having *some* usability engineering work performed, even though the methods needed to achieve this result may not always be the absolutely "best" method and will not necessarily give perfect results.

It will be easy for the knowledgeable reader to dismiss the methods proposed here with various well-known counter-examples showing important usability aspects that will be missed under certain circumstances. Some counter-examples are no doubt true and I do agree that better results can be achieved by applying more careful methodologies. But remember that such more careful methods are also more expensive—often in terms of money and always in terms of required expertise (leading to the intimidation factor discussed above). Therefore, the simpler methods stand a much better chance of actually being used in practical design situations, and they should thus be viewed as a way of serving the user community.

The "discount usability engineering" [Nielsen 1989b, 1990b, 1994c] method is based on the use of the following four techniques:

- User and task observation
- Scenarios
- Simplified thinking aloud
- Heuristic evaluation

First, the basic principle of early focus on users should of course be followed. It can be achieved in various ways, including simple visits to customer locations. The main rules for "discount task analysis" are simply to observe users, keep quiet, and let the users work as they normally would without interference.

Scenarios

Scenarios are an especially cheap kind of prototype. The entire idea behind prototyping is to cut down on the complexity of implementation by eliminating parts of the full system. Horizontal prototypes reduce the level of functionality and result in a user interface surface layer, while vertical prototypes reduce the number of features and implement the full functionality of those chosen (i.e., we get a part of the system to play with).

Scenarios are the ultimate reduction of both the level of functionality and of the number of features: They can only simulate the user interface as long as a test user follows a previously planned path. See Figure 9 (page 94).

Since the scenario is small, we can afford to change it frequently, and if we use cheap, small thinking-aloud studies, we can also afford to test each of the versions. Therefore, scenarios are a way of getting quick and frequent feedback from users.

Scenarios can be implemented as paper mock-ups [Nielsen 1990d] or in simple prototyping environments [Nielsen 1989a], which may be easier to learn than more advanced programming environments [Nielsen *et al.* 1991]. This is an additional savings compared to more complex prototypes requiring the use of advanced software tools.

Simplified Thinking Aloud

The thinking-aloud method is discussed further in Section 6.8. Basically, it involves having one test user at a time use the system for a given set of tasks while being asked to "think out loud." By verbalizing their thoughts, users allow an observer to determine not just *what* they are doing with the interface, but also *why* they are doing it. This additional insight into a user's thought process can help pinpoint concrete interface elements that cause misunderstandings, so that they can be redesigned.

Traditionally, thinking-aloud studies are conducted with psychologists or user interface experts as experimenters who videotape the subjects and perform detailed protocol analysis. This kind of method is certainly intimidating for ordinary developers. Those developers who have used the thinking-aloud method seem [Jørgensen 1989] to be happy with it, however. My studies [Nielsen 1992a] show that computer scientists are indeed able to apply the thinking-aloud method effectively to evaluate user interfaces with a minimum of training and that even methodologically primitive experiments will succeed in finding many usability problems.

Another major difference between simplified and traditional thinking aloud is that data analysis can be done on the basis of the notes taken by the experimenter instead of by videotapes. Recording, watching, and analyzing the videotapes is expensive and takes a lot of time that is better spent on running more subjects and on testing more iterations of redesigned user interfaces. Videotaping should only be done in those cases (such as research studies) where absolute certainty is needed. In discount usability engineering we don't aim at perfection; we just want to find most of the usability problems. A survey of 11 software engineers [Perlman 1988] found that they rated simple tests of prototypes as almost twice as useful as video protocols.

Heuristic Evaluation

Current collections of usability guidelines typically have on the order of a thousand rules to follow and are therefore seen as intimidating by developers. For the discount method I advocate cutting the complexity by two orders of magnitude, to just 10 rules, relying on a small set of broader heuristics such as the basic usability principles listed in Table 2 and discussed in Chapter 5, Usability Heuristics.

These principles can be used to explain a very large proportion of the problems one observes in user interface designs. Unfortunately,

• *Simple and natural dialogue:* Dialogues should not contain information that is irrelevant or rarely needed. Every extra unit of information in a dialogue competes with the relevant units of information and diminishes their relative visibility. All information should appear in a natural and logical order.

• *Speak the users' language:* The dialogue should be expressed clearly in words, phrases, and concepts familiar to the user, rather than in system-oriented terms.

• *Minimize the users' memory load:* The user should not have to remember information from one part of the dialogue to another. Instructions for use of the system should be visible or easily retrievable whenever appropriate.

• *Consistency:* Users should not have to wonder whether different words, situations, or actions mean the same thing.

• *Feedback:* The system should always keep users informed about what is going on, through appropriate feedback within reasonable time.

• *Clearly marked exits:* Users often choose system functions by mistake and will need a clearly marked "emergency exit" to leave the unwanted state without having to go through an extended dialogue.

• *Shortcuts:* Accelerators—unseen by the novice user—may often speed up the interaction for the expert user such that the system can cater to both inexperienced and experienced users.

• *Good error messages:* They should be expressed in plain language (no codes), precisely indicate the problem, and constructively suggest a solution.

• *Prevent errors:* Even better than good error messages is a careful design that prevents a problem from occurring in the first place.

• *Help and documentation:* Even though it is better if the system can be used without documentation, it may be necessary to provide help and documentation. Any such information should be easy to search, be focused on the user's task, list concrete steps to be carried out, and not be too large.

Table 2 *These usability principles should be followed by all user interface designers. This specific list was developed by the author and Rolf Molich [Molich and Nielsen 1990], but it is similar to other usability guidelines. See [Nielsen 1994d] for several lists of similar heuristics.*

it does require some experience with the principles to apply them correctly in all cases. On the other hand, even nonexperts can find many usability problems by heuristic evaluation, and many of the remaining problems would be revealed by the simplified thinking-aloud test. It can also be recommended to let several different people perform a heuristic evaluation as different people locate different usability problems.

1.5 Recipe For Action

As discussed on page 8, the demand for usability is growing rapidly these years. This book presents many steps that can be taken to increase usability. The most important advice to remember is that usability does not appear just because you wish for it. Get started on a systematic approach to usability—the sooner, the better. From a management perspective, the action items are

1. Recognize the need for usability in your organization.
2. Make it clear that usability has management support (this includes promoting a culture where it is seen as positive for developers to change their initial design ideas to accommodate demonstrated user needs).
3. Devote specific resources to usability engineering (you can start out small, but you need a minimal amount of *dedicated* resources for usability to make sure that it does not fall victim to deadline pressures).
4. Integrate systematic usability engineering activities into the various stages of your development lifecycle (see Chapter 4), including the early ones.
5. Make sure that all user interfaces are subjected to user testing.

If you think this 5-step plan is too much, then try this 1-step plan for a start:

1. Pick one of your existing user interfaces. Subject it to a simple user test by defining some typical test tasks, getting hold of a few potential customers who have not used the system before, and observing them as they try performing the tasks with the system (without *any* help or interference from you). If no usability problems are found, then be happy that you have been lucky. In the more likely case that problems are found, you already have your first usability project defined: get rid of them in the next release by using iterative design.

Chapter 2 *What Is Usability?*

Back when computer vendors first started viewing users as more than an inconvenience, the term of choice was "user friendly" systems. This term is not really appropriate, however, for several reasons. First, it is unnecessarily anthropomorphic—users don't need machines to be friendly to them, they just need machines that will not stand in their way when they try to get their work done. And second, it implies that users' needs can be described along a single dimension by systems that are more or less friendly. In reality, different users have different needs, and a system that is "friendly" to one may feel very tedious to another.

Because of these problems with the term "user friendly," user interface professionals have tended to use other terms in recent years. The field itself is known under names like CHI (computer–human interaction), HCI (human–computer interaction, which is preferred by some who like "putting the human first" even if only done symbolically), UCD (user-centered design), MMI (man–machine interface), HMI (human–machine interface), OMI (operator-machine interface), UID (user interface design), HF (human factors), ergonomics,[1] etc.

I tend to use the term "usability" to denote the considerations that can be addressed by the methods covered in this book. As shown in the following section, there are also broader issues to consider within the overall framework of traditional "user friendliness."

2.1   Usability and Other Considerations

To some extent, usability is a narrow concern compared to the larger issue of system acceptability, which basically is the question of whether the system is good enough to satisfy all the needs and requirements of the users and other potential stakeholders, such as the users' clients and managers. The overall acceptability of a computer system is again a combination of its social acceptability and its practical acceptability. As an example of social acceptability, consider a system to investigate whether people applying for unemployment benefits are currently gainfully employed and thus have submitted fraudulent applications. The system might do this by asking applicants a number of questions and searching their answers for inconsistencies or profiles that are often indicative of cheaters. Some people may consider such a fraud-preventing system highly socially desirable, but others may find it offensive to subject applicants to this kind of quizzing and socially undesirable to delay benefits for people fitting certain profiles. Notice that people in the latter category may not find the system acceptable even if it got high scores on practical acceptability in terms of identifying many cheaters and were easy to use for the applicants.

Given that a system is socially acceptable, we can further analyze its practical acceptability within various categories, including traditional categories such as cost, support, reliability, compatibility with existing systems, etc., as well as the category of usefulness. *Usefulness* is the issue of whether the system can be used to achieve some desired goal. It can again be broken down into the

---

1. Human factors and ergonomics have a broader scope than just human–computer interaction. In fact, many usability methods apply equally well to the design of other complex systems, and even to simple ones that are not simple enough.

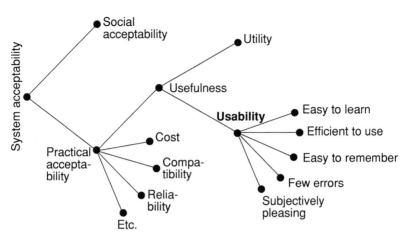

Figure 1 *A model of the attributes of system acceptability.*

two categories of utility and usability [Grudin 1992], where utility is the question of whether the functionality of the system in principle can do what is needed, and usability is the question of how well users can use that functionality. Note that the concept of "utility" does not necessarily have to be restricted to the domain of hard work. Educational software ("courseware") has high utility if students learn from using it, and an entertainment product has high utility if it is fun to use. Figure 1 shows the simple model of system acceptability outlined here. It is clear from the figure that system acceptability has many components and that usability must trade off against many other considerations in a development project.

Usability applies to all aspects of a system with which a human might interact, including installation and maintenance procedures. It is very rare to find a computer feature that truly has no user interface components. Even a facility to transfer data between two computers will normally include an interface to trouble-shoot the link when something goes wrong [Mulligan *et al.* 1991]. As another example, I recently established two electronic mail addresses for a committee I was managing. The two addresses were `ic93-papers-administrator` and `ic93-papers-committee` (for mail to my assistant and to the entire membership, respectively). It turned out that several people sent email to the wrong address, not realizing where their mail would go. My mistake was twofold: first in not realizing that even a pair of email addresses constituted a user interface of sorts, and second in breaking the well-known usability principle of avoiding easily confused names. A user who was taking a quick look at the "To:" field of an email message might be excused for thinking that the message was going to one address even though it was in fact going to the other.

2.2   Definition of Usability

It is important to realize that usability is not a single, one-dimensional property of a user interface. Usability has multiple components and is traditionally associated with these five usability attributes:

- *Learnability*: The system should be easy to learn so that the user can rapidly start getting some work done with the system.
- *Efficiency*: The system should be efficient to use, so that once the user has learned the system, a high level of productivity is possible.
- *Memorability*: The system should be easy to remember, so that the casual user is able to return to the system after some period of not having used it, without having to learn everything all over again.
- *Errors*: The system should have a low error rate, so that users make few errors during the use of the system, and so that if they do make errors they can easily recover from them. Further, catastrophic errors must not occur.
- *Satisfaction*: The system should be pleasant to use, so that users are subjectively satisfied when using it; they like it.

Each of these usability attributes will be discussed further in the following sections. Only by defining the abstract concept of "usability" in terms of these more precise and measurable components can we arrive at an engineering discipline where usability is not just argued about but is systematically approached, improved, and evaluated (possibly measured). Even if you do not intend to run formal measurement studies of the usability attributes of your system, it is an illuminating exercise to consider how its usability could be made measurable. Clarifying the measurable aspects of usability is much better than aiming at a warm, fuzzy feeling of "user friendliness" [Shackel 1991].

Usability is typically measured by having a number of test users (selected to be as representative as possible of the intended users) use the system to perform a prespecified set of tasks, though it can also be measured by having real users in the field perform whatever tasks they are doing anyway. In either case, an important point is that usability is measured relative to certain users and certain tasks. It could well be the case that the same system would be measured as having different usability characteristics if used by different users for different tasks. For example, a user wishing to write a letter may prefer a different word processor than a user wishing to maintain several hundred thousands of pages of technical documentation. As further discussed in Section 6.5 (page 185), usability measurement therefore starts with the definition of a representative set of test tasks, relative to which the different usability attributes can be measured.

To determine a system's overall usability on the basis of a set of usability measures, one normally takes the mean value of each of the attributes that have been measured and checks whether these means are better than some previously specified minimum (see the section on *Goal Setting* on page 80). Since users are known to be very different, it is probably better to consider the entire distribution of usability measures and not just the mean value. For example, a criterion for subjective satisfaction might be that the mean value should be at least 4 on a 1–5 scale; that at least 50% of the users should have given the system the top rating, 5; and that no more than 5% of the users gave the system the bottom rating, 1.

Learnability

Learnability is in some sense the most fundamental usability attribute, since most systems need to be easy to learn, and since the first experience most people have with a new system is that of

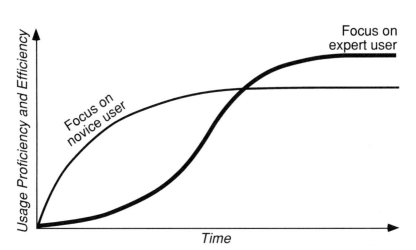

Figure 2 *Learning curves for a hypothetical system that focuses on the novice user, being easy to learn but less efficient to use, as well as one that is hard to learn but highly efficient for expert users. See also Section 2.4 (page 40) for a discussion of how to ride the best parts of both curves.*

learning to use it. Certainly, there are some systems for which one can afford to train users extensively to overcome a hard-to-learn interface, but in most cases, systems need to be easy to learn.

Ease of learning refers to the novice user's experience on the initial part of the learning curve, as shown in Figure 2. Highly learnable systems have a steep incline for the first part of the learning curve and allow users to reach a reasonable level of usage proficiency within a short time. Practically all user interfaces have learning curves that start out with the user being able to do nothing (have zero efficiency) at time zero (when they first start using it). Exceptions include the so-called walk-up-and-use systems such as museum information systems that are only intended to be used once and therefore need to have essentially zero learning time, allowing users to be successful from their very first attempt at using them.

The standard learning curve also does not apply to cases where the users are transferring skills from previous systems, such as when they upgrade from a previous release of a word processor to the new release [Telles 1990]. Assuming that the new system is reasonably consistent with the old, users should be able to start a fair bit up on the learning curve for the new system [Polson *et al.* 1986].

Initial ease of learning is probably the easiest of the usability attributes to measure, with the possible exception of subjective satisfaction. One simply picks some users who have not used the system before and measures the time it takes them to reach a specified level of proficiency in using it. Of course, the test users should be representative of the intended users of the system, and there might be a need to collect separate measurements from complete novices without any prior computer experience and from users with some typical computer experience. In earlier years, learnability studies focused exclusively on users without any computer experience, but since many people now have used computers, it is becoming more and more important to include such users in studies of system learnability.

The most common way to express the specified level of proficiency is simply to state that the users have to be able to complete a certain task successfully. Alternatively, one can specify that users need to be able to complete a set of tasks in a certain, minimum time before one will consider them as having "learned" the system. Of course, as shown in Figure 2, the learning curve actually represents a continuous series of improved user performance and not a dichotomous "learned"/"not learned" distinction. It is still common, however, to define a certain level of performance as indicating that the user has passed the learning stage and is able to use the system, and to measure the time it takes the user to reach that stage.

When analyzing learnability, one should keep in mind that users normally do not take the time to learn a complete interface fully before starting to use it. On the contrary, users often start using a system as soon as they have learned a part of the interface. For example, a survey of business professionals who were experienced personal computer users [Nielsen 1989e] found that 4 of the 6 highest-rated usability characteristics (out of 21 characteristics in the survey) related to exploratory learning: easy-to-understand error messages, possible to do useful work with program before having learned all of it, availability of undo, and confirming questions before execution of risky commands. Because of users' tendency to jump right in and start using a system, one should not just measure how long it takes users to achieve complete mastery of a system but also how long it takes to achieve a sufficient level of proficiency to do useful work.

Efficiency of Use

Efficiency refers to the expert user's steady-state level of performance at the time when the learning curve flattens out (again, see Figure 2). Of course, users may not necessarily reach that final level of performance any time soon. For example, some operating systems are so complex that it takes several years to reach expert-level performance and the ability to use certain composition operators to combine commands [Doane *et al.* 1990, 1992]. Also, some users will probably continue to learn indefinitely, though most users seem to plateau once they have learned "enough" [Rosson 1984, Carroll and Rosson 1987]. Unfortunately, this steady-state level of performance may not be optimal for the users who, by learning a few additional advanced features, sometimes would save more time over the course of their use of the system than the time it took to learn them.

To measure efficiency of use for experienced users, one obviously needs access to experienced users. For systems that have been in use for some time, "experience" is often defined somewhat informally, and users are considered experienced either if they say so themselves or if they have been users for more than a certain amount of time, such as a year. Experience can also be defined more formally in terms of number of hours spent using the system, and that definition is often used in experiments with new systems without an established user base: Test users are brought in and asked to use the system for a certain number of hours, after which their efficiency is measured. Finally, it is possible to define test users as experienced in terms of the learning curve itself: A user's performance is continuously measured (for example, in terms of number of seconds to do a specific task), and when the performance has not increased for some time, the user is assumed to have reached the steady-state level of performance for that user [Nielsen and Phillips 1993].

A typical way to measure efficiency of use is thus to decide on some definition of expertise, to get a representative sample of users with that expertise, and to measure the time it takes these users to perform some typical test tasks.

Memorability

Casual users are the third major category of users besides novice and expert users. Casual users are people who are using a system intermittently rather than having the fairly frequent use assumed for expert users. However, in contrast to novice users, casual users have used a system before, so they do not need to learn it from scratch, they just need to remember how to use it based on their previous learning. Casual use is typically seen for utility programs that are only used under exceptional circumstances, for supplementary applications that do not form part of a user's primary work but are useful every now and then, as well as for programs that are inherently only used at long intervals, such as a program for making a quarterly report.

Having an interface that is easy to remember is also important for users who return after having been on vacation or who for some other reason have temporarily stopped using a program. To a great extent, improvements in learnability often also make an interface easy to remember, but in principle, the usability of returning to a system is different from that of facing it for the first time. For example, consider the sign "Kiss and Ride" seen outside some Washington, DC, Metro stations. Initially, the meaning of this sign may not be obvious (it has poor learnability without outside assistance), but once you realize that it indicates a drop-off zone for commuters arriving in a car driven by somebody else, the sign becomes sufficiently memorable to allow you to find such zones at other stations (it is easy to remember).[2]

---

2. "Kiss and Ride" is an analogy with "Park and Ride" areas where people can leave their cars. The sign refers to commuters who are driven by their spouses and will kiss them before getting out of the car to take the train.

Interface memorability is rarely tested as thoroughly as the other usability attributes, but there are in principle two main ways of measuring it. One is to perform a standard user test with casual users who have been away from the system for a specified amount of time, and measure the time they need to perform some typical test tasks. Alternatively, it is possible to conduct a memory test with users after they finish a test session with the system and ask them to explain the effect of various commands or to name the command (or draw the icon) that does a certain thing. The interface's score for memorability is then the number of correct answers given by the users.

The performance test with casual users is most representative of the reason we want to measure memorability in the first way. The memory test may be easier to carry out but does have the problem that many modern user interfaces are built on the principle of making as much as possible visible to the users. Users of such systems do not need to be actively able to remember what is available, since the system will remind them when necessary. In fact, a study of one such graphical interface showed that users were unable to remember the contents of the menus when they were away from the system, even though they could use the same menus with no problems when they were sitting at the computer [Mayes *et al.* 1988].

Few and Noncatastrophic Errors

Users should make as few errors as possible when using a computer system. Typically, an error is defined as any action that does not accomplish the desired goal, and the system's error rate is measured by counting the number of such actions made by users while performing some specified task. Error rates can thus be measured as part of an experiment to measure other usability attributes.

Simply defining errors as being any incorrect user action does not take the highly varying impact of different errors into account. Some errors are corrected immediately by the user and have no other effect than to slow down the user's transaction rate somewhat. Such errors need not really be counted separately, as their effect is included in the efficiency of use if it is measured the normal way in terms of the user's transaction time.

Other errors are more catastrophic in nature, either because they are not discovered by the user, leading to a faulty work product, or because they destroy the user's work, making them difficult to recover from. Such catastrophic errors should be counted separately from minor errors, and special efforts should be made to minimize their frequency.

Subjective Satisfaction

The final usability attribute, subjective satisfaction, refers to how pleasant it is to use the system. Subjective satisfaction can be an especially important usability attribute for systems that are used on a discretionary basis in a nonwork environment, such as home computing, games, interactive fiction, or creative painting [Virzi 1991]. For some such systems, their entertainment value is more important then the speed with which things get done, since one might *want* to spend a long time having fun [Carroll and Thomas 1988]. Users should have an entertaining and/or moving and/or enriching experience when using such systems since they have no other goal.

Note that the notion of subjective satisfaction as an attribute of usability is different from the issue of the public's general attitudes toward computers. Even though it is likely that a person's feelings toward computers as a general phenomenon will impact the extent to which that person likes interacting with a particular system, peoples' attitudes toward computers in general should probably be seen as a component of the social acceptability of computers rather than their usability. See [LaLomia and Sidowski 1991] for a survey of such computer attitude studies. Computer enthusiasts may hope that steady improvements in computer usability will result in more positive attitudes toward computers. Little is currently known about the relation between attributes of individual computer systems and users' general attitudes, though users who perceive that they have a high degree of control over the computer have been found also to have positive attitudes toward computers [Kay 1989].

In principle, certain objective measures might be used instead of asking the users' subjective preference to assess the pleasing nature of an interface. In a few cases, psychophysiological measures such as EEGs, pupil dilation, heart rate, skin conductivity, blood pressure, and level of adrenaline in the blood have been used to estimate the users' stress and comfort levels [Mullins and Treu 1991; Schleifer 1990; Wastell 1990]. Unfortunately, such measures require intimidating experimental conditions such as wiring the user to an EEG machine or taking blood samples. Since test users are normally nervous enough as it is and since a relaxed atmosphere is an important condition for much user testing (see page 181), the psychophysiological approach will often be inappropriate for usability engineering studies.

Alternatively, subjective satisfaction may be measured by simply *asking* the users for their subjective opinion. From the perspective of any single user, the replies to such a question are subjective, but when replies from multiple users are averaged together, the result is an objective measure of the system's pleasantness. Since the entire purpose of having a subjective satisfaction usability attribute is to assess whether users like the system, it seems highly appropriate to measure it by asking the users, and this is indeed what is done in the overwhelming number of usability studies.

To ensure consistent measurements, subjective satisfaction is normally measured by a short questionnaire that is given to users as part of the debriefing session after a user test. Of course, questionnaires can also be given to users of installed systems in the field without the need to have them go through a special test procedure first. For new systems, however, it is important not to ask the users for their subjective opinions until after they have had a chance to try using the system for a real task. The answers users give to questions before and after having used a system are unfortunately not very highly correlated [Root and Draper 1983].

Users have been known to refuse to use a program because the manual was too big [Nielsen *et al.* 1986], without even trying to read it to see whether it was in fact as difficult as they thought. Therefore it is certainly reasonable to study the approachability of a

*Please indicate the degree to which you agree or disagree with the following
statements about the system:*
"It was very easy to learn how to use this system."
"Using this system was a very frustrating experience."
"I feel that this system allows me to achieve very high productivity."
"I worry that many of the things I did with this system may have been wrong."
"This system can do all the things I think I would need."
"This system is very pleasant to work with."

Table 3 *Questions users might be asked to measure subjective satisfaction using a Likert scale. Users would typically indicate their degree of
agreement on a 1–5 scale for each statement. One would normally refer to
the system by its name rather than as "this system."*

system (this is especially important from a marketing perspective)
[Angiolillo and Roberts 1991]. To do so, one can show the system to
users and ask them, "How difficult do you think it would be to
learn to use this?"—just don't expect the answers to have much
relation to the *actual* learnability of the system.

Even when users do have experience using a system, their subjective ratings of its difficulty are much more closely related to the
peak difficulty they experienced than to mean difficulty; the most
difficult episode a user experienced is the most memorable for that
user. In one experiment, the peak experienced difficulty while
performing a task accounted for 31% of the users' subjective rating
of the system's difficulty whereas the task time only accounted for
7% [Cordes 1993]. One conclusion is that one cannot rely solely on
user ratings if the goal is to improve overall system performance.
On the other hand, sales considerations imply a need to have users
believe that the system is easy to generate positive word-of-mouth,
and such impressions might be improved more by a bland interface with no extreme peak in difficulty than by a system that is
mostly excellent but has one really hard part for users to overcome.

Subjective satisfaction questionnaires are typically very short,
though some longer versions have been developed for more
detailed studies [Chin *et al.* 1988]. Typically, users are asked to rate
the system on 1–5 or 1–7 rating scales that are normally either
Likert scales or semantic differential scales [LaLomia and Sidowski
1990]. For a *Likert scale*, the questionnaire postulates some state-

Please mark the positions that best reflect your impressions of this system:

Pleasing	_ _ _ _ _ _ _	Irritating
Complete	_ _ _ _ _ _ _	Incomplete
Cooperative	_ _ _ _ _ _ _	Uncooperative
Simple	_ _ _ _ _ _ _	Complicated
Fast to use	_ _ _ _ _ _ _	Slow to use
Safe	_ _ _ _ _ _ _	Unsafe

Table 4 *Some semantic differential scales to measure subjective satisfaction with computers. See [Coleman et al. 1985] for a list of 17 such scales.*

ment (e.g., "I found this system very pleasant to use") and asks the users to rate their degree of agreement with the statement. When using a 1–5 rating scale, the reply options are typically 1 = strongly disagree, 2 = partly disagree, 3 = neither agree nor disagree, 4 = partly agree, and 5 = strongly agree.

A *semantic differential scale* lists two opposite terms along some dimension (for example, very easy to learn vs. very hard to learn) and asks the user to place the system on the most appropriate rating along the dimension. Table 3 and Table 4 list some sample questions that are often asked to measure subjective satisfaction. One could add a few questions addressing issues of special interest, such as "the quick reference card was very helpful," but it is normally best to keep the questionnaire short to maximize the response rate. A final rating for subjective satisfaction is often calculated simply as the mean of the ratings for the individual answers (after compensating for any use of reverse polarity), but it is also possible to use more sophisticated methods, drawing upon rating scale theory from sociology and psychometrics.

No matter what rating scales are used, they should be subjected to pilot testing (see page 174) to make sure that the questions are interpreted properly by the users. For example, a satisfaction questionnaire for a point-of-sales system used a dimension labelled "human contact vs. cold technology" to assess whether users felt that it was impersonal to be served by a machine. However, since no humans were present besides the user, many users felt that it was logically impossible to talk about "human contact," and did not answer the question in the intended manner.

When rating scales are used, one needs an anchor or baseline to calibrate the scale before it is possible to assess the results. If subjective satisfaction ratings are available for several different systems or several different versions of the same system, it is possible to consider the ratings in relation to the others and thus to determine which system is the most pleasant to use. If only a single user interface has been measured, one should take care in interpreting the ratings, since people are often too polite in their replies. Users normally know that the people who are asking for the ratings have a vested interest in the system being measured, and they will tend to be positive unless they have had a really unpleasant experience. This phenomenon can be partly counteracted by using reverse polarity on some of the questions, that is, having some questions to which an agreement would be a negative rating of the system.

Nielsen and Levy [1994] found that the median rating of subjective satisfaction for 127 user interfaces for which such ratings had been published was 3.6 on a 1–5 scale with 1 being the worst rating and 5 the best. Ostensibly, the rating 3 is the "neutral" point on a 1–5 rating scale, but since the median is the value where half of the systems were better and half were poorer, the value 3.6 seems to be a better estimate of "neutral" or "average" subjective satisfaction.

If multiple systems are tested, subjective satisfaction can be measured by asking users which system they would prefer or how strongly they prefer various systems over others. Finally, for systems that are in use, one can measure the extent that users choose to use them over any available alternatives. Data showing voluntary usage is really the ultimate subjective satisfaction rating.

2.3   Example: Measuring the Usability of Icons

To clarify the slightly abstract definition of usability in the previous section, this section gives several examples of how to measure the usability of a concrete user interface element: icons. Icons have become very popular elements in graphical user interfaces, but not all icons have equally good usability characteristics.

A systematic approach to icon usability would define measurable criteria for each of the usability attributes of interest to the system being developed. It is impossible to talk about the usability of an icon without knowing the context in which it will be shown and the circumstances under which it will be used. This section presents a few of the approaches to icon usability that have been published in the user interface literature. For some other examples, see [Green and Barnard 1990; Hakiel and Easterby 1987; Magyar 1990; Nolan 1989; Salasoo 1990; Stammers and Hoffman 1991; Zwaga 1989].

A classic study of icon usability was described by Bewley *et al.* [1983]. Four different sets of icons were designed for a graphical user interface with 17 icons. All of the icons were tested for ease of learning, efficiency of use, and subjective satisfaction. Ease of learning was assessed by several means: First, the intuitiveness[3] of the individual icons was tested by showing them to the users, one at a time, asking the user to describe "what you think it is." Second, since icons are normally not seen in isolation, the understandability of sets of icons was tested by showing the users entire sets of icons (one out of the four sets that had been designed). Users were then given the name of an icon and a short description of what it was supposed to do, and asked to point to the icon that best matched the description. Users were also given the complete set of names and asked to match up all the icons with their name. The score for all these learning tests was the proportion of the icons that were correctly described or named.

Two efficiency tests were conducted. In the first test, users who had already learned the meaning of the icons through participation in the learning tests were given the name of an icon and told that it might appear on the computer display. A random icon then

---

3. An early activity aimed at getting intuitive icons is to ask some users to draw icons they would like for each of the concepts that need to be depicted. The results will probably not look very good, but they can serve as a pool of ideas for the graphic designer.

appeared, and the users pressed a "yes" button if it was one they were looking for and a "no" button if it was some other icon. In the second test, users were shown a randomized display of icons and asked to click on a specific icon. Both these tests were timed, and the score for an icon was the users' reaction time in seconds.

Subjective satisfaction was measured in two ways. First, users were asked to rate each icon one at a time for how easy it was to pick out. Second, for each of the 17 concepts, the users were shown the four possible icons and asked to choose the one they preferred. The subjective score for an icon was the user rating for the first test and the proportion of users who preferred it for the second test.

Given the results from all these tests, it was possible to compare the four icon sets. One set that included the names of the commands as part of the icon got consistently high scores on the test where users had to describe what the icon represented. This result may not be all that surprising and has indeed been confirmed by later research on other interfaces [Egido and Patterson 1988; Kacmar and Carey 1991]. Unfortunately, this set of icons was not very graphically distinct, and many of the icons were hard to find on a screen with many similar icons. For the final system, a fifth set of icons was designed, mostly being based on one of the four original sets, but with some variations based on lessons from the tests as well as the aesthetic sensibilities of the graphic designers.

Icons are probably easier to design for objects than for operations since many objects can be depicted representationally. Rogers [1986] studied the usability of icon sets for operations by testing gradually more complex icons with more and more elements. The only usability parameter measured was comprehensibility, which was assessed by a matching test. For each level of icon complexity (for example, icons with few elements), an entire set of icons was designed to represent the commands in the system. For each such set, 10 users were shown all the icons as they went through a list of textual descriptions of the command functions.[4] For each textual description, the users picked the one icon they believed matched it best, and the total comprehension score for an icon set was then calculated as the number of correct matches.

The best icons showed both the concrete object being operated upon (for example a sheet of paper) and an abstract representation of the operation (for example an arrow). Icons with only one of these elements were harder to understand as were icons with even more information (such as replacing the arrow with a pointing finger with little cartoon-like lines denoting movement). So a medium level of complexity was best for comprehension. Also, icons for commands with a visual outcome (such as the movement of text in a word processor) were much easier to comprehend than were icons for commands with a nonvisual outcome (such as "save a file").

Icons that are intended for critical or widely used applications may need to satisfy more stringent quality criteria than other icons. International standards is certainly one area where one would want a high level of usability. Lindgaard *et al.* [1987] report on a case where the International Standards Organization (ISO) required that icons should be correctly interpreted by at least 66% of the subjects in a test for the icon to be considered for adoption as an international standard. Only half of the proposed icons actually passed this criterion when they were tested with technically knowledgeable users, and for naive subjects, only 1 out of 12 icons was good enough. Iterative design resulted in improved icons, but the important lesson from this study is the benefit of deciding on a reasonable criterion for measurable usability and then testing to see whether the goal has been met before releasing a product.

The examples in this section have shown that icon usability can be defined and measured in many different ways. The main conclusion from the examples is the need to refine the basic usability criteria listed in Section 2.2 with respect to the circumstances of each concrete project. There are many different ways of measuring usability, and no single measure will be optimal for all projects.

---

4. Users were shown the command descriptions one at a time, thus preventing them from matching icons to descriptions by exclusion. If the users had been able to see all the command descriptions at the same time as they were seeing all the icons, they could have assigned the last (and probably most difficult) icon to the remaining, unmatched command description.

2.4   Usability Trade-Offs

The learning curves in Figure 2 (page 28) may give the impression that one can have *either* a system that is easy to learn *or* one that is eventually efficient, though initially hard to learn. In fact, often a system that will give good novice learning will also be good for the experts. Also, it is often possible to ride the best parts of both learning curves by providing a user interface with multiple interaction styles, such that the user starts by learning one interaction style that is easy to learn and later changes to another that is more efficient for frequently used operations.

The typical way to achieve this "best-of-both-worlds" effect is to include *accelerators* in the user interface. Accelerators are user interface elements that allow the user to perform frequent tasks quickly, even though the same tasks can also be performed in a more general, and possibly slower, way. Typical examples of accelerators include function keys, command name abbreviations, and the use of double-clicking to activate an object. Section 5.7 (page 139) provides more examples of dialogue shortcuts that can serve as accelerators for the expert user.

Users of such a dual interface who are on the part of the learning curve where they are changing to expert mode may suffer a small dip in performance, so the learning curve will not necessarily be continuously increasing. Also, one should keep in mind that the increased interface complexity inherent in having both novice and expert modes can be a problem in itself. It is therefore important to design the interface in such a way that the novice users can use it without being confronted with the expert mode and the accelerators. For example, a command language system that allows abbreviations should always spell out the full name of the commands in any help and error messages. Also, any operation that is activated by double-clicking should also be made available as a menu choice or in some other visible fashion.

The trade-off between learnability for novice users and efficiency of use for expert users can sometimes be resolved to the benefit of both user groups without employing dual interaction styles. For example, unless the application involves a very large number of fields, one might as well use descriptive field labels in a dialog box, even though they would make it a little larger than if cryptic abbreviations were used. The expert users would not be hurt by such a concession to the novices.[5] Similarly, both user groups would benefit from appropriate choice of default values—experts because they would need to change the value less often, and novices because the system would conform to their typical needs without the need for them to learn about the nondefault options.

Even so, it is not always possible to achieve optimal scores for all usability attributes simultaneously. Trade-offs are inherent in any design process and apply no less to user interface design. For example, the desire to avoid catastrophic errors may lead to the decision to design a user interface that is less efficient to use than otherwise possible: typically because extra questions are asked to assure that the user is certain about wanting a particular action.

In cases where a usability trade-off seems necessary, attempts should first be made at finding a win–win solution that can satisfy both requirements. If that is not possible, the dilemma should be resolved under the directions set out by the project's usability goals (see page 79), which should define which usability attributes are the most important given the specific circumstances of the project.

Furthermore, considerations other than usability may lead to designs violating some usability principles. For example, security considerations often require access controls that are decidedly non-user friendly, such as not providing constructive error messages in case of an erroneously entered password. As another example, museum information systems and other publicly used systems may have hidden options, such as a command to reboot the system

---

5. Actually, Fitts' Law implies that it would be a little slower to move the mouse between fields in the larger version of the dialog box, since the time to point at an object is proportional to the logarithm of the distance to the object [Card *et al.* 1978]. However, expert users would be likely to move between the fields in the dialog box with the Tab key (another accelerator) if speed was of the essence, and they would therefore not be subject to Fitts' Law.

in case of trouble, in cases where the options are not intended to be used by the regular users.

2.5 Categories of Users and Individual User Differences

The two most important issues for usability are the users' task and their individual characteristics and differences. An analysis of 92 published comparisons of usability of hypertext systems found that 4 of the 10 largest effects (including all of the top 3 effects) in the studies were due to individual differences between users and that 2 were due to task differences [Nielsen 1989d]. It is therefore an important aspect of usability engineering to know the user. Understanding the major ways of classifying users may also help [Potosnak *et al.* 1986], though often the same system design will be good for many categories of users.

Figure 3 shows the "user cube" of the three main dimensions[6] along which users' experience differs: experience with the system, with computers in general, and with the task domain.

The users' experience with the specific user interface under consideration is the dimension that is normally referred to when discussing user expertise, and users are normally considered to be either novices or experts, or somewhere in-between. The transition from novice to expert user of a system often follows a learning curve somewhat like those shown in Figure 2.

Most of the usability principles discussed in this book will help make systems easier to learn, and thus allow users to reach expert status faster. In addition to general learnability, there are several

---

6. Note that the classification dimensions used here are different from those used in the "user cube" of Cotterman and Kumar [1989]. Their dimensions concerned the degree to which the user was the producer or consumer of information, whether the user had any part in developing the system, and the user's degree of decision-making authority over the system. These dimensions are certainly also of interest.

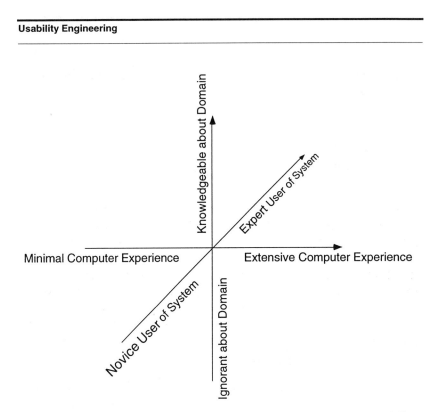

Figure 3 *The three main dimensions on which users' experience differs: knowledge about computers in general, expertise in using the specific system, and understanding of the task domain.*

user interface elements that can prod users to acquire expertise. A classic example is the way many menu systems list the appropriate shortcut for menu options as part of the menu itself. Such shortcuts are often function keys or command name abbreviations but, in any case, they can be mentioned in a way that does not hurt novice users while still encouraging them to try the alternative interaction technique. Online help systems may encourage users to broaden their understanding of a system by providing hypertext links to information that is related to their specific queries. It may even be possible for the system to analyze the user's actions and suggest alternative and better ways of achieving the same goal.

Some user interfaces are only intended to be used by novices, in that almost nobody will use them more than a few times. This is true for most walk-up-and-use systems, like a kiosk for making dinner reservations in an amusement park, but also for interfaces that may require a little reading of the instructions, such as installation programs, disk formatting routines, and tax return programs that change every year. Most interfaces, however, are intended for both novice and expert users and thus need to accommodate both usage styles.

As discussed in Section 2.4, a common way to cater to both expert and novice users is to include accelerators in the interface to allow expert users to use faster, but less obvious, interaction techniques. Several widely used systems come with two sets of menus, one for novice users (often called "short menus" to avoid any stigma) and one for expert users ("long menus"). This allows the system to offer a wide range of features to the experts without confusing the novices. Similarly, as discussed in Section 5.10, online help can assist the novice users without getting in the way of the experts. Interfaces that are solely intended for novices may not need special help systems, as they should include all the necessary user assistance in the primary interface itself.

In spite of the common simplistic distinction between expert and novice users, the reality is that most people do not acquire comprehensive expertise in all parts of a system, no matter how much they use it. Almost all systems of some complexity have so many features and so many uses that any given user only makes extensive use of a small subset [Draper 1984]. Thus, even an "expert" user may be quite novice with respect to many parts of the system not normally used by that user. As a consequence, expert users still need access to help systems for those parts of the interface that they do not use as often, and they will benefit from increased learnability of these features.

The users' general experience with computers also has impact on user interface design. As a simple example, consider a utility program distributed to mainframe systems administrators as compared with one that is to be used by home computer owners. Even though the two utilities may be intended for somewhat the same purpose, such as disk defragmentation, the interfaces should be very different. Even with more application-oriented interfaces, users with extensive experience from many other applications will normally be better off than users who have only used a single system, since experienced users will have some idea of what features to look for and how a computer normally deals with various situations. For example, a user with experience of a spreadsheet and a database program might try to look for a "sort" command in a new word processor. Furthermore, a user's programming experience will to a large degree determine the extent to which that user can use macro languages and other complex means of combining commands, and whether the resulting structures will be easily maintainable and modifiable when the user's needs change at a later date.

The final important dimension is the user's knowledge of the task domain addressed by the system. Interfaces for users with extensive domain knowledge can use specialized terminology and a higher density of information in the screen designs. Users with little domain knowledge will need to have the system explain what it is doing and what the different options mean, and the terminology used should not be as abbreviated and dense as for domain specialists. Consider, for example, the design of a financial planning system. The interface obviously needs to be very different depending on whether the intended users are finance professionals or whether the system is intended to help professionals from other fields invest and keep track of their money.

Users also differ in other ways than experience. Some differentiating factors are easy to observe, like age [Czaja 1988] and gender [Fowler and Murray 1987; Teasley et al. 1994]. Other factors are less immediately obvious, like differences in spatial memory and reasoning abilities [Gomez et al. 1986] and preferred learning style [Sein and Bostrom 1989], where some people learn better from abstract descriptions, and others learn better from concrete examples. The important lesson from studies of these and other differences is that one needs to consider the entire spectrum of intended users and make sure that the interface is usable for as many as possible, and not just for those who happen to have the same characteristics as the developers themselves. For example, the developers may find it easy to remember where everything is located in a hierarchical file system, but users with lower spatial memory abilities may find the user interface significantly easier to use if it included an overview map [Vincente and Williges 1988].

In addition to differences between groups of users, there are also important differences between individual users [Egan 1988]. The most extreme example may be in programming, where the difference in productivity between the best and the worst programmers typically is a factor of 20 [Curtis 1981]. That is, the program that one person can write in two weeks will take another a year—and the two-week program will often be of better quality. A practical implication of this result that has been found in several studies is that the most important aspect of improving software projects is to employ fewer, but better programmers. Even for nonprogramming tasks, the ratio between the best and the worst users' performance is typically a factor of between 4 and 10.

Since the ratio between best and worst users reflects the extremes and also depends on the number of users tested, one also commonly uses quartile ratios to express the magnitude of individual differences. Quartiles divide a sorted range of observations, such as a set of user performance data, into four equally large sets. The Q_3/Q_1 ratio indicates how much better the best 25% (the top, or fourth quartile)[7] of the users are compared with the worst 25% (the bottom, or first quartile). Q_3 indicates the level of performance where 25% of the users are better and 75% are worse. Similarly, Q_1 indicates the level of performance where 25% of the users are worse and 75% are better. For example, assume that 8 users had been measured as having task throughputs of 2, 3, 3, 4, 4, 5, 6, and 9 transactions per minute. Since there are 8 users, the bottom quartile will cut between the second worst and third worst users, or a level of 3. Similarly, the top quartile will cut between the second best and

---

7. The reason Q_3 is used to represent the performance of top users even though they are the *fourth* quartile is that Q_3 is the level separating the third and the fourth quartile. It would not be as representative to use Q_4 which is the other endpoint of the interval representing the top quartile, since Q_4 is the performance achieved by the single-best user.

third best, corresponding to a level of 5.5. Thus, the Q_3/Q_1 ratio is 5.5/3=1.8. For many computer tasks, the Q_3/Q_1 ratio is about two.

Attitude differences can also impact how people use computers. For whatever reason, some people simply love using computers and will go to extreme efforts to learn all about their system. I once interviewed a business professional who said that she liked to learn a new software package every month just to stay in shape, and many other "super-users" spend as much time as many hackers learning about obscure details in their computers, even though they are business professionals and not programmers [Nielsen *et al.* 1986]. Such super-users (also known as "power users" or "gurus") often serve an important function as liaisons between the regular users and new computer developments as introduced by an information management department or outside software vendors. The super-users' role as technology champions not only helps introduce new systems, but also provides the regular users with a local means of finding sympathetic and task-specific help [Gantt and Nardi 1992; Nardi and Miller 1991]. Since they often like to talk, super-users can also serve as a way for software developers to get feedback about changing user needs before the majority of users have reached a stage where these new needs have become apparent. Just remember that most users will be different from the super-users, so do not design the user interface purely on the basis of their desires.

Given the many differences between groups of users and between individual users, it might be tempting to give up and just allow the users to customize their interfaces to suit their individual preferences. However, as discussed under the heading *Users Are Not Designers* on page 12, it is not a good idea to go too far in that direction either. Most often, it is possible to design user interfaces to accommodate several kinds of users as long as attention is paid to all of the relevant groups during the design process. It is rare that an interface change that is necessary to help one group will be a major problem for another, or that it is at least not possible to work around the second group's difficulties.

Chapter 3   *Generations of User Interfaces*

User interface design is still too new a field to have attracted much historical analysis. People have mostly been too busy building interfaces to worry where they came from, even though a few historical treatments are starting to emerge [Anonymous 1990; Card and Moran 1988; Gaines 1984; Gaines and Shaw 1986a and b; Goldberg 1988; Grudin 1990a; Nielsen 1990a, Chapter 3; Nyce and Kahn 1991; Perry and Voelcker 1989; Rheingold 1985; Teitelman 1986]. See also [Ramsey and Grimes 1983] for a survey of early research in the user interface field.

In the computer field, the term "generation" is often used to refer to the changes in the underlying hardware component technology. However, user interface technology has also been through a series of generations that roughly parallels the generations of hardware [Tesler 1991], and there are also other elements of the history of computing that have seen considerable change, such as the categories of people using the computers. Table 5 summarizes the generations of computers and user interfaces so far. The summary of the advertising image of computers is based on [Aspray and Beaver 1986]. The dates given for each generation in Table 5 indicate the time from when early adapters started using that generation to the time when they started using the next. Certainly, pioneers in leading research laboratories started using many technologies

Generation	Hardware technology	Operating mode	Programming languages	Terminal technology	User types	Advertising image	User interface paradigm
0 −1945 Pre-history	Mechanical, electromecha-nical (Babbage, Zuse Z3)	Not really being "used" except for calculations	Moving cables around	Reading blinking lights and punch cards	The inventors themselves	None (computers had not left the lab yet)	None (direct hands-on access to the hardware only important thing)
1 1945–1955 Pioneer	Vacuum tubes, huge machines, short mean time between failures	One user at a time "owns" machine (but for a limited time only)	Machine language 0011001111101	TTY, typewriter. Only used in the computer center	Experts, pioneers	Computer as calculator	Programming, Batch
2 1955–1965 Historical	Transistors; more reliable. Computers start seeing use out-side the lab.	Batch (central-ized "computer as temple," not accessed directly)	Assembler ADD A,B	Line-oriented terminals ("glass-TTY")	Technocrats, professional computerists	Computer as information processor	Command languages
3 1965–1980 Traditional	Integrated circuits. Businesses can cost-justify buying computers for many needs.	Time-sharing (online transac-tion processing systems)	High-level lan-guages, For-tran, Pascal, C **if** expense > income **then**...	Full-screen ter-minals, alphanu-meric characters only. Remote access common	Specialized groups without computer knowl-edge (e.g., bank tellers)	Mechanization of white-collar labor	Full-screen strictly hierarchi-cal menus and form fill-in
4 1980–1995 Modern	VLSI. Individuals can buy their own per-sonal computer	Single-user personal com-puters	Problem-ori-ented lan-guages, spreadsheets	Graphical dis-plays. Desktop workstations, heavy portables	Business professionals, hobbyists	Personal pro-ductivity (com-puter as tool)	WIMP (Win-dows, Icons, Menus, and a Pointing device)
5 1995–? Future	Wafer-scale integration. Individuals can buy *many*.	Networked single-user and embedded systems	Nonimperative, possibly graphical	"Dynabook," mul-timedia I/O, eas-ily portable, with cellular modem	Everybody	Computer as appliance	Noncommand–based interfaces

Table 5 *Summary of the generations of computers and user interfaces.*

earlier, and many innovation laggards stayed safely a generation or so behind the early adapters.

The historical development of user interfaces is interesting because each generation seems to contain the previous ones as special cases. Even as communication bandwidth has grown, previous communication methods remain useful, and the addition of new user populations does not mean that the previous users disappear. Many other technological developments involve the replacement of older technology with newer inventions, but a good designer of modern user interfaces still needs to know how to best use interaction techniques from several generations ago.

3.1 Batch Systems

The first generation of user interfaces was not even interactive. Batch systems can be said to involve zero-dimensional interfaces in that the interaction between the system and the user was restricted to a single point in time: the submission of the batch job as a single unit. All the user's commands had to be specified before the result of any of them was made known to the user. Obviously, this "interaction style" was not highly usable for most purposes.

Batch jobs did have an advantage in being able to run without user supervision in cases where the same thing had to be done over and over again, such as the archetypal case of payroll processing. Therefore, many modern computers have retained some form of batch capability to supplement their interactive mode. It is recommended, however, that such batch modes provide some opportunity for the user to continuously monitor the progress of the batch job if desired, such that the user can interrupt and/or modify the job. It is very frustrating to have a long computation run almost to the end only to have to be discarded because the last command should have been modified.

Batch interfaces have enjoyed a renaissance recently in the form of systems accessed through the exchange of electronic mail messages, such as the bibliography server described on page 303.

For example, the ephemeral interest group system [Brothers *et al.* 1992] allowed users to set up informal discussion groups that were maintained by a central server. If they wanted to get a copy of the discussion so far, users could send an email message to the server specifying the number of the group as well as a special keyword. The server would reply with a return message containing its records of the specified discussion group. In a similar manner, users could join and leave interest groups and get a list of the other members of a group by sending specialized messages to the server. Many other services exist on various email systems, all based on batch-style interaction, and some computer systems can even be accessed through fax messages [Johnson *et al.* 1993]. The difference from traditional batch systems is that email and fax interfaces often can be accessed from anywhere in the world.

3.2   Line-Oriented Interfaces

Time-sharing systems were invented around 1960 [Lee *et al.* 1992] as a way to allow several users simultaneous interactive access to a single mainframe computer. A major problem with time-sharing is the small amount of computational resources available to support the user interface for any given user, so early time-shared user interfaces often used line-oriented interfaces.

In spite of the primitive interfaces to early time-shared computers, the very introduction of such a major feature for the sole benefit of the human users gave rise to an increased awareness of user interface issues. J. C. R. Licklider, who played a central role in early work on time-sharing, also wrote a very influential paper, "Man–Computer Symbiosis" [Licklider 1960], which was an early call to arms for getting computers to reflect the user's needs and abilities more closely.

As shown in Figure 4, line-oriented interfaces were basically one-dimensional interfaces, where the user could only interact with the computer on the single line that served as the command line. Once the user had hit the return key, the input could be modified no further. Similarly, once the computer had output a line of informa-

Figure 4 *Examples of a line-oriented, a full-screen, and a graphical user interface. The line-oriented interface allows the user to modify the last line only and is thus one dimensional. The full-screen interface allows the user to move about in two dimensions, and the graphical interface almost adds a third dimension through the overlapping windows.*

tion to the user, it was frozen and could not be modified to reflect any changes in the data. Line-oriented interfaces were originally implemented on tele-typewriters (TTYs), where the interaction was printed on an endless roll of paper passing through the typewriter. Later versions did use terminal screens, but continued to treat the text as frozen once it had scrolled above the command line. Such an interface is often called a "glass-TTY." Even though glass-TTYs represented a more advanced technology than the paper-based TTYs, they were somewhat of a step backwards in terms of usability, as the user could no longer read more than the last 24 lines or so of text. The endless scroll of paper at least had the advantage of keeping a permanent record of the entire interaction and allowing the user access to large amounts of information.

Since line-oriented interfaces did not allow users to move about the screen, their interaction techniques were mostly limited to question–answer dialogues and the typing of commands with parameters. Question–answer dialogues involve exchanges prompted by the computer, where the user answers the computer's questions one at a time. Such dialogues are thus especially suited for situations where the dialogue is well structured with a small number of options that can be predicted in advance, and where it is acceptable to have the user be directed by the computer rather than having freedom to structure the task in alternative ways. These characteristics are true of many walk-up-and-use systems for novice or casual users, and question–answer dialogues are therefore still being used, even in systems that have otherwise left the line-oriented interaction style. Two problems with question–answer dialogues are that users may want to change earlier answers and that they need to answer the current question without knowing what the following questions will be. A typical example of both these problems is the question "Enter city" as part of a dialogue to elicit a user's address. Many people will answer something like "Morristown, NJ 07960" without knowing that the next question will be "State" or "ZIP." This example obviously indicates the need to offer the user facilities for editing previous replies in a question–answer dialogue.

Most line-oriented user interfaces were built on command languages of various sorts, and much early research in the user interface field involved the proper selection of command names. Some command languages are very powerful and allow the construction of very complicated sequences of commands with huge sets of modifiers and parameters. Unfortunately, command languages are normally also quite unforgiving of user errors since they require the user to specify the desired command in exactly the required format, which the user has to remember without much help from the computer.

To speed up interactions and reduce the risk of spelling errors, most command languages allow the user to abbreviate the command names. There are many reasonable ways to abbreviate commands, including truncation and vowel removal [Ehrenreich 1985]. The most important abbreviation guideline is to choose a single, consistent rule for generating the abbreviations [Streeter *et al.* 1983] and then explaining that rule in the manual.

3.3   Full-Screen Interfaces

After some time with glass-TTYs, where only the bottom line of the terminal could be modified, computers started taking advantage of the modifiable nature of the entire screen, and full-screen interfaces were introduced, changing the space of interface design from one to two dimensions. A classic use of the full screen is form-filling dialogues, where the user is presented with a number of labelled fields that can be edited in any sequence desired by the user. Form fill-in still exists in modern interfaces in the form of dialog boxes, even though dialog boxes are more dynamic than traditional forms since they can contain pop-up menus and other ways to make the computer help the user while the form is being filled out.

In addition to menus, which are discussed further in the subsection below, many full-screen interfaces also use function keys as a primary interaction style. In principle, a function key is just a packaging of a complete command into a single lexical user operation. Two main advantages of function keys are that they serve as interaction accelerators and that there are so few of them that users often are able to learn them by heart. Since the exact interpretation of a function key can depend on the screen object pointed to by the cursor, some uses of function keys allowed an early approximation to the point-and-click interaction style of modern mouse-based interfaces.

Menu Hierarchies

Full-screen interfaces often depend heavily on hierarchically nested menus, with each menu taking up the full screen. In principle, menus can also be used in line-oriented interfaces, since it is possible for the user to choose from a menu by typing an indication of the desired option on the command line, even if the menu itself has scrolled up into the inactive area of the screen. In practice, however, menus seem to be used more in full-screen systems, and they are of course also being used extensively in most modern window systems.

The design of hierarchical menus [Paap and Roske-Hofstrand 1988] is especially important in many full-screen interfaces and has indeed been studied extensively. The best advice is obviously to avoid hierarchical menus since they hide options from the user and require the introduction of an extra set of interaction techniques for navigating the hierarchy. Therefore, it is often better to overload a nonhierarchical menu slightly than to split it into a hierarchy. Even

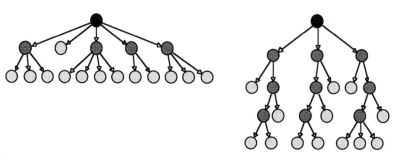

Figure 5 *Example of broad and deep menu hierarchies, both providing the user access to 13 commands (the leaf nodes of the trees).*

so, many systems do include so many features that a menu hierarchy is necessary to access them all.

The basic trade-off in hierarchical menu design is between depth and breadth. As shown in Figure 5, a flat, broad menu does not require the user to go through as many levels as a deep menu, thereby reducing the need for user navigation. At the same time, each node in the menu hierarchy becomes more complex in a flat menu structure, making the user choose between more options at each level. Since both navigation and decisions take time, neither too deep nor too broad menu trees are desirable in general.

If one assumes that users will make no errors in selecting the correct option at each menu level, and if one knows the probability with which the user will select each menu option, then one can mathematically determine the optimal menu structure [Landauer and Nachbar 1985; Fisher *et al.* 1990]. These assumptions may be somewhat reasonable if the menus are only intended to be used by expert users or if the menu items have an "obvious" structure known to all users (such as alphabetical or numerical order). For nonexpert users, however, the need to consider errors leads to a requirement for having the various submenus contain "natural" groupings of options, such that their names on the higher levels are as understandable as possible. For example, Tullis [1985] used cluster analysis to group the 271 functions in an operating system based on similarity ratings for the various functions from experienced users.

In recent years, many telephone-operated interfaces have been designed to allow users to access various forms of information and services, such as their bank account balance, over regular push-button telephones [Halstead-Nussloch 1989]. These systems are very often menu-based, but are otherwise closer to the line-oriented generation of user interfaces since the dialogue is completely linear. Telephone-operated interfaces are thus an example of the hybrid nature of menu interfaces and also indicate that the concept of "generations" of interfaces presented in this chapter should be seen more as a way to conceptualize the history of user interface design than as a sequential progression of interfaces replacing each other.

3.4   Graphical User Interfaces

Even though graphical user interfaces have a history going back to Ivan Sutherland's Sketchpad system from 1962 [Sutherland 1963], Douglas Engelbart's mouse from 1964 [Engelbart 1988], and several research systems from the 1970s [Goldberg 1988], they did not see widespread commercial use until the 1980s [Perry and Voelcker 1989]. Most current user interfaces belong to the category of graphical user interfaces sometimes referred to as WIMP systems (windows, icons, menus, and a pointing device) after their basic components. As can be seen in Figure 4, window interfaces almost add a third dimension to the two dimensions inherent in each window because of the possibility for overlapping windows. Of course, overlapping windows are not truly three-dimensional since it is not possible to see the content of obscured windows without moving them to the top, so it would be more accurate to refer to these interfaces as having two-and-a-half dimensions.

The primary interaction style used in many graphical user interfaces is direct manipulation [Shneiderman 1983], which is based on visual representation of the dialogue objects of interest to the user. Such a continuously updated representation allows the user to control the dialogue by moving objects around on the screen and otherwise manipulating them with the mouse. As an example, the traditional way of specifying a margin indentation in a word processor would be to issue a command to indent by a certain number of spaces. Such a command is an indirect manipulation of the margin, however, and the user may have to try several times before the desired layout is achieved. In contrast, direct manipulation of a margin would involve dragging the margin itself or a margin marker to the desired position. Since the user is getting continuous feedback about the positioning of the margin as it is being moved, the result should be less of a surprise. Of course, this example does show that direct manipulation may not be optimal for all tasks, in that it would be easier to achieve a very precise margin setting by typing in the number.

Let's move from the interaction techniques to the structure of the interface. Many graphical user interfaces can be said to be *object-oriented*.[1] Object-oriented interfaces are in contrast to the function-oriented interfaces that were the traditional structure for character-based interfaces. In a function-oriented interface, the interaction is structured around a set of commands issued by the user in various combinations to achieve the desired result. The main interface issue is how to provide easy access to these commands and their parameters, and typical solutions include command-line interfaces with various abbreviation options as well as full-screen menus.

Object-oriented interfaces are sometimes described as turning the application inside–out as compared to function-oriented interfaces. The main focus of the interaction changes to become the users' data and other information objects that are typically represented graphically on the screen as icons or in windows. Users achieve their goals by gradually massaging these objects (using various modification features that are of course similar to the concept of

---

1. Note that I am talking about object-oriented *interfaces*. These interfaces may or may not be implemented using object-oriented *programming* which is a completely different issue. Once the interface has been structured around objects, it may feel natural to implemented these objects using object-oriented programming, but one can also implement object-oriented interfaces using traditional programming methods.

commands) until their state, as shown on the screen, matches the desired result. Unfortunately, experience shows that developers who are used to designing function-oriented user interfaces have serious difficulties in changing over to designing object-oriented interfaces [Nielsen *et al.* 1992].

An example may clarify the distinction between function- and object-oriented interfaces and show why not just any graphical user interface is object-oriented. Consider the task of selecting certain information from a database, formatting the data, and printing the resulting report. A function-oriented interface that was designed by participants in our study started by asking the user to specify the query criteria in a (graphical) dialog box. Then, the user had to select formatting options from a (graphical) pull-down menu and, finally, the user could click on a (graphical) print button. Only after the last step would the user be shown any actual data from the database. All these steps were centered around the operations to be performed by the user and not around the actual data to be manipulated by the user. An alternative, object-oriented design would start by showing the user a window with sample records from the database. Observing this data would make it much easier for the user to remember the nature of the database contents and would simplify the task of constructing an appropriate query. As the user modified the query, the system would dynamically update the content of the data window to show samples of records satisfying the query. Formatting would be done by modifying the window layout, thus providing immediate feedback on how typical records would look in the revised formatting. Issuing the print command would still be the final step, but the output would not be a surprise to the user, since it would only reflect the data-centered modifications for which incremental feedback had already been observed by the user.

Most interface specialists assume that graphical user interfaces have better usability characteristics in general than character-based interfaces, especially with respect to learnability for novice users. In spite of this common belief, there is not much hard experimental evidence to prove the superiority of graphical interfaces. One of the few experiments [Margono and Shneiderman 1987] compared a graphical file system with a command-line file system and found that novice users could perform a set of file manipulation tasks in 4.8 minutes while making 0.8 errors with the graphical interface, whereas the same tasks took 5.8 minutes and involved 2.4 errors with the command-line interface. Users also strongly preferred the graphical interface, giving it a satisfaction rating of 5.4 on a 1–6 scale, whereas the command-line interface rated at 3.8.

Another experiment [Rauterberg 1992] compared two versions of a widely sold database package that was available for both character-based and graphical computer systems. Novice users were able to perform 5 test tasks in 82 minutes with the character-based user interface and in 49 minutes with the graphical user interface. Expert users performed the same tasks in 25 and 10 minutes, respectively, showing that the graphical user interface was better for both user categories.

One of the questions I get asked the most is the extent to which graphical user interfaces have been measured to be better than character-based user interfaces. Studies like the two mentioned here are pitting concrete implementations against each other, and therefore do not really answer the general question of whether graphical user interfaces are really better. To some extent, the question is meaningless since one will always be able to design an atrocious graphical interface that will test out worse than a highly polished character-based interface. In one study comparing two graphical interfaces, two command-line interfaces and one full-screen menu interface, Whiteside *et al.* [1985] concluded that there were no systematic differences in usability between the interaction paradigms but that the care with which the interface is crafted was more important.

Even so, it does seem that graphical user interfaces enjoy an advantage over character-based interfaces, if for no other reason than the potential they offer for richer interface designs. Anything that can be done in a character-based user interface can also be done in a graphical user interface just by refraining from using the graphics, whereas the reverse is obviously not true. Also, the large screens and multiple windows, while not inherently restricted to graphics screens, offer better possibilities for users to interact with multiple applications and data objects at the same time, thus better matching the task requirements of busy business professionals, process control operators, and many other user groups. Finally, the use of an independent pointing device such as the mouse offers the user a sense of control over the interface and a natural way to move about screens which can be made more compelling through the use of graphic design.

In fact, graphical interfaces can sometimes be *too* natural and compelling, especially if the actual system does not support user expectations. For example, novice users of systems where file manipulation is performed by dragging icons can sometimes be observed trying to perform text editing operations by (unsuccessfully) dragging pieces of text around on the screen [Nielsen 1987b]. These novice users quite reasonably transferred their knowledge of how to move objects from the file system to the text editor, but unfortunately, the two parts of the system did not view "moving things" as a single, generic command that could be accomplished by a single interaction technique.[2]

Another example of the abductive nature of graphical interfaces is seen in the calculator example in Figure 6. When I asked 24 experienced users of a graphical user interface how they could operate the Calculator utility in their system (having an interface similar to the one in Figure 6), 13 stated that it could only be operated by the mouse, and 11 stated that it could be operated either by mouse clicks or through the keyboard [Nielsen 1987b]. In fact, the calculator could be operated through either interaction technique. In other words, more than half of the users had formed an erroneous functional mental model [Nielsen 1990c] of the Calculator utility because the direct manipulation part of the interface was so convincing that it kept them from discovering the other part of the interface.

---

2. Based on these and other research results, some later systems have introduced a "drag and drop" feature for moving word processor selections and spreadsheet cells by direct manipulation.

Figure 6 *A simple calculator operated by direct manipulation.*

Unfortunately, direct manipulation interfaces may be harder to use for some disabled users than the traditional, text-only interfaces were [Newell 1993]. Users with motor difficulties may have no problems operating a keyboard with its discrete nature: Even if you do not hit a key exactly right, the character still appears perfectly on the screen (and you can backspace if you hit the wrong key). In contrast, direct manipulation is much more dependent on fine control of a continuous input device, the mouse. As another example, blind users cannot see icons and objects on the screen and will thus have trouble manipulating them [Griffith 1990]. Considerable research efforts are underway to solve or alleviate these problems, using various techniques like audible representations of the various windows on a screen [Edwards 1988; Mynatt and Edwards 1992], but in general it does seem that graphical user interfaces are a detriment to this particular category of users.

3.5   Next-Generation Interfaces

The next generation of user interfaces is already under development in laboratories around the world [Nielsen 1993a]. It is likely that the trend from the previous generations will continue, and that the dimensionality of user interfaces will increase from the current 2.5 to a full 3 (or more) dimensions. Common ways to add a dimension to user interfaces include adding time (in the form of animation [Baecker *et al.* 1991; Robertson *et al.* 1993]), sound [Gaver 1989] or voice [Tucker and Jones 1991], as well as a true third spatial dimension in the form of virtual reality systems [Biocca 1992; Mercurio and Erickson 1990; Pausch 1991; Rheingold 1991; Thomas and Stuart 1992].

Much of the original vision of highly personal and portable computing was described in a pioneering article introducing a hypothetical "dynabook" (dynamic book) computer [Kay and Goldberg 1977]. Even though current personal computers have achieved graphical user interfaces and even some portability, they are still far from the early ideal, where computers would be as easy to use and to carry around as books.

The two easiest predictions regarding the next generation of user interfaces are thus that they will include higher dimensionality with more media types and that they will be highly portable and personal, while utilizing cellular modems and other communications technology to achieve tight connectivity.

In addition, it is likely that next-generation user interfaces will be more object-oriented in terms of their functionality and not just in terms of information manipulation, as has been the case with many graphical user interfaces as discussed on page 58.

Traditional operating systems were based on the notion of applications that were used by the user one at a time. Even window systems and other attempts at application integration typically forced the user to "be" in one application at a time, even though other applications were running in the background. Also, any given document or data file was only operated on by one application at a time. Some systems allow the construction of pipelines connecting multiple applications, but even these systems still basically have the applications act sequentially on the data.

The application model is constraining to users who have integrated tasks that require multiple applications. Approaches to alleviate this mismatch in the past have included integrated software [Nielsen *et al.* 1986] and composite editors that could deal with multiple data types in a single document. No single program is likely to satisfy all computer users, however, no matter how tightly integrated it is, so other approaches have also been invented to break the application barrier. Cut-and-paste mechanisms have been available for several years to allow the inclusion of data from one application in a document belonging to another application. Recent systems even allow live links back to the original application such that changes in the original data can be reflected in the copy in the new document. However, these mechanisms are still constrained by the basic application model that require each document to belong to a specific application at any given time.

An alternative model is emerging in object-oriented operating systems where the basic object of interest is the user's document. Any given document can contain subobjects of many different types, and the system will take care of activating the appropriate code to display, print, edit, or email these data types as required [Banning 1984; Dreger *et al.* 1992; Gates 1990]. The main difference is that the user no longer needs to think in terms of running applications, since the data knows how to integrate the available functionality in the system. In some sense, such an object-oriented system is the ultimate composite editor, but the difference compared to traditional, tightly integrated multi-media editors is that the system is open and allows plug-and-play addition of new or upgraded functionality as the user desires without changing the rest of the system.

Because I am still using a system based on the traditional applications model, I currently have about six spell checkers on my personal computer, since each application has its own. This profusion of spell checkers leads to problems with inconsistent interfaces and the resulting increase in learning time and usage errors, and it requires me to update six different "personal" dictionaries with the specialized terms and proper names used in my writing. Also, my wealth of spell checking functionality is restricted to work within some applications and does not help me when I am using others, such as my electronic mail package.

Future object-oriented software structures might allow me to add various types of "language servers" to my system as needed, including a high-powered spell checker, a thesaurus, and a grammar assistant. The increasing need to design user interfaces for international and multilingual use certainly implies major benefits from an ability to change the language of the "language server" in the system and have the new language apply to all other system features without the need to reprogram them.

A major dialogue style for next-generation user interfaces may be noncommand user interfaces [Nielsen 1993a]. All user interface styles until now have at least had the concept of commands in common and were based on the principle of an explicit dialogue between the user and the computer in which the user ordered the computer to do certain specific actions. In contrast, many current research efforts aim at systems that allow the user to focus on the domain instead of having to control the computer explicitly. In these future systems, the computer will take over responsibility for the interaction, basing its actions on its observations of the user, using technologies like active badges [Want *et al.* 1992], eyetracking [Jacob 1991], gesture recognition [Kurtenbach and Hulteen 1990; Rhyne and Wolf 1993], and semi-intelligent analyses of the user's actions. Some systems go so far as to immerse the user in a simulated world with devices like headmounted displays [Steuer 1992], but it is also possible to achieve much of the same effect while staying with the basic workstation model of computing.

For example, the Portholes system for connecting work groups at remote locations displays miniature images of each participant's office as well as meeting areas [Dourish and Bly 1992]. These images are refreshed every few minutes and thus allow people at each location to get a general idea of which colleagues are around and what they are doing, but without the privacy intrusion that might follow from broadcasting live video. For the purposes of the current discussion, an important point about Portholes is that the various participants do not need to take any action to inform their co-workers that they are in their office or that they are meeting with somebody and should not be disturbed. This information is communicated to the system by virtue of the regular activities the users would do anyway, thus allowing them to focus on their real-world task and not on using a computer. Experience with other systems for computer-supported cooperative work has shown that people are reluctant to expend effort on entering information into a computer for the sole purpose of helping others [Grudin 1988], so this type of interface design to allow users to focus on their work is probably the only one that would work in the long term.

When the computer is allowed to change the user interface, it can adapt the interaction to the user's specific usage circumstances and location. For example, if the computer knows where the user is, it can enlarge the text on the display if the user is standing up, or it could speak out important alert messages by speech synthesis if the user was in the other end of the office. Furthermore, the computer could act on important electronic mail arriving while the user was out of the office by one of several means: activating the user's beeper, ringing a phone in the office where the user was, downloading the message to the user's notebook computer over the wireless network, or sending a fax to the user's hotel. The exact delivery mechanism would be chosen by the computer based on knowledge of the user's whereabouts and preferences.

Computer control of the interface may be resented by some users if it is not designed carefully. Many forms of adaptive interfaces may be readily accepted because they simply cause the computer to behave the way one would naturally expect it to do if it were part of the traditional physical world. For example, the organization of kitchen tools in drawers and cabinets adapts by itself to cause the most frequently used tools to be on top and in front, whereas less frequently used tools are hidden [Hill and Hollan 1992]. In a similar manner, several current applications augment their " File" menu with lists of the last five or so files used by the user in that application, under the assumption that recently used files are likely to be among the more frequently used ones in the future and thus should be made more easily accessible. This assumption seems reasonable, and a study of somewhat similar adaptive menus found them to be an improvement over static menus [Greenberg and Whitten 1985]. Given the observation that users tend to have several working sets of data and tools that are used together [Henderson and Card 1986], it might be better, though, to have the computer build cross-application object lists that can be associated with the user's various tasks.

3.6   Long-Term Trends in Usability

Gould *et al.* [1991] discuss the long-term trends in usability and conclude that they are not known with the same certainty as the long-term trends of many other industries. For example, statistics on accidents per person-kilometer are readily available to chart progress in automobile and highway design as well as aircraft and airport design. Even within the computer industry, we have well-known measures of the progress in some system components such as density and price of memory chips and speed of CPUs.

In contrast, usability has not been measured over the years, and it is not even certain that such measures would have been meaningful, had they been made. Given that the user populations have expanded dramatically from the early computers to mainframes to personal computers, it would not be reasonable to use the same metric to compare a 1950s line-oriented interface with a 1970s full-screen interface with a 1990s graphical user interface, since each interface hopefully had been designed with the user population and the typical tasks of that year in mind. Happ [1994] uses the term "usability foresight" to refer to the potential for extending these changes in usability to predict future interface needs: if, for example, we expect the changing user population to require learning times of no more than 10% of the current learning time for a certain system, we can start speculating about the kinds of interface changes that would be needed to achieve that goal.

In spite of the lack of concrete data, there are no doubts that usability has improved over the years to the extent that a broader and less technically inclined part of the population can now learn to use computers. Unfortunately, it does not seem that user productivity has improved to the same extent that system learnability has [Landauer 1994]. Users can certainly do *more* things with computers than they ever could, and the richness of the interfaces has increased from zero and one dimensions to two and a half and three, but users may not always get their job done much faster as a result.

A side effect of the increased emphasis on usability in modern systems and their enhanced user interface capabilities has been to raise users' expectations. Since *some* software has highly polished user interfaces, users have grown to expect decent usability from *all* their systems, and people's patience with poor user interfaces has been reduced. Some shrink-wrap applications are now designed by vendors with a staff of 30 or more crack usability specialists, and users are now judging other interfaces, including internally developed systems, by the standards set by the best of these applications.

One potential opportunity for long-term progress in usability is that new user interface generations can build on the capabilities of earlier generations, while adding new interaction capabilities. For example, graphical user interfaces include textual user interfaces as a special case and may have function keys, command languages, and hierarchical menus to the extent that these interaction techniques are better than direct manipulation for part of an interface. Thus, a new generation of user interfaces need not sacrifice whatever usability has already been achieved. It may not always be possible to transfer research results from the earlier user interface generations without modifications, however, since interaction techniques change by the context in which they are placed.

Table 6 shows a summary of the most important interaction styles discussed in this chapter. It can be seen that several interaction styles are used across multiple generations of user interfaces, though their relative importance may vary. Shneiderman [1991] lists some common sense rules for choosing an appropriate interaction style for a system. For example, systems that involve dealing with data from paper forms should probably be designed using a form fill-in dialogue, and if the user is furthermore expected to be an expert, the interface can be designed as a dense display with multiple fields crammed into as few screens as possible. Unfortunately, it is currently impossible to give very firm rules of this kind. There are too many exceptions, where the detailed characteristics of the domain, the users, or their task dictate other approaches.

Interaction Style	Mainly Used In	Main Characteristics
Batch	Batch processing, email servers	Does not require user intervention, works even when user and computer are in different time or place.
Question–Answer	Line-oriented	Computer controls the user, so suited for casual use.
Command Language	Line-oriented	Easy to edit and reuse command history. A powerful language can support very complex operations.
Function Keys	Full-screen, WIMP	Fast entry of a few standard commands, but limited flexibility.
Form Fill-in	Full-screen, WIMP	Many fields can be seen and edited at once.
Menus	Full-screen, WIMP, Telephone-based interfaces	Frees the user from remembering options, at cost of potentially being slow or having confusing hierarchy.
Direct Manipulation	WIMP, Virtual reality	User in control. Enables metaphors from real world. Good for graphics.
Non-Command	Future systems, Virtual reality	The user is freed to concentrate on the domain and need not control the computer. Computer monitors users and interprets their actions, so suited for cases where misinterpretations are unlikely or without serious consequences.
Natural Language	Future systems	Ideally, allows unconstrained input to handle frequently changing problems.

Table 6 *Summary of the main interaction styles.*

Natural-language interfaces are not discussed much in this book. Certainly, these interfaces have their own usability problems and need usability engineering efforts to be successful, and even a computer with perfect natural-language capabilities could be hard to use. Just consider how difficult it sometimes is to get another human to understand the way you want things done. Also, of course, a natural-language interface restricted to a single or a few languages would have poor international usability as it is more difficult for people to construct complete sentences in a foreign language than to type a few command keywords or to pick from a menu. The main reason natural language is not considered in greater detail in this book is that it is still not a practical interaction style except for some constrained database applications. In any case, there is no reason to believe that the usability engineering methods for natural language would be much different from those needed for traditional interfaces. For example, the "Wizard of Oz" method (see page 96) would seem ideal for the testing of preliminary prototypes.

Chapter 4

The Usability Engineering Lifecycle

Usability engineering is not a one-shot affair where the user interface is fixed up before the release of a product. Rather, usability engineering is a set of activities that ideally take place throughout the lifecycle of the product, with significant activities happening at the early stages before the user interface has even been designed. The need to have multiple usability engineering stages supplement each other was recognized early in the field, though not always followed on development projects [Gould and Lewis 1985].

Usability cannot be seen in isolation from the broader corporate product development context where one-shot projects are fairly rare. Indeed, usability applies to the development of entire product families and extended projects where products are released in several versions over time. In fact, this broader context only strengthens the arguments for allocating substantial usability engineering resources as early as possible, since design decisions made for any given product have ripple effects due to the need for subsequent products and versions to be backward compatible. Consequently, some usability engineering specialists [Grudin *et al.* 1987] believe that "human factors involvement with a particular product may ultimately have its greatest impact on future product releases." Planning for future versions is also a prime reason to follow up the release of a product with field studies of its actual use.

1. Know the user
   a. Individual user characteristics
   b. The user's current and desired tasks
   c. Functional analysis
   d. The evolution of the user and the job
2. Competitive analysis
3. Setting usability goals
   a. Financial impact analysis
4. Parallel design
5. Participatory design
6. Coordinated design of the total interface
7. Apply guidelines and heuristic analysis
8. Prototyping
9. Empirical testing
10. Iterative design
    a. Capture design rationale
11. Collect feedback from field use

Table 7 *The stages of the usability engineering lifecycle model.*

For a company that sells software or other products on the open market, the usability of each product will contribute to the company's general reputation as a quality supplier, and just a single product with poor usability can cause severe damage to the sales of the entire product family.

Table 7 shows a summary of the lifecycle stages discussed in this chapter. It is important to note that a usability engineering effort can still be successful even if it does not include every possible refinement at all of the stages. Section 4.13, *Prioritizing Usability Activities*, on page 112 contains a discussion of how to choose usability methods under varying levels of resource constraints.

The lifecycle model emphasizes that one should not rush straight into design. The least expensive way for usability activities to influence a product is to do as much as possible before design is started, since it will then not be necessary to change the design to comply with the usability recommendations. Also, usability work done before the system is designed may make it possible to avoid developing unnecessary features. Several of the pre-design usability activities might be considered part of a market research or product planning process as well, and may sometimes be performed by marketing groups. However, traditional market research does not usually employ all the methods needed to properly inform usability design, and the results are often poorly communicated to developers. But there should be no need for duplicate efforts if management successfully integrates usability and marketing activities [Wichansky *et al.* 1988]. One outcome of such integration could be the consideration of product usability attributes as features to be used by marketing to differentiate the product. Also, marketing efforts based on usability studies can sell the product on the basis of its benefits as perceived by users (*what* it can do that they want) rather than its features as perceived by developers (*how* does it do it).

4.1   Know the User

The first step in the usability process is to study the intended users and use of the product. At a minimum, developers should visit a customer site so that they have a feel for how the product will be used. Individual user characteristics and variability in tasks are the two factors with the largest impact on usability, so they need to be studied carefully. When considering users, one should keep in mind that they often include installers, maintainers, system administrators, and other support staff in addition to the people who sit at the keyboard. The concept of "user" should be defined to include everybody whose work is affected by the product in some way, including the users of the system's end product or output even if they never see a single screen.

Even though "know the user" is the most basic of all usability guidelines, it is often difficult for developers to get access to users. Grudin [1990b, 1991a and b] analyzes the obstacles to such access, including

- The need for the development company to protect its developers from being known to customers, since customers may bypass established technical support organizations and call developers directly, sidetracking them from their main job.
- The reluctance of sales representatives to let anybody else from the company talk to "their" customers, fearing that the devel-

opers or usability people may offend the customer or create dissatisfaction with the current generation of products.

• User organizations only making users available for a short time, either because they are highly paid executives or because they are unionized and dislike being studied.

All these issues are real and need to be addressed when trying to get to "know the user." No universal solutions are available, except to recommend an explicit effort to get direct access to representative users and not be satisfied with indirect access and hearsay. It is amazing how much time is wasted on certain development projects by arguing over what users *might* be like or what they *may* want to do. Instead of discussing such issues in a vacuum, it is much better (and actually less time-consuming) to get hard facts from the users themselves.

Individual User Characteristics

It is necessary to know the class of people who will be using the system. In some situations this is easy since it is possible to identify these users as concrete individuals. This is the case when the product is going to be used in a specific department in a particular company. For other products, users may be more widely scattered such that it is possible to visit only a few, representative customers. Alternatively, the products might be aimed toward the entire population or a very large subset.

By knowing the users' work experience, educational level, age, previous computer experience, and so on, it is possible to anticipate their learning difficulties to some extent and to better set appropriate limits for the complexity of the user interface. Certainly one also needs to know the reading and language skills of the users. For example, very young children have no reading ability, so an entirely nontextual interface is required. Also, one needs to know the amount of time users will have available for learning and whether they will have the opportunity for attending training courses: The interface must be made much simpler if users are expected to use it with minimum training.

The users' work environment and social context also need to be known. As a simple example, the use of audible alarms, "beeps," or more elaborate sound effects may not be appropriate for users in open office environments. In a field interview I once did, a secretary complained strongly that she wanted the ability to shut off the beep because she did not want others to think that she was stupid because her computer beeped at her all the time.

A great deal of the information needed to characterize individual users may come from market analysis or from the observational studies one may conduct as part of the task analysis. One may also collect such information directly through questionnaires or interviews. In any case, it is best not to rely totally on written information since new insights are almost always achieved by observing and talking to actual users in their own working environment.

Task Analysis

A task analysis [Diaper 1989a; Fath and Bias 1992; Johnson 1992] is essential as early input to system design. The users' overall goals should be studied as well as how they currently approach the task, their information needs, and how they deal with exceptional circumstances or emergencies. For example, systematic observation of users talking to their clients may reveal input and output needs for a transactions-processing system. Sometimes, interviewing or observing the users' clients or others who interact with them can provide additional task analysis insights [Garber and Grunes 1992].

The users' model of the task should also be identified, since it can be used as a source for metaphors for the user interface (see page 126). Also, seek out and observe especially effective users and user strategies and "workarounds" as hints of what a new system could support. Such "lead users" are often a major source of innovations [von Hippel 1988]. Finally, one should identify the weaknesses of the current situation: points where users fail to achieve goals, spend excessive time, or are made uncomfortable. These weaknesses present opportunities for improvements in the new product.

A typical outcome of a task analysis is a list of all the things users want to accomplish with the system (the goals), all the information they will need to achieve these goals (the preconditions), the steps that need to be performed and the interdependencies between these steps, all the various outcomes and reports that need to be produced, the criteria used to determine the quality and acceptability of these results, and finally the communication needs of the users as they exchange information with others while performing the task or preparing to do so.

When interviewing users for the purpose of collecting task information, it is always a good idea to ask them to show concrete examples of their work products rather than keeping the discussion on an abstract level. Also, it is preferable to supplement such interviews with observations of some users working on real problems, since users will often rationalize their actions or forget about important details or exceptions when they are interviewed.

Often, a task analysis can be decomposed in a hierarchical fashion [Greif 1991], starting with the larger tasks and goals of the organization and breaking each of them down into smaller subtasks, that can again be further subdivided. Typically, each time a user says, "then I do *this*," an interviewer could ask two questions: "*Why* do you do it?" (to relate the activity to larger goals) and "*How* do you do it?" (to decompose the activity into subtasks that can be further studied). Other good questions to ask include, "why do you *not* do this in such and such a manner?" (mentioning some alternative approach), "Do errors ever occur when doing this?," and "How do you discover and correct these errors?" [Nielsen *et al.* 1986].

Finally, users should be asked to describe exceptions from their normal work flow. Even though users cannot be expected to remember *all* the exceptions that have ever occurred, and even though it will be impossible to predict all the future exceptions, there is considerable value to having a list indicating the *range* of exceptions that must be accommodated. Users should also be asked for remarkable instances of notable successes and failures, problems, what they liked best and least, what changes they would like, what ideas they have for improvements, and what currently annoys them. Even though not all such suggestions may be followed in the final design, they are a rich source of inspiration.

Functional Analysis

A new computer system should not be designed simply to propagate suboptimal ways of doing things that may have been instituted because of limitations in previous technologies. Therefore, one should not analyze just the way users currently do the task, but also the underlying functional reason for the task: What is it that really needs to be done, and what are merely surface procedures which can, and perhaps should, be changed [Schmidt 1988].

For example, many projects in the *computer-supported cooperative work* (CSCW) field assume that face-to-face interaction is the ultimate in communication and that computers should emulate *physically proximate reality* (PPR) as closely as possible. In contrast, the "beyond being there" approach [Hollan and Stornetta 1992; Brothers *et al.* 1992] separates the needs of human communication from the media through which communication has been achieved so far. Computerized communication tools might be built to take advantage of the strengths of the computer medium, such as asynchronism, anonymity, searchable archives, and automated replies and filters, even if the resulting communication mechanisms do not resemble the way people talk when they are in the same room.

As a more mundane example, initial observations of people reading printed manuals could show them frequently turning pages to move through the document. A naive design of online documentation might take this observation to imply really good and fast paging or scrolling mechanisms. A functional analysis would show that manual users really turn pages this much to find specific information, but they have a hard time locating the correct page. Based on this analysis, one could design an online documentation interface that first allowed users to specify their search needs, then used an outline of the document to show locations with high search scores, and finally allowed users to jump directly to these locations, highlighting their search terms to make it easier to judge the relevance of the information [Egan *et al.* 1989].

Of course, there is a limit to how drastically one can change the way users currently approach their task, so the functional analysis should be coordinated with a task analysis.

The Evolution of the User

Users will not stay the same. Using the system changes the users, and as they change they will use the system in new ways. Carroll and Rosson [1991] refer to this dialectic phenomenon as the "coevolution of tasks and artifacts." For example, spreadsheets were initially invented as aids for calculation, but having such a malleable computerized medium available encouraged users to integrate noncalculation data in a spreadsheet. Users have often been known to use spreadsheets for databases [Nielsen *et al.* 1986], and these and other uses have led spreadsheet vendors to include noncalculation features in later versions.

It is impossible to forecast these changes completely as users will always discover new uses for computer systems after some period of use, but a flexible design will stand a better chance of supporting these new uses. Try to make an educated guess based on your knowledge about how other users have changed in the past. One way of getting such knowledge is through the post-deployment field studies discussed on page 109.

A typical change is that users become experts after some time and want interaction shortcuts (sometimes called accelerators). For example, a business graphics package might lead novice users through a series of question–answer screens to specify the main characteristics of the main types of charts, but expert users will probably want to be able to change the charts by direct manipulation and maybe even to be given access to a kind of specialized programming language for the construction of graphics. It is important not to design just for the way users will use the system in the first short period after its release.

4.2   Competitive Analysis

As discussed in Section 4.8, prototyping is an important part of the usability process, and existing, perhaps competing, products are often the best prototypes we can get of our own product [Byrne 1989]. It is desirable to analyze existing products heuristically according to established usability guidelines and to perform empirical user tests with these products. A competing product is already fully implemented and can therefore be tested very easily [Bachman 1989]. Also, the developers of the existing systems often have put a reasonable amount of effort into their development process so that the competing products may work fairly well. This again means that user testing with existing products can be more realistic than a test of other prototypes. Users can perform real tasks on the competing system, making it possible to learn how well its functionality and interaction techniques support the kinds of tasks the planned new product is expected to support based on the initial analysis of the intended users.

If several competing products are available for analysis, one can furthermore perform a comparative analysis of their differing approaches to the various user interface design issues for the kind of product being studied. This will provide ideas for the new design and will give a list of ad hoc guidelines for approaches that seem to work and those that should be avoided. Also, reading trade press reviews can provide some insights into the usability characteristics and different approaches of a large number of competing products. Such reviews should be complemented with more thorough and principled analysis and testing of a smaller number of important products. Sometimes, competitive analysis will involve the study of non-computer interfaces. For example, an electronic reference book project should first studying how people use traditional printed encyclopedia [Marchionini 1989].

Note that a competitive analysis does not imply stealing other people's copyrighted user interface designs. One would hope to be able to do better than the previous designs as a result of the analyses of their strengths and weaknesses.

4.3 Goal Setting

As discussed in Chapter 2, usability is not a one-dimensional attribute of a system. Usability comprises several components that can sometimes conflict. Normally, not all usability aspects can be given equal weight in a given design project, so you will have to make your priorities clear on the basis of your analysis of the users and their tasks. For example, learnability would be especially important if new employees were constantly being brought in on a temporary basis, and the ability of infrequent users to return to the system would be especially important for a reconfiguration utility that was used once every three or four months.

As also discussed in Chapter 2, the different usability parameters can be operationalized and expressed in measurable ways. Before starting the design of a new interface, it is important to discuss the usability metrics of interest to the project and to specify the goals of the user interface in terms of measured usability [Chapanis and Budurka 1990]. One may not always have the resources available to collect statistically reliable measures of the usability metrics specified as goals, but it is still better to have some idea of the level of usability to be strived for.

For each usability attribute of interest, several different levels of performance can be specified as part of a goal-setting process [Whiteside *et al.* 1988]. One would at least specify the minimum level which would be acceptable for release of the product, but a more detailed goal specification can also include the planned level one is aiming for as well as the current level of performance. Additionally, it can help to list the current value of the usability attribute as measured for existing or competing interfaces, and one can also list the theoretically best possible value, even though this value will typically not be attained. Figure 7 shows one possible notation, called a *usability goal line*, for representing the range of specification levels for one usability goal.

In the example in Figure 7, the number of user errors per hour is counted. When using the current system, users make an average of 4.5 errors per hour, and the planned number of user errors is 2.0 per hour. Furthermore, the theoretical optimum is obviously to have no errors at all. If the new interface is measured at anything between 1.0 and 3.0 user errors per hour, it will be considered on target with respect to this usability goal. A performance in the interval of 3–5 would be a danger signal that the usability goal was

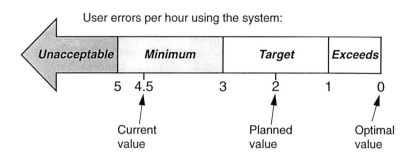

Figure 7 *An example of a usability goal line in a notation similar to that used by Rideout [1991].*

not met, even though the new interface could still be released on a temporary basis since a minimal level of usability had been achieved. It would then be necessary to develop a plan to reduce user errors in future releases. Finally, more than 5.0 user errors per hour would make this particular product sufficiently unusable to make a release unacceptable.

Usability goals are reasonably easy to set for new versions of existing systems or for systems that have a clearly defined competitor on the market. The minimum acceptable usability would normally be equal to the current usability level, and the target usability could be derived as an improvement that was sufficiently large to induce users to change systems. For completely new systems without any competition, usability goals are much harder to set. One approach is to define a set of sample tasks and ask several usability specialists how long it "ought" to take users to perform them. One can also get an idea of the minimum acceptable level by asking the users, but unfortunately users are notoriously fickle in this respect; countless projects have failed because developers believed users' claims about what they wanted, only to find that the resulting product was not satisfactory in real use.

Financial Impact Analysis

At about the same time as usability goals are being specified, it is a good idea to make an analysis of the financial impact of the usability of the system. Such an analysis involves estimating the number of users who will be using the system, their loaded salaries or other costs, and the approximate time they will be using the system. The cost of the users' time is not just their salary but also other costs, such as various pensions and benefits, employment taxes or fees charged by the government, and general overhead costs like the rent of office space. This total cost will be referred to as the *loaded salary* or *loaded cost* of a user.

Financial impact analyses are easiest to make for software that is being developed in-house or under contract directly from the user organization, as the savings are readily available as true bottom-line benefits. For example, consider the development of a software system for a group of 3,000 specialized staff processing some kind of service orders. If the loaded cost of the technicians is assumed to be $25 per hour, and the technicians can be assumed to be using the system about a third of their working day, we immediately[1] find that the annual financial impact of the user interface is approximately $47,000,000. Furthermore, let us assume that the system is planned for introduction in two years and that it will then be used for four years until it is replaced by a new system or a major redesign. Under these assumptions, the annual impact translates into a total financial impact of $129,000,000, when considering the time value of money and deflating the impact of money spent in future years by 10% per year.[2]

Usability activities that might improve the learnability of the user interface sufficiently to cut down learning-time by one day would be worth $600,000, corresponding to a present value of $500,000. Similarly, usability improvements leading to a 10% increase in user

---

1. By multiplying by 8 hours per day and 236 working days per year.

2. The deflator should be derived from the expected real return from alternative investments. A 10% deflator for the real value of money corresponds to an investment return of 13% per year (the stock market average) minus an inflation rate of 3%. A more elaborate financial model might use a deflator that has not been adjusted for inflation and then increase the annual estimates of various cost categories by their expected rate of increase. This latter approach is more accurate if the increase in salaries and overhead is expected to differ significantly from the inflation rate.

productivity would be worth $4,700,000 per year, or $12,900,000 over four years (again deflating the value of money saved in later years).[3] We would normally find it worthwhile to invest a reasonable amount in usability work in this kind of development project. Also, this calculation makes it clear that productivity improvements would be worth more than learning time savings for this product, assuming that the one day and 10%, respectively, are approximately the magnitude of improvement that can be expected.

In the case of software being developed for sale on the open market, user savings are not directly available as profits for the development organization. Therefore, the financial impact analysis should have two components: an estimate of the impact on the development organization (to help determine the magnitude of the usability budget) and an estimate of the impact on the user organizations (to help prioritize the focus of the available usability resources). Analyses of the financial impact of usability on the development organization should include estimates of revenue loss or enhancements as well as cost estimates like the expense of servicing calls to customer support lines. Unfortunately, specific data about these two aspects is usually considered highly secret proprietary information, since user interfaces now constitute a major aspect of a company's competitive advantage.

Anecdotal evidence indicates that some vendors have found that a product with a usability level below a certain point is simply not worth selling, since one can predict that it will fail in the market. Alternatively, customers may buy the product, but they will then make such excessive demands on the vendor's technical support staff that each sale ends up losing money. One example was an upgrade to a spreadsheet, where the installed base of customers

---

3. Calculations of present value for this example assume that the savings in training costs are realized on the first day after the introduction of the system (that is, 2 years from the present). Productivity savings are realized throughout the year but for simplicity's sake, they are calculated as occurring on a single day half-way through the year. Thus, for example, savings in the system's first year of use are deflated by the compound value of 10% over 2.5 years = 27%.

guaranteed the "success" (in terms of sheer number of sales) of the upgrade. The installation program supplied with the upgrade had such a horrible user interface that the customers needed on average two 20-minute calls to the vendor's toll-free support line before they had succeeded in installing their upgrade. Given that it costs about $20 to service a more typical, 5-minute support call, the installation user interface (which could probably have been fixed with a minimum of usability engineering effort) ended up costing the vendor more than the $70 per user they made selling the upgrade.[4] In general, the need to save on customer support is a driving force for usability engineering in many companies. The median loaded cost of servicing a customer support call was $23.33 according to a 1993 survey of 148 software vendors in the industry newsletter *Soft Letter*.

As an example analysis of the financial impact of a user interface on the customers, assume that you were developing a word processor that is expected to sell one million copies. About half of the users are expected to be secretaries who will be using the word processor about half of their working day, and the other half of the users are expected to be business professionals who will be using the word processor about 10% of their working day. Furthermore, assume that the loaded cost of a secretary is $20 per hour and that the loaded cost of a business professional is $100 per hour. This means that the amount of money spent by users while using the word processor is about $19,000,000,000 annually (calculated at 8 hours per day and 236 working days per year). This amount is an indication of the potential value being influenced by the usability engineer in charge of the word processor's user interface, even though it will never show up on the development organization's budget.

Assume that we are considering the potential benefits from improving the efficiency of the word processor's editing features

---

4. This example also indicates the necessity of paying attention to the total user interface in the usability engineering lifecycle. The spreadsheet itself might have had perfect usability, but the install utility ended up destroying the product.

by 5%. To calculate the savings from such an improvement, we furthermore need to estimate the proportion of the users' time spent editing as opposed to just entering text. Such data should preferably be gathered from field studies or by logging data from instrumented copies of installed versions of previous systems. For the sake of argument, we will assume that 10% of the secretaries' word processor use is editing and that the corresponding proportion for the business professional users is 25%. This means that total annual value of the time spent editing by the users of the word processor is $3,300,000,000, and that the value[5] of a 5% savings would be $165,000,000. Of course, the vendor of the word processor package will not get this money, but there is still *some* value to having the users save $165,000,000, and the usability work that could bring about such savings would be worthy of a larger part of the budget than work on some other feature that might save users no more than a few million dollars.

Much of the information needed for the financial impact analysis should be available from the marketing department. Specifically, they should have data about the current or projected number of users in different markets and perhaps be able to provide estimates of the users' salary levels.

4.4   Parallel Design

It is often a good idea to start the design with a parallel design process, in which several different designers work out preliminary designs [Nielsen *et al.* 1993, 1994]. The goal of parallel design is to explore different design alternatives before one settles on a single approach that can then be developed in further detail and subjected to more detailed usability activities. Figure 8 is a conceptual chart of the relation between parallel and iterative design.

---

5.   In principle, the value of saved time is not the average cost of the employees' time, but the *marginal* value of their time, necessitating the use of a so-called hedonic wage model [Sassone 1987], but for practical purposes one can use average values for the type of rough estimate we are making here.

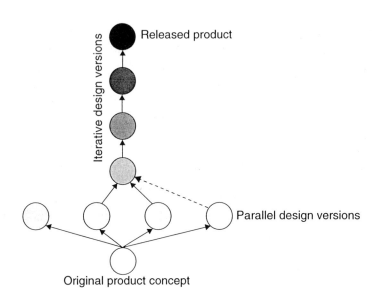

Figure 8 *Conceptual illustration of the relation between parallel and iterative design. Normally, the first prototype would be based on ideas from several of the parallel design sketches.*

Typically, one can have three or four designers involved in parallel design. For critical products, some large computer companies have been known to devote entire teams to developing multiple alternative designs almost to the final product stage, before upper management decided on which version to release. In general, though, it may not be necessary for the designers to spend more than a few hours or at the most one or two days on developing their initial designs. Also, it is normally better to have designers work individually rather than in larger teams, since parallel design only aims at generating rough drafts of the basic design ideas.

In parallel design, it is important to have the designers (or the design teams) work independently, since the goal is to generate as much diversity as possible. Therefore, the designers should not discuss their designs with each other until after they have produced their draft interface designs.

When the designers have completed the draft designs, one will often find that they have approached the problem in at least two drastically different ways that would give rise to fundamentally different user interface models. Even those designers who are basing their designs on the same basic approach almost always have different details in their designs. Usually, it is possible to generate new combined designs after having compared the set of initial designs, taking advantage of the best ideas from each design. If several fundamentally different designs are available, it is best to pursue each of the main lines of design a little further in order to arrive at a small number of prototypes that can be subjected to usability evaluation before the final approach is chosen.

A variant of parallel design is called *diversified parallel design* and is based on asking the different designers to concentrate on different aspects of the design problem. For example, one designer could design an interface that was optimized for novice users, at the same time as another designer designed an interface optimized for expert users and a third designer explored the possibilities of producing en entirely nonverbal interface. By explicitly directing the design approach of each designer, diversified parallel design drives each of these approaches to their limit, leading to design ideas that might never have emerged in a unified design. Of course, some of these diversified design ideas may have to be modified to work in a single, integrated design.

It is especially important to employ parallel design for novel systems where little guidance is available for what interface approaches work the best. For more traditional systems, where competitive products are available, the competitive analysis discussed in Section 4.2 can serve as initial parallel designs, but it might still be advantageous to have a few designers create additional parallel designs to explore further possibilities.

The parallel design method might at first seem to run counter to the principle of cost-effective usability engineering, since most of the design ideas will have to be thrown away without even being implemented. In reality, though, parallel design is a very cheap way of exploring the design space, exactly *because* most of the ideas will not need to be implemented, the way they might be if some of them were not tried until later as part of iterative design. The main financial benefit of parallel design is its parallel nature, which allows several design approaches to be explored at the same time, thus compressing the development schedule for the product and bringing it to market more rapidly. Studies have shown that about a third of the profits are lost when products ship as little as half a year late [House and Price 1991], so anything that can speed up the development process should be worth the small additional cost of designing in parallel rather than in sequence.

4.5 Participatory Design

Even though the advice to "know the user" may have been followed before the start of the design phase, one still cannot know the user sufficiently well to answer all issues that come up in doing the design [Kensing and Munk-Madsen 1993]. Instead of guessing, designers should have access to a pool of representative users after the start of the design phase. It is important to have access to the people who will actually be using the system, and not just to their managers or union representatives. Even well-intentioned managers will often not know the exact issues facing users in their everyday work, and they will normally have different characteristics from the real users in many ways. Elected union leaders may not be typical workers either, and they may also have spent too much time in administration.

Users often raise questions that the development team has not even dreamed of asking. This is especially true with respect to potential mismatches between the users' actual task and the developers' model of the task. Therefore, users should be involved in the design process through regular meetings between designers and users. Users participating in a system design process are sometimes referred to as *subject matter experts*, or SMEs.

Users are not designers, so it is not reasonable to expect them to come up with design ideas from scratch. However, they are very good at reacting to concrete designs they do not like or that will not work in practice. To get full benefits from user involvement, it is necessary to present these suggested system designs in a form the users can understand. Instead of voluminous system specifications, concrete and visible designs, preferably in the form of prototypes, should be employed for this purpose. In early stages of the design where functional prototypes are not yet available, paper mock-ups or simply a few screen designs can be used to prompt user discussion.[6] Even simple, guided discussion can elicit ideas from users.

It is important to realize that participatory design should not just consist of asking users what they want, since users often do not know what they want or what they need, or even what the possibilities are. For example, in one study users were first asked to rate the usefulness of some new features of an editor on the basis of a description of the features and then asked the same question after they had tried out the actual features [Root and Draper 1983]. It turned out that the correlation between the users' ratings before and after actual experience with the features was as low as 0.28, indicating essentially no relation between the two sets of ratings. See also the discussion of the usability slogan, *The User Is Not Always Right*, on page 11.

For larger development projects, thought should be given to periodically refreshing the pool of users who participate in the project since they risk becoming less representative of the average user population as their involvement with system development grows. A user representative who has been to too many design meetings will be steeped in the developers' way of thought and will understand the proposed system structure and possibly have a tendency to accept the rationale for awkward design elements. Fresh users who are brought in later in the project are more likely to question such potential problems since they will not know the history of the design. Furthermore, of course, users are different, so it is dangerous to rely too much on information from a small set of users

---

6. I once gave a presentation to a group of users about a proposed user interface using (then) new terminal technology. They listened politely and did not say anything, until the time when I put a screen dump on the overhead—after which the audience erupted with questions and comments [Nielsen 1987a].

that never changes. On the other hand, there are trade-offs involved in changing user representatives, since one also does not want to spend time explaining the project to new people, so such changes should not be made more than a few times during a project.

4.6   *Coordinating the Total Interface*

Consistency is one of the most important usability characteristics (see Section 5.4 on page 132). Consistency should apply across the different media which form the total user interface, including not just the application screens but also the documentation, the online help system, and any online or videotaped tutorials [Perlman 1989] as well as traditional training classes. For example, in one case studied by Poltrock [1994], training materials described an obsolete way of using an interface because the training department had not been informed about the introduction of a redesigned, and presumably better, interface.

Consistency is not just measured at a single point in time but should apply over successive releases of a product so that new releases are consistent with their predecessors. Also, since very few companies produce only a single product, efforts should be made to promote consistency across entire product families. Corporate user interface standards are one common way of promoting that goal. In spite of the general desirability of consistency, it is obviously not the only desirable usability characteristic, and consistency may sometimes conflict with other interface desiderata [Grudin 1989]. It is necessary to maintain some flexibility so that bad design is not forced upon users for the sake of consistency alone.

To achieve consistency of the total interface it is necessary to have some centralized authority for each development project to coordinate the various aspects of the interface. Typically this coordination can be done by a single person, but on very large projects or to achieve corporate-wide consistency, a committee structure may be more appropriate. Also, interface standards (discussed further in Chapter 8) are an important approach to achieving consistency. In addition to such general standards, a project can develop its own ad hoc standard with elements like a dictionary of the appropriate terminology to be used in all screen designs as well as in the other parts of the total interface.

In addition to formal coordination activities, it is helpful to have a shared culture in the development groups with common understanding of what the user interface should be like. Many aspects of user interface design (especially the dynamics) are hard to specify in written documents but can be fairly easily understood from looking at existing products following a given interface style. Actually, prototyping also helps achieve consistency, since the prototype is an early statement of the kind of interface toward which the project is aiming. Having an explicit instance of parts of the design makes the details of the design more salient for developers and encourages them to follow similar principles in subsequent design activities [Bellantone and Lanzetta 1991].

Furthermore, consistency can be increased through technological means such as code sharing or a constraining development environment. When several products use the same code for parts of their user interface, then those parts of the interfaces automatically will be consistent. Even if identical code cannot be used, it is possible to constrain developers by providing development tools and libraries that encourage user interface consistency by making it easiest to implement interfaces that follow given guidelines [Tognazzini 1989; Wiecha *et al.* 1989].

4.7 Guidelines and Heuristic Evaluation

Guidelines list well-known principles for user interface design which should be followed in the development project. In any given project, several different levels of guidelines should be used: *general guidelines* applicable to all user interfaces, *category-specific guidelines* for the kind of system being developed (e.g., guidelines for window-based administrative data processing or for voice interfaces accessed through telephone keypads), and *product-*

specific guidelines for the individual product. All these guidelines can be used as background for heuristic evaluation as discussed in Section 5.11 on page 155.

For example, a general guideline could be to "provide feedback" to the user about the system's state and actions. This general advice could be made more specific in a category-specific guideline for graphical user interfaces: Ensure that the main objects of interest to the user are visible on the screen and that their most important attributes are shown. Finally, this guideline could be further developed into a product-specific guideline for the design of a graphical file system: Have each file and subdirectory represented by an icon and use different icon shapes to represent different classes of objects (data files, executable files, and subdirectories). It would then be possible to check that each aspect of the file system complied with this latter rule.

As another example, the same general guideline, "provide feedback," could be applied to hypermedia navigation to recommend that users be informed about the transition that takes place when they move from one node to another. Experience with existing products or reading of the research literature [Merwin *et al.* 1990] could then lead to a further ad hoc guideline for a particular hypertext document stating that an animated visual effect should be used to signify navigational transitions rather than having an instantaneous change to the destination screen.

The difference between standards and guidelines is that a standard specifies how the interface should appear to the user, whereas a set of guidelines provides advice about the usability characteristics of the interface. Standards are discussed further in Chapter 8 and have interface consistency as one of their major objectives. Hopefully a given standard will follow most of the traditional usability guidelines so that the interfaces designed according to the standard will also be as usable as possible. For example, a guideline may state that users should always be able to back out from any undesired system state. One standard might instantiate that general guideline by specifying that an undo command should always be available and that it should be shown as an icon at the top right of the screen. Another standard might follow the same guideline by returning to the previous system state whenever the user hits the escape key.

Several very extensive collections of general user interface guide-lines exist, including

- [Brown 1988] with 302 guidelines
- [Marshall *et al.* 1987] with 162 guidelines
- [Mayhew 1992] with 288 guidelines
- [Smith and Mosier 1986] with 944 guidelines

It is thus normally possible to rely on the international user inter-face community for general guidelines, whether expressed individ-ually in research papers or collected in larger guidelines reports. Chapter 5 in this book provides a short list of the most important general guidelines. Some category-specific guidelines can also be found in the research literature, but they are also often a product of corporate memory, to the extent that lessons from previous projects are generalized and made available to future projects. Finally, product-specific guidelines are often developed as part of indi-vidual projects as project members gain a better understanding of the special usability aspects of their system. Such understanding can be gathered early on through competitive analysis as discussed on page 78, and additional insights typically come from user testing of prototypes of the new system.

4.8   Prototyping

One should not start full-scale implementation efforts based on early user interface designs. Instead, early usability evaluation can be based on prototypes of the final systems that can be developed much faster and much more cheaply, and which can thus be changed many times until a better understanding of the user inter-face design has been achieved.

In traditional models of software engineering most of the develop-ment time is devoted to the refinement of various intermediate

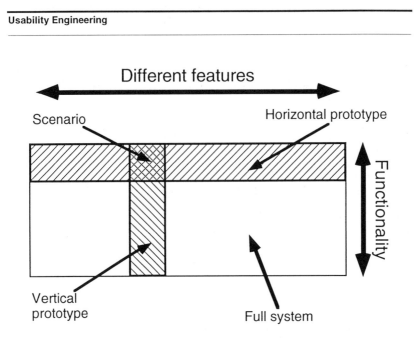

Figure 9 *The two dimensions of prototyping: Horizontal prototyping keeps the features but eliminates depth of functionality, and vertical prototyping gives full functionality for a few features.*

work products, and executable programs are produced at the last possible moment. A problem with this "waterfall" approach is that there will then be no user interface to test with real users until this last possible moment, since the "intermediate work products" do not explicitly separate out the user interface in a prototype with which users can interact. Experience also shows that it is not possible to involve the users in the design process by showing them abstract specifications documents, since they will not understand them nearly as well as concrete prototypes.

The entire idea behind prototyping is to save on the time and cost to develop something that can be tested with real users. These savings can only be achieved by somehow reducing the prototype compared with the full system: either cutting down on the number of features in the prototype or reducing the level of functionality of the features such that they *seem* to work but do not actually *do* anything. These two dimensions are illustrated in Figure 9.

Cutting down on the number of features is called *vertical prototyping* since the result is a narrow system that does include in-depth functionality, but only for a few selected features. A vertical prototype can thus only test a limited part of the full system, but it will be tested in depth under realistic circumstances with real user tasks. For example, for a test of a videotex system, in-depth functionality would mean that a user would actually access a database with some real data from the information providers.

Reducing the level of functionality is called *horizontal prototyping* since the result is a surface layer that includes the entire user interface to a full-featured system but with no underlying functionality. A horizontal prototype is a simulation [Life *et al.* 1990] of the interface where no real work can be performed. In the videotex example, this would mean that users should be able to execute all navigation and search commands but without retrieving any real information as a result of these commands [Nielsen 1987a]. Horizontal prototyping makes it possible to test the entire user interface, even though the test is of course somewhat less realistic, since users cannot perform any real tasks on a system with no functionality. The main advantages of horizontal prototypes are that they can often be implemented fast with the use of various prototyping and screen design tools and that they can be used to assess how well the entire interface "hangs together" and feels as a whole.

Finally, one can reduce both the number of features and the level of functionality to arrive at a scenario that is only able to simulate the user interface as long as the test user follows a previously planned path. Scenarios are extremely easy and cheap to build, while at the same time not being particularly realistic. Scenarios are discussed further on page 99.

In addition to reducing the proportion of the system that is implemented, prototypes can be produced faster by:

- Placing less emphasis on the efficiency of the implementation. For example, it will not matter how much disk space the prototype uses since it will only be used for a short time. Similarly, test users may be able to cope with slow response times that would never be acceptable in the final product. Note, however, that response times are an important aspect of usability and that test users may get very frustrated and make errors if the prototype is *too* slow. Of course, efficiency measures of the users' performance will be invalid if the prototype slows them down too much, so inefficient prototypes are better suited for early evaluation of interface concepts than for measurement studies.

- Accepting less reliable or poorer quality code. Even though bugs and crashes do distract users during testing, they can often be compensated for by the experimenter.

- Using simplified algorithms that cannot handle all the special cases (such as leap years) that normally require a disproportionately large programming effort to get right.

- Using a human expert operating behind the scenes to take over certain computer operations that would be too difficult to program. This approach is often referred to as the *Wizard of Oz technique* after the "pay no attention to that man behind the curtain" scene in this story. Basically, the user interacts normally with the computer, but the user's input is not relayed directly to the program. Instead, the input is transmitted to the "wizard" who, using another computer, transforms the user's input into an appropriate format. A famous early Wizard of Oz study was the "listening typewriter" [Gould *et al.* 1983] simulation of a speech recognition interface where the user's spoken input was typed into a word processor by a human typist located in another room.[7] When setting up a Wizard of Oz simulation, experience with previously implemented systems is helpful in order to place realistic bounds on the Wizard's "abilities" [Maulsby *et al.* 1993].

- Using a different computer system than the eventual target platform. Often, one will have a computer available that is faster or otherwise more advanced than the final system and which can therefore support more flexible prototyping tools and require less programming tricks to achieve the necessary response times.

- Using low-fidelity media [Virzi 1989] that are not as elaborate as the final interface but still represent the essential nature of the

---

7. Dye *et al.* [1990] survey additional simulations of listening typewriters.

interaction. For example, a prototype hypermedia system could use scanned still images instead of live video for illustrations.

- Using fake data and other content. For example, a prototype of a hypermedia system that will include heavy use of video could use existing video material, even though it did not exactly match the topic of the text, in order to get a feel for the interaction techniques needed to deal with live images. A similar technique is used in the advertising industry, where so-called ripomatics are used as rudimentary television commercials with existing shots from earlier commercials to demonstrate concepts to clients before they commit to pay for the shooting of new footage.

- Using paper mock-ups instead of a running computer system. Such mock-ups are usually based on printouts of screen designs, dialog boxes, pop-up menus, etc., that have been drawn up in some standard graphics or desktop publishing package. They are made into functioning prototypes by having a human "play computer" and find the next screen or dialog element from a big pile of paper whenever the user indicates some action. This human needs to be an expert in the way the program is intended to work since it is otherwise difficult to keep track of the state of the simulated computer system and find the appropriate piece of paper to respond to the user's stated input.

  Paper mock-ups have the further advantage that they can be shown to larger groups on overhead projectors [Rowley and Rhoades 1992] and used in conditions where computers may not be available, such as customer conference rooms. Portable computers with screen projection attachments confer some of the same advantages to computerized prototypes, but also increase the risk of something going wrong.

- Relying on a completely imaginary prototype where the experimenter describes a possible interface to the user orally, posing a series of "what if (the interface did this or that) . . ." questions as the user steps though an example task. This verbal prototyping technique has been called "forward scenario simulation" [Cordingley 1989] and is more akin to interviews or brainstorming than a true prototyping technique.

Obviously, several prototyping techniques can be combined either in one, especially cheap prototype, or as alternative prototypes, each exploring one aspect of the usability of the total system. For example, one could create one prototype hypermedia interface with scanned still images of the actual topic material, and another prototype interface with "ripomatic" live video from an existing system on another topic. The still-image prototype could then be used to test the integration of text and images to support learning the domain of the hyperdocument, and the live-video prototype could be used to test interaction mechanisms for controlling the time-variant media, such as super–fast-forwarding as a way to scan a long video clip in a short amount of time. Of course, one would ultimately have to produce a single, integrated prototype with domain-specific live video to test the integration of text and video, but that more expensive version could be put off while the cheaper prototypes were used to clean up the interface and help decide the types of new video material one would need to film.

Special prototyping tools [Hix and Schulman 1991] and languages are a major means of fast implementation of user interface proto-types. In addition to specialized prototyping tools, fast prototyping is often achieved by the use of hypertext systems [Hartson and Smith 1991; Nielsen 1989a; Young *et al.* 1990], courseware authoring tools, database systems [Lee *et al.* 1990], so-called fourth-generation application generators, specialized screen generator tools, and the features some spreadsheets have for constructing general user interfaces as a front-end to an underlying spreadsheet.

Prototypes may sometimes be used for a special form of participa-tory design called *interactive prototyping*, where the prototype is developed and modified on the fly as a test user comments on its weak spots. If a crack programmer is available and a flexible inter-face construction system is used, such interactive prototyping can be a powerful experience for the users who get the immediate grat-ification of seeing their design suggestions implemented. Also, the design may proceed rapidly as multiple variations are tested and modified in a single test session.

Unfortunately, reality is often less ideal, since even a true wizard programmer will often make mistakes when hacking code in real time. Programming errors and system difficulties will sidetrack the test session from the focus on the user's task and the interface, and the user may feel severely alienated by the many extra windows popping up for split-second editing by the programmer. These problems may be avoided by using paper mock-ups for interactive prototyping sessions and allow the users to modify the paper designs. One such technique is PICTIVE (Plastic Interface for Collaborative Technology Initiatives through Video Exploration) [Muller 1991, 1992] where designs are put together as multiple layers of sticky notes and overlays that can be changed by simple colored pens. A final PICTIVE design may be somewhat of a mess of loose paper and plastic, which is why the two last characters of the acronym imply using a videotape of the design session to convey the result to the implementers. PICTIVE is especially suited for prototyping activities carried out as part of a participatory design process since the low-tech nature of the materials make them equally accessible to users and to developers.

A prototype is a form of design specification and is often used as a major way of communicating the final design to developers. Unfortunately, the prototype can be *over*specified in some aspects that are not really intended to be part of the design. Whenever something is made concrete, there is a need to instantiate a multitude of representational details that might not have been explicitly designed by anybody. For example, a screen design will have to use certain colors and fonts, even though the designer's focus may have been on the wording and positioning of the dialogue elements. Basically, one needs to be aware that not every aspect of the prototype should be replicated in the final system, and the designers should inform developers about which aspects of the prototype are intentional and which are arbitrary.

Scenarios

Scenarios are the ultimate minimalist prototype in that they describe a single interaction session without any flexibility for the user. As such, they combine the limitations of both horizontal prototypes (users cannot interact with real data) and vertical prototypes (users cannot move freely through the system).

The term "scenario" has seen widespread use in the user interface community with slightly different meanings [Campbell 1992; Karat and Karat 1992]. Carroll and Rosson [1990] give examples of the term in at least seven different meanings. Therefore, I will try to clarify the terminology by the following definition [Nielsen 1990d]:

A scenario is an encapsulated description of

- an individual *user*
- using a specific set of computer *facilities*
- to achieve a specific *outcome*
- under specified *circumstances*
- over a certain *time interval* (this in contrast to simple static collections of screens and menus: The scenario explicitly includes a time dimension of what happens when).

As such, scenarios have two main uses: First, scenarios can be used during the design of a user interface as a way of expressing and understanding the way users eventually will interact with the future system. Second, scenarios can be used during early evaluation of a user interface design to get user feedback without the expense of constructing a running prototype.

For example, a scenario for the use of an automated teller machine (ATM) might read as follows for used during the design phase:

1. The user approaches the machine and inserts a bank card. No matter what side is up, the machine reads the card correctly.
2. The machine asks the user to input a four-digit personal identification number, and the user does so using the numeric keypad.
3. The machine presents the user with a menu of four options, "withdraw $100," "withdraw other amounts," "make a deposit," and "other transactions." There is a button next to each of the menu options.
4. The user presses the button for "withdraw $100," and the machine pays out that amount, deducting it from the user's account. If the user has more than one account tied into the bank card, the amount is deducted from the account with the largest balance.

5. The machine returns the bank card to the user.

This scenario immediately raises some questions for the design of the user interface to this machine. For example, is $100 the best amount to have available as a single-button choice?[8] Is it even a good idea to have this accelerated option for a pay-out at a single push of a button, or should the user always be asked to specify the account in case there are several possibilities? And so on. In general, scenario descriptions are good tools in early design stages because they can be generated and edited before the user interface has been fully designed [Carroll and Rosson 1992]. Scenarios describing possible uses of envisioned future systems are also helpful for early participatory design exercises, since users will find it easier to relate to the task-oriented nature of the scenarios than to the abstract, and often function-oriented, nature of systems specifications.

Scenarios can also be used for user testing if they are developed with slightly more detail than a pure narrative. In the previous example, it would be possible to make mock-up drawings of the ATM screens with the buttons and menus, and present them to users, asking them to "use" the screens to withdraw money, and asking them what they would think should happen in each step.

Elaborate scenarios are sometimes produced in the form of "day-in-the-life" videotapes [Vertelney 1989]. These videos show enactments of "users" (actors) interacting with a simulated system in the course of their daily activities. Because the interactions are shown on video, the simulated system can be produced using all kinds of special effects and can be made to look quite sophisticated [Dubberly and Mitsch 1987]. These videos can then be shown to users; for example, to prompt discussions in focus groups.

---

8. One way of empirically answering this question would be to analyze the bank's database of previous ATM withdrawals. If it turned out that most withdrawals were for the amount of $50, then the $100 should be changed to $50.

4.9   *Interface Evaluation*

The most basic advice with respect to interface evaluation is simply to *do it*, and especially to conduct some user testing. The benefits of employing some reasonable usability engineering methods to evaluate a user interface rather than releasing it without evaluation are much larger than the incremental benefits of using exactly the right methods for a given project.

Whitefield *et al.* [1991] provide a classification of evaluation methods on two dimensions: whether or not real users are involved and whether or not the interface has actually been implemented. One would certainly expect the best results from testing real users and real systems, but doing so may not always be feasible. The prototyping methods described above provide a means of performing evaluations early enough to influence a project while it can still change direction, and the heuristic evaluation method discussed in Chapter 5 allows you to assess usability without the expense of a user test.

User testing is covered in more detail in Chapter 6.

Severity Ratings

From whatever evaluation methods are used, a major result will be a list of the usability problems in the interface as well as hints for features to support successful user strategies. It is normally not feasible to solve all the problems, so one will need to prioritize them. Priorities are best based on experimental data about the impact of the problems on user performance (e.g., how many people will experience the problem and how much time each of them will waste because of it), but sometimes it is necessary to rely on intuitions only.

Severity ratings are usually gathered by sending a group of usability specialists a list of the usability problems discovered in the interface and asking them to rate the severity of each problem. Sometimes, the severity raters are given access to use the system while making their estimates, and sometimes they are asked to judge the problems based only on written description. Note that the latter approach is possible because the severity raters are supposed to be usability specialists. They should therefore be able to visualize the interface based on the written description (and possibly some screen dumps) in a way that regular users would normally not be able to do. Typically, evaluators need only spend about 30 minutes to provide their severity ratings, though more time may of course be needed if the list of usability problems is extremely long. It is important to note that each usability specialist should provide his or her individual severity ratings independently of the other evaluators.

Unfortunately, severity ratings derived purely by subjective judgment from usability specialists are not very reliable. People have too different opinions about usability. I therefore recommend that you never rely on severity ratings from any single usability specialist (especially not yourself!). Instead, collect ratings from several independent evaluators. Even with just three to four evaluators, the mean of their ratings is much better than the ratings from any single one of them. In one case study, the probability for getting within ±0.5 rating unit from the true severity of a problem on a 5-point rating scale was only 55% with ratings from a single usability specialist, but 95% with the mean of ratings from 4 independent specialists [Nielsen 1994b].

Two common approaches to severity ratings are either to have a single scale or to use a combination of several orthogonal scales. A single rating scale for the severity of usability problems might be

0 = this is not a usability problem at all

1 = cosmetic problem only—need not be fixed unless extra time is available on project

2 = minor usability problem—fixing this should be given low priority

3 = major usability problem—important to fix, so should be given high priority

4 = usability catastrophe—imperative to fix this before product can be released

		Proportion of users experiencing the problem	
		Few	*Many*
Impact of problem on the users who experience it	*Small*	Low severity	Medium severity
	Large	Medium severity	High severity

Table 8 *Table to estimate the severity of usability problems based on the frequency with which the problem is encountered by users and the impact of the problems on those users who do encounter it.*

Alternatively, severity can be judged as a combination of the two most important dimensions of a usability problem: how many users can be expected to have the problem, and the extent to which those users who do have the problem are hurt by it. A simple example of such a rating scheme is given in Table 8. Of course, both dimensions in the table can be estimated at a finer resolution, using more categories than the two shown here for each dimension. Both the proportion of users experiencing a problem and the impact of the problem can be measured directly in user testing. A fairly large number of test users would be needed to measure reliably the frequency and impact of rare usability problems, but from a practical perspective, these problems are less important than more commonly occurring usability problems, so it is normally acceptable to have lower measurement quality for rare problems.

If no user test data is available, the frequency and impact of each problem can be estimated heuristically by usability specialists, but such estimates are probably best when made on the basis of at least a small number of user observations.

One can add a further severity dimension by judging whether a given usability problem will be a problem only the first time it is encountered or whether it will persistently bother users. For example, consider a set of pull-down menus where all the menus are indicated by single words in the menubar except for a single menu that is indicated by a small icon (as, for example, the Apple menu on the Macintosh). Novice users of such systems can often be observed not even trying to pull down this last menu, simply because they do not realize that the icon is a menu heading. As soon as somebody shows the users that there is a menu under the icon (or if they read the manual), they immediately learn to overcome this small inconsistency and have no problems finding the last menu in future use of the system. This problem is thus not a persistent usability problem and would normally be considered less severe than a problem that also reduced the usability of the system for experienced users.

4.10 Iterative Design

Based on the usability problems and opportunities disclosed by the empirical testing, one can produce a new version of the interface. Some testing methods such as thinking aloud provide sufficient insight into the nature of the problems to suggest specific changes to the interface in many cases. Log files of user interaction sequences often help by showing where the user paused or otherwise wasted time, and what errors were encountered most frequently. It often also helps if one is able to understand the underlying cause of the usability problem by relating it to established usability principles such as those discussed in Chapter 5, or by using a formal classification scheme for different categories of problems [Booth 1990]. In other cases alternative potential solutions need to be designed based solely on knowledge of usability guidelines, and it may be necessary to test several possible solutions before making a decision. Familiarity with the design options, insight gained from watching users, creativity, and luck are all needed at this point.

Houde [1992] presents an interesting case study of iterative design of a graphical user interface for the manipulation of three-dimensional objects on a two-dimensional computer screen. One of the issues that was addressed in the iterative design was the design of cursors and handles for movement and rotation. The initial design used a single picture of a grasping hand, but users were soon seen to be disturbed by having the cursor seem to grasp empty air next to the object they wanted to move rather than the object itself. The second iteration replaced the static image of the cursor with an active area on each movable object, such that a customized picture of a hand grasping the object in an appropriate manner for the object would appear when the user clicked in the active area. Unfortunately, the concept of an active area frustrated users who had to click all over the objects to find the spot where the picture of the grabbing hand would appear. The third iteration therefore introduced multiple customized hands that would appear on an object when it was selected. Users could then move these hands as handles to manipulate the object. Again, user testing indicated problems, this time because the way people would want to use hands to move objects was very individual and would depend on the shape of the object (for example, lifting a lamp would be done differently than lifting a chair). Finally, the fourth, successful, solution was to surround each selected object by a wire-frame bounding box and attach the hands to the box. Because of the regular shape of the box, users were less confused about how to use the hands to move it.

As shown by this example, some of the changes made to solve certain usability problems may fail to solve the problems. A revised design may even introduce new usability problems [Bailey 1993]. This is yet another reason for combining iterative design and evaluation. In fact, it is quite common for a redesign to focus on improving one of the usability parameters (for example, reducing the user's error rate), only to find that some of the changes have adversely impacted other usability parameters (for example, transaction speed).

In some cases, solving a problem may make the interface worse for those users who do not experience the problem. Then a trade-off analysis is necessary as to whether to keep or change the interface, based on a frequency analysis of how many users will have the problem compared to how many will suffer because of the proposed solution. The time and expense needed to fix a particular problem is obviously also a factor in determining priorities. Often, usability problems can be fixed by changing the wording of a menu item or an error message. Other design fixes may involve fundamental changes to the software (which is why they should be discovered as early as possible) and will only be implemented if they are judged to impact usability significantly.

Furthermore, it is likely that additional usability problems appear in repeated tests after the most blatant problems have been corrected. There is no need to test initial designs comprehensively since they will be changed anyway. The user interface should be changed and retested as soon as a usability problem has been detected and understood, so that those remaining problems that have been masked by the initial glaring problems can be found.

I surveyed four projects that had used iterative design and had tested at least three user interface versions [Nielsen 1993b]. The median improvement in usability per iteration was 38%, though with extremely high variability. In fact, in 5 of the 12 iterations studied, there was at least one usability metric that had gotten *worse* rather than better. This result certainly indicates the need to keep iterating past such negative results and to plan for at least three versions, since version two may not be any good. Also, the study showed that considerable additional improvements could be achieved after the first iteration, again indicating the benefits of planning for multiple iterations.

During the iterative design process it may not be feasible to test each successive version with actual users. The iterations can be considered a good way to evaluate design ideas simply by trying them out in a concrete design. The design can then be subjected to heuristic analysis and shown to usability experts and consultants or discussed with expert users (or teachers in the case of learning systems). One should not "waste users" by performing elaborate tests of every single design idea, since test subjects are normally hard to come by and should therefore be conserved for the testing of major iterations. Also, users get "worn out" as appropriate test subjects as they get more experience with the system and stop being representative of novice users seeing the design for the first time. Users who have been involved in participatory design are especially inappropriate as test subjects, since they will be biased.

Capture the Design Rationale

The rationale for the various user interface design decisions can be made explicit and recorded for later reference [Moran and Carroll 1994]. Having access to an audit trail through the design rationale is important during iterative development and during development of any future releases of the product. Since changes to the interface will often have to be made, it is helpful to know the reasons underlying the original design so that important usability principles are not sacrificed to attain a minor objective. Similarly, the design rationale can help technical writers develop documentation and translators develop foreign versions. Furthermore, the design rationale can help in maintaining user interface consistency across successive product versions.

Design rationales can be captured either in traditional written form or in a hypertext [Nielsen 1990a] structure such as the gIBIS system [Conklin and Begeman 1988; Conklin and Yakemovic 1991] with links between alternative design options and the supporting evidence or arguments leading to the choice of one of them. Figure 10 shows an example of a design rationale in hypertext, using a QOC-notation (questions, options, and criteria) similar to that suggested by MacLean *et al.* [1989, 1991a and b]. Future repositories for design rationales may even include video records of design meetings and selected user tests [Hodges *et al.* 1989].

During the development process, a design rationale can also be captured by a low-tech solution on the walls of the design team's meeting room. Karat and Bennett [1990, 1991b] used such a technique by taping notepaper on the walls, using different walls for different perspectives on the design. One wall was used for design sketches, one for design constraints, one for scenarios (cf. page 99), and one for open questions. The scenarios are interaction examples illustrating the flow of specific user actions needed for some result, concentrating on what the user will see, what the user must know, and what the user can do [Karat and Bennett 1991a]. Since design

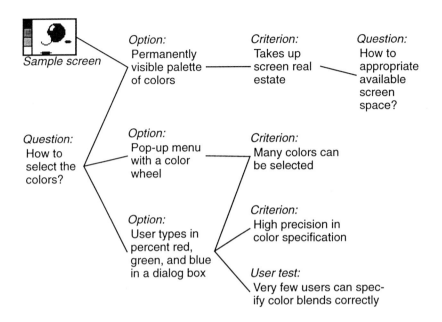

Figure 10 *A partial example of a design rationale for a small part of an interface design for a hypothetical color paint program. The full design rationale might include more sample screens and links to additional design questions like the "How to appropriate..." question hinted at here. The lines might denote hypertext links in an online representation, or they could be supported by simple proximity in a paper document.*

issues are often difficult to understand fully in the abstract, the concreteness of the scenarios adds value to a design rationale.

4.11 Follow-Up Studies of Installed Systems

The main objective of usability work after the release of a product is to gather usability data for the next version and for new, future products: In the same way that existing and competing products were the best prototypes for the product in the initial competitive analysis phase, a newly released product can be viewed as a prototype of future products. Studies of the use of the product in the field assess how real users use the interface for naturally occurring tasks in their real-world working environment and can therefore provide much insight that would not be easily available from laboratory studies.

Sometimes, field feedback can be gathered as part of standard marketing studies on an ongoing basis. As an example, an Australian telephone company collected customer satisfaction data on a routine basis and found that overall satisfaction with the billing service had gone up from 67% to 84% after the introduction of a redesigned bill printout format developed according to usability engineering principles [Sless 1991]. If the trend in customer satisfaction had been the opposite, there would have been reason to doubt the true usability of the new bill outside the laboratory, but the customer satisfaction survey confirmed the laboratory results.

Alternatively, one may have to conduct specific studies to gather follow-up information about the use of released products. Basically, the same methods can be used for this kind of field study as for other field studies and task analysis, especially including interviews, questionnaires, and observational studies. Furthermore, since follow-up studies are addressing the usability of an existing system, logging data from instrumented versions of the software becomes especially valuable for its ability to indicate how the software is being used across a variety of tasks.

In addition to field studies where the development organization actively seeks out the users, information can also be gained from the more passive technique of analyzing user complaints, modification requests, and calls to help lines (see Section 7.5, *User Feedback*, on page 221). Even when a user complaint at first sight might seem to indicate a programming error (for example, "data lost"), it can sometimes have its real roots in a usability problem, causing users to operate the system in dangerous or erroneous ways. Defect-tracking procedures are already in place in many software organizations and may only need small changes to be useful for usability engineering purposes [Rideout 1991]. Furthermore, information about common learnability problems can be gathered instructors who teach courses in the use of the system.

Finally, economic data on the impact of the system on the quality and cost of the users' work product and work life are very important and can be gathered through surveys, supervisors' opinions, and statistics for absenteeism, etc. These data should be compared with similar data collected before the introduction of the system.

4.12 Meta-Methods

To ensure the successful application of the usability engineering methods discussed here, it is important to supplement each of them with the following *meta-methods* (methods that apply to methods):

- Write down an explicit plan for what to do when using the method. For example, a plan for empirical user testing would include information about how many users to test, what kind of users to test (and how to get hold of them), what test tasks these users would be asked to perform (which itself should be based on task analysis and user observation), and a time schedule for the studies.
- Subject this plan to an independent review by a person who is not otherwise on your team and who can critique it from a fresh perspective. This person should preferably be experienced with respect to usability engineering.
- Perform a pilot activity by investing about 10–15% of the total resources budgeted for the use of the method. Then revise your plan for the remaining 85–90% to fix the difficulties that invariably will be found during the pilot activity. For example, with empirical user testing, the original test instructions are often misinterpreted by the users; you want the main test to focus on the usability of your system and not on your ability to write readable test instructions. See page 174 for more information about pilot tests.

Furthermore, as early as possible in the project, an overall usability plan should be established listing the usability activities to be performed throughout the lifecycle. Not all projects can afford to use all the methods, and the exact methods to use will depend on the characteristics of the project.

These meta-methods may involve a little extra work up front, but they save work in the long term and ensure that your efforts are on the right track to increase usability, thereby reducing the risk of truly wasting the main effort.

4.13 Prioritizing Usability Activities

It is not always possible to perform all the recommended usability activities in any given project. My own approach to budget constraints or time pressures is outlined in Section 1.4, *Discount Usability Engineering* (page 16), and stresses

- visit to user sites (see page 73)
- prototyping through scenarios (see page 99)
- simplified thinking aloud (see page 195)
- heuristic evaluation (see page 155)

To get additional prioritizing advice, I surveyed 13 usability engineering specialists and asked them to rate 33 different usability methods for their importance to the usability of the final interface [Nielsen 1992b]. The ratings were on a scale from one (no impact on usability) to five (absolutely essential for usability).

The top six methods according to rated impact on usability were

1–2 Iterative design and task analysis of the user's current task. Both rated 4.7.

3 Empirical tests with real users. Rated 4.5.

4 Participatory design. Rated 4.4.

5–6 Visit to customer location before start of design and field study to find out how system is actually used after installation. Both rated 4.3.

The usability specialists were also asked to what extent they had actually used the 33 methods on their most recent project. There was a fairly high correlation between the ratings of the usability impact of the various methods and the extent to which the methods were actually being used in projects ($r = 0.71$). A regression analysis (indicating the match between the scores on the two scales) found that the following two usability activities seemed to be significantly underused in real projects:

- Coordination of the total interface (not just screens but also manuals, training, etc.) was given an impact rating of 4.1. From this rating, the regression analysis would "predict" 64% use, even though total consistency currently was part of only 38% of the projects.
- Field studies at customer locations after installation of the system were given an impact rating of 4.3. From this rating, the regression analysis would "predict" 69% use, even though post-installation studies currently were performed in only 46% of the projects.

4.14 Be Prepared

Even though it is preferable to use usability engineering methods throughout the software lifecycle, practical considerations sometimes dictate the need for emergency human factors to help projects that have gone astray or are especially pressed for time. In these cases, better results may be expected if the usability specialists have prepared for such eventualities in advance [Mulligan *et al.* 1991]. The following precautions can be taken during any less hectic periods that may be available between urgent projects:

- Get a good user interface prototyping tool and acquire proficiency in using it. If you develop interfaces mostly for a certain platform (say, phone-based interfaces, or hypermedia with lots of color video), you may even consider developing a specialized prototyping tool tailored to your special needs, but there are also several good general tools available. In any case, *learning* to use such tools and all their advanced features can take several weeks or even months [Nielsen and Richards 1989; Nielsen *et al.* 1991], which will not be available when the emergency project starts. An expert user can tweak a prototyping tool and throw together initial interfaces for user testing in a very short time, and this may be the only way you will ever get time to test anything.

- Learn appropriate techniques for usability inspection and heuristic evaluation (see page 155), and get familiar with the relevant interface standards and guidelines. Use of these methods can improve interface designs in just a few hours, but they may take almost two weeks to learn for some methods [Jeffries *et al.* 1991].

- Build up an understanding of the types of users, tasks, applications, and computer platforms that are typical for your organization. Generalizing the specific experience from previous user tests, field visits, and studies of installed systems will help you make more informed judgments about the new interface.

- Set up procedures that will allow you to recruit test users easily when they are needed. For example, cultivate relationships with major nearby customer sites and local colleges, set up contracts with temporary employment agencies, or build a database of interested volunteers (retired staff can often form a valuable source of volunteers with substantial domain knowledge). One of the major impediments to conducting user testing when it is needed is the time it may take to find appropriate users if one is not prepared.

- Find and train a usability champion in each project group that does not have its own full-time usability specialist [Mrazek and Rafeld 1992]. Such usability champions should know enough about usability to handle the everyday usability needs of their projects, including activities like heuristic evaluation and quick user testing of design ideas. Since the usability champions are not full-time usability specialists, they will function best if they have access to usability specialists who can keep them up-to-date with developments in the user interface field and take care of more specialized jobs like the building of a usability laboratory or the finding and scheduling of test users.

- Read more usability books and articles (see the bibliography on page 283 for ideas for further reading) and attend conferences (see page 284). Also try out a lot of different systems with different kinds of interfaces to get experience with alternative interaction styles: Many good design ideas come from knowing how analogous design problems were solved in other interfaces.

Chapter 5   *Usability Heuristics*

This chapter presents some basic characteristics of usable interfaces. The principles are fairly broad and apply to practically any type of user interface, including both character-based and graphical interfaces [Nielsen 1990e]. The principles are summarized in Table 2 (page 20). After detailed sections for each of the ten basic heuristics, Section 5.11 (page 155) concludes the chapter with information on how to use usability heuristics as a basis for a systematic inspection of a user interface to find its usability problems (the *heuristic evaluation* method).

5.1   *Simple and Natural Dialogue*

User interfaces should be simplified as much as possible, since every additional feature or item of information on a screen is one more thing to learn, one more thing to possibly misunderstand, and one more thing to search through when looking for the thing you want. Furthermore, interfaces should match the users' task in as natural a way as possible, such that the mapping between computer concepts and user concepts becomes as simple as possible and the users' navigation through the interface is minimized.

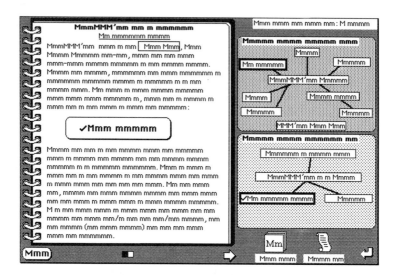

Figure 11 *Mumble screen layout for a hypertext system. The actual system is described in [Nielsen 1990a, 1990i]. The screen could be made to abstract even further from the information content in the full system by replacing the icons with generic shapes.*

The ideal is to present exactly the information the user needs—and no more—at exactly the time and place where it is needed. Information that will be used together should be displayed close together, and at a minimum on the same screen. Also, both information objects and operations should be accessed in a sequence that matches the way users will most effectively and productively do things. Sometimes such sequences are enforced by the user interface, but it is normally better to allow the user to control the dialogue as much as possible such that the sequence can be adjusted by the individual user to suit that user's task and preferences. Even so, the system may ease the user's understanding of the dialogue by indicating a suggested or preferred sequence, such as the sequence implied by the listing of fields in a dialog box from top to bottom.

Graphic Design and Color

Good graphic design is an important element in achieving a simple and natural dialogue for modern computer systems with graphical user interfaces [Marcus 1992]. In addition to getting help from a graphics designer, there are several simple considerations that may lead to simpler dialogues. By prototyping screen layouts using "mumble screens" like that shown in Figure 11 where all text has been replaced with the letter "m," one can abstract away from the detailed information content in the system and focus on layout issues.[1]

Screen layouts should use the gestalt rules for human perception [Rock and Palmer 1990] to increase the users' understanding of relationships between the dialogue elements. These rules say that things are seen as belonging together, as a group, or as a unit, if they are close together, are enclosed by lines or boxes, move or change together, or look alike with respect to shape, color, size, or typography. For example, in Figure 12, most people will perceive two major groups of objects due to the closeness of the objects within the groups compared with the distance between the groups. Then, most people would think that the left set of objects contained two sets of objects that were even more closely related, due to the enclosure of the six objects in the upper right corner and the highlighting of the four objects in the lower left corner. Also, the right set of objects will be perceived as containing three groups, and the middle one will be seen as standing out from the background since it is smaller.

These principles of graphic structure should be used to help the user understand the structure of the interface. For example, menus can use a dividing line or color coding [McDonald et al. 1988] to split options into related groups, each of which will be easier to understand because each option will be seen in a relevant context.

---

1. Mumble text has also been used as a task analysis technique for finding out whether users gain information simply from the way information is presented on a form without reading the detailed data [Nygren et al. 1992]. If they do, then one should design similar capabilities for users in a computerized information environment.

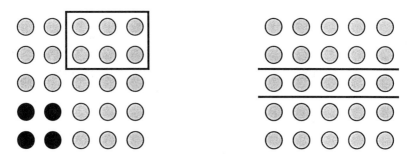

Figure 12 *Example of objects structured according to the gestalt principles of closeness, closure, and similarity.*

Similarly, dialog boxes can group related features and enclose them in boxes or separate them by lines or white space. Also, since users will perceive structure based on these principles, care should be taken not to separate out unrelated objects in ways that make them seem as belonging together. For example, consider a bank statement with the following layout:

```
Balance                                    $1,000.00
$2,000.00
```

What is the balance? One or two thousand dollars? The closeness rule will make many people perceive the label Balance as being matched with the number $2,000, even though it may have been intended as a label for the line containing the number $1,000.

Principles of graphic design can also help users prioritize their attention to a screen by making the most important dialogue elements stand out. As shown by the right part of Figure 12, a small delineated area will stand out from the background, and one can also make objects stand out by highlighting them in various ways, including the use of bolder colors or typefaces, and by making them larger. Also, information that is presented "first," given the usual reading direction (that is, at the top and to the left in many cultures) normally gets more attention. It is even possible to attract the users' attention by using blinking objects, but blinking is so distracting and annoying that it should only be used in extreme cases. On alphanumeric terminals, UPPERCASE TEXT CAN ALSO BE USED TO GET THE USERS' ATTENTION, but upper case should be used sparingly as it is about 10% slower to read than mixed-case text.

With respect to the use of color in screen designs [Rice 1991; Travis 1991], the three most important guidelines are

- Don't over-do it. An interface should not look like an angry fruit salad of wildly contrasting, highly saturated colors. It is better to limit the design to a small number of consistently applied colors. Color-coding should be limited to no more than 5 to 7 different colors since it is difficult to remember and distinguish larger numbers, even though highly trained users can cope with about 11 colors [Durrett and Trezona 1982]. Also, light grays and muted pastel colors are often better as background colors than screaming colors are.

- Make sure that the interface can be used without the colors. Remember that many people (about 8% of males) are colorblind, so any color-coding of information should be supplemented by redundant cues that make it possible to interpret the screens even without being able to differentiate the colors. For example, icons that are about to be deleted could be turned red for fast identification by users with full color vision and they could also be marked with an X. The best test would be to have a selection of colorblind users try out the system, but it would be difficult to do so comprehensively as there are many different types of color blindness.[2] In addition to having at least some colorblind test users, one can also check how the interface looks on a mono-chrome screen. In many cases, some users will be limited to monochrome displays anyway.

---

2. Being "colorblind" normally does not mean than one cannot distinguish any colors at all, so the expression is somewhat inaccurate. About 6% of males and 0.4% of females are partially red–green colorblind (and so can distinguish yellows and blues as well as some shades of green and red), 2% of males and 0.03% of females are fully red–green colorblind, and only 0.005% of males and 0.003% of females are yellow–blue or completely colorblind [Silverstein 1987]. Therefore, a test with a single colorblind user (while much better than no such test) will not guarantee that all types of users with color-deficient vision will be able to use the interface without problems.

- Try to use color only to categorize, differentiate, and highlight, not to give information, especially quantitative information.

It is true that some colors and color combinations are more visible than others [Durrett 1987], and you certainly would not want to present your help screens in light blue text on a bright yellow background.[3] If the most obviously horrible color combinations are avoided, however, there is normally only a small additional benefit to be gained from searching out the absolutely optimal choice of colors.

Less Is More

The great rune stone in Jelling, Denmark (from the last half of the tenth century), bears the following inscription: *"King Harald ordered these memorials raised to Gorm, his father, and Thyre, his mother; that Harald who won for himself all Denmark and Norway and made the Danes Christian."* The stone does seem to focus excessively on King Harald, and the last half of the text distracts from the message regarding King Gorm and Queen Thyre.[4] Similarly, adding information and data fields to a user interface can distract the user from the primary information.

Based on a proper task analysis, it is often possible to identify the information that is truly important to users and which will enable them to perform almost all of their tasks. It will then normally be better to design a single screen with this information and relegate less important information to auxiliary screens than to cram all the information that might possibly be useful into a set of screens that will require the user to switch screens for even the most simple tasks.

Other information may not even be necessary at all. For example, many programs follow the example of King Harald and dedicate

---

3. Detailed guidelines for choosing screen colors can be found in part 8 of ISO 9241 (an international standard for user interface issues). The content of this standard is discussed further by Smith [1988].

4. Compare with the inscription on the small Jelling rune stone from the first half of the tenth century: *"King Gorm raised these memorials to his wife Thyre, the joy of Denmark."* The runes are fewer, but the message is focused.

large amounts of screen space to a display of the name of the program, the vendor's logo, the version number, and other similar information. Even though this information is potentially important and should be available for users making bug reports, it normally only takes up screen space that could have been used for other purposes (maybe even as white space to make for a better layout). And of course, *any* piece of information is something users will have to look at when they search the screen, and it will therefore slow down their performance by some fraction of a second. It is better to provide identifying information as part of a startup screen that can be extravagantly eye-catching and serve as feedback to the user that the appropriate program is being entered. Also, of course, identifying information about the program, its version, and its status should be accessible through the help system. As another example, headers with address and message routing information can be eliminated from displays of electronic mail and network news [Andersen *et al.* 1989] to be shown only in the rare case when a user actually needs this system-oriented information.

Extraneous information not only risks confusing the novice user, but also slows down the expert user. For example, a study of experienced telephone company directory assistance operators showed that finding a target that appeared in the top quarter of the screen took 5.3 seconds when the screen was half full of information and 6.2 seconds when the screen was full of information [Springer 1987]. Saving 0.9 seconds may not seem like a lot, but for this specific application, it was estimated to reduce call processing costs by more than 40 million dollars per year.

The "less is more" rule does not just apply to the information contents of screens but also to the choice of features and interaction mechanisms for a program. A common design pitfall is to believe that "by providing lots of options and several ways of doing things, we can satisfy everybody." Unfortunately, you do have to make the hard choices yourself. Every time you add a feature to a system, there is one more thing for users to learn (and possibly use erroneously) and the manual gets bigger, more intimidating, and harder to search. One study found that the users' planning time for formula entry was 2.9 seconds in one spreadsheet and 4.6 in another [Olson and Nilsen 1987–88]. The first spreadsheet was faster because it only provided a single method for formula entry and therefore did not require users to think about which method to use. In contrast, the second spreadsheet provided multiple methods, with the result that the users were slowed down more by having to choose between methods than the amount of time they sometimes gained from being able to use a "faster" method for certain formulas.

This does not mean that one should never provide alternative interaction techniques. On the contrary, they are often a good idea as further discussed in Section 5.7, on Shortcuts, on page 139. Alternatives can be provided if users can easily recognize the conditions under which each one is optimal so that they can consistently choose the optimal interaction technique without additional planning. For training, users should at first be taught only the single, general method that is preferable in most common situations. Other methods can be taught later but should not be introduced at a stage when they will only confuse the novice user.

Sometimes, one can design an especially simple interface for novice users and shield them from any necessary complexity that may be needed by advanced users. Most systems doing this have only two levels of interface complexity: novice mode and expert mode, but in principle it might be possible to provide multiple nested levels of increased complexity. This nested design strategy is sometimes referred to as *training wheels* [Carroll 1990a].

Since novice users are often observed spending too much time recovering from errors, the training wheels approach can give them a system where they are blocked from even entering potential error situations. Of course, this limits the available functionality, but novice users probably do not need the advanced features anyway. In one experiment, novice users were able to learn basic use of a word processor and type a letter in 116 minutes when they were faced with the full system and in 92 minutes when they were given the training wheels system where actions leading to the most common errors were not available [Carroll and Carrithers 1984]. Not only did the training wheels users get started faster, but they also liked the system better and scored slightly higher on a comprehension exam after the study. Even better, the initial use of the training wheels interface did not impair users when they later graduated to the full system. On the contrary, users who had learned the basics of the system with the training wheels interface learned advanced features *faster* than users who had been using the full system all the time [Catrambone and Carroll 1987].

5.2   Speak the Users' Language

As a part of user-centered design, the terminology in user interfaces should be based on the users' language and not on system-oriented terms. For example, a user interface for foreign currency transactions should not require users to specify British pounds with a code like `317`, even if it is the one used internally in the system. Instead, terms like `GBP` or simply `Pounds` should be used, depending on whether the system was intended for professional currency traders or for the general public.

As far as possible, dialogues should be in the users' native language and not in a foreign language (see Chapter 9 for a discussion of translation and other internationalization issues). Of course, concerns for the users' "language" should not be limited to the words in the interface but should include nonverbal elements like icons (see page 38 for a discussion of how to elicit ideas for intuitive icons).

As part of the general principle of speaking the users' language, one should take care not to use words in nonstandard meanings, unless, of course, a word meaning that would be nonstandard in the general population happens to be the standard use of the word in the user community. Special dictionaries exist to help distinguish common meanings of words from less common meanings. For example, [Dale and O'Rourke 1981] lists 44,000 English word meanings and provides statistics on how many Americans know each meaning. Even though such statistics are only valid in the country where they were collected, one can normally assume that the avoidance of unusual word meanings will also be a way to improve international understandability of an interface.

To speak the users' language does not always imply limiting the interface vocabulary to a small set of commonly used words. On the contrary, when the user population has its own specialized terminology for its domain, the interface had better use those specialized terms rather than more commonly used, but less precise, everyday language [Brooks 1993]. Even for the general population, specific, distinguishing words are better than bland words.

Speaking the users' language also involves viewing interactions from the users' perspective. For example, a security transactions statement should read, "You have bought 100 shares of XYZ Corp." and not, "We have sold you 100 shares of XYZ Corp." As another example, consider a computer utility, such as a virus guard, that is continuously active, running in the background, but which might periodically need to be deactivated for whatever reason. One approach might be to introduce an "override mode" with a command that could be activated whenever the user needed to perform a task that conflicted with the background utility. Unfortunately, the override would be *on* when the user wanted the utility to be *off*, so using this model would conflict with the user-oriented perspective, even though it might in fact be a perfect reflection of the internal workings of the operating system. A better choice would be a reverse model using a dialog box with a checkbox for "XYZ-utility active: ❏." This design also simplifies the interface since it has no concept of a special override mode.

The system should not force naming conventions or restrictions on objects named by the user. For example, users should be allowed to use as long names as they want, even though the system may not always be able to show very long names without scrolling. If the system for some reason cannot handle names longer than a certain number of characters, it should not just truncate without warning the user's input after that number of characters. Instead, it should offer a constructive error message and allow the user to edit the name to be as meaningful as possible within the limitations imposed by the system.

Given the advice to speak the users' language, an obvious idea is simply to ask users what words and concepts they would like to see in the interface. Unfortunately, the verbal disagreement phenomenon guarantees the failure of that approach: There are so many different words in common use for the same things that the probability is very low that a user will mention the most appropriate name when asked. Furnas *et al.* [1987] found that the probability that two users would mention the same name was no more than 7–18%, depending on the phenomenon being named. Even if one asked several users and then picked the name mentioned by most of them, one would still only match 15–36% of the users. In other words, the majority of users will be dissatisfied anyway, even if words are chosen by asking the users themselves.

A much better alternative is to let the users vote on the names, based on a shortlist of possible names. This list can be generated by several means, including suggestions from the developers, from usability specialists, and from asking a few users. In one experiment [Bloom 1987–88] names for the features in a mail merge facility were chosen in three different ways:

- Technical terms as suggested by the original developers of the system: variable field, token character, record, delimiter, etc.
- The terms suggested by the most users when they were given a short description of the concepts: part, marker, unit, period, etc.
- The winners when users were given a list of several alternative terms and asked to vote: component, placeholder, information package, separator, etc.

Not only do the winners of the user vote seem more descriptive, they also tested much better in a user test. Test users learning the system made 11.1 errors on average when using the original system with the technical terms, 10.3 errors when using the system with the terms suggested by the most users, and only 8.3 errors when using the system with the vote-winning terms. For a second test, only the technical terms and the vote winners were compared. Users made 14.7 errors when learning the system with the technical terms and only 4.6 errors when learning the system with the vote-winning terms, confirming that the vote-winners made the system easier to learn. However, continued testing after the users had learned the system found exactly the same error rate (2.0 errors) for both sets of names, indicating that people can learn basically anything eventually. The test users were finally asked to perform a new set of tasks with the system without being allowed access to the documentation. During this transfer test, the users of the system with the technical terms made 23.6 errors, whereas the users of the system with the vote-winning terms made only 5.8 errors. This latter result shows that the vote-winning terms enabled the users to understand the system better in that they could generalize their knowledge to correctly use it in new ways.

Given that there are so many ways to refer to the same concepts, computers should allow for rich use of synonyms in interpreting command languages and in documentation indexes. It should also be possible for the users to define *aliases* (user-defined terms that are translated by the system). Not only may an alias be easier to remember for the user who defined it, but it can also serve as a shortcut for complex sequences such as commands with multiple parameters or electronic mail addresses. For some applications, such as the searching of online documentation or database queries, the system itself may build up a list of aliases over time through the use of adaptive indexing [Furnas 1985], where new names for objects are added every time a user tries a query term that is not known by the system, but where the user eventually succeeds in finding the relevant information anyway.

Mappings and Metaphors

A more general way of approaching the goal of a user-oriented dialogue is to aim at good mappings between the computer display of information and the user's conceptual model of the information. Such mappings are not always easy to discover, as exemplified by the case one would naively imagine to be the simplest of all: that of producing a world map [Monmonier 1991].

Unfortunately, the world is round, and the map is flat, leading to all kinds of geographical distortions and the need to select a mapping projection suitable for the user's task.

To discover such mappings, the first step is to perform a task analysis and build up an understanding of the users and their domain. In addition to talking with users and observing them, it is also possible to use more complex methods to build an understanding of the users' knowledge representation and the way they model their domain. Typically, users are asked to list or group concepts in the domain, and the orderings or groupings are assumed to correspond to the users' model of the domain. Some commonly used techniques include ordered recall (users are allowed to freely associate and mention as many concepts as they can think of, with concepts that are mentioned close together assumed to be associated in the user's mind), card sorting (each concept is written on a card, and the user sorts the cards into piles), and paired similarity ratings (users are given a questionnaire listing all possible pairs of concepts and asked to rate their similarity) [McDonald and Schvaneveldt 1988]. The outcome of these tests can either be used directly or be subjected to multidimensional scaling or cluster analysis, using a statistics program. For example, Loshe *et al.* [1991] used card sorting to elicit the users' mental models of a set of graphics and charts. Subjects who were graphic artists were found to structure the graphics significantly differently than other subjects, indicating the need to structure user interfaces to graphics and charting software differently for these two categories of users.

User interface metaphors [Carroll *et al.* 1988; Wozny 1989] are a possible way to achieve a mapping between the computer system and some reference system known to the users in the real world. For example, consider the task of installing or updating new software on a personal computer. The traditional user interface to this task is very system-oriented, listing files, features, disks, etc., from which the user has to choose. Alternatively, a mail-order catalog could be used as a metaphor to structure the interface and allow the users to utilize their existing knowledge about how one selects and previews options [Card and Henderson 1987].

Unfortunately, metaphors may mislead users, or users' understanding of the computer may be limited to those aspects that can be inferred from the metaphor [Halasz and Moran 1982]. For example, the metaphor "a word processor is like a typewriter" will help users discover features like backspace and scrolling, but may prevent them from looking for a global replace feature.

As another example, the operation "delete file" has often been metaphorized in graphical user interfaces, with icons like a trash can, a paper shredder, and even a black hole used to represent deletion. Even though the black hole cannot be said to be very user-oriented, all these icons represent ways to draw upon the users' non-computer-related experience and knowledge and they thus serve as good metaphors for the concept of file deletion. A problem arises when considering data security. Most current operating systems do not delete the *contents* of a file from the disk when the file is deleted. Often, the only result of a file deletion is to make the storage space occupied by the file available for use by other files at a later date. This means that as long as no other files have overwritten the ostensibly deleted storage blocks, it will be possible to read the contents of the deleted file. Users with sensitive data on their disks can therefore not rely on file deletion to safeguard their data in cases where others have access to the disk—for example because it is sold or sent in for repair. The paper-shredder icon may give users a false sense of security due to the connotations of physical paper shredders with respect to the destruction of confidential paper documents. In contrast, the trash-can icon at least implicitly suggests that others might look through the discarded documents.

The lesson from these examples is that one should take care when "speaking the users' language" not to inadvertently imply more than one intended. Specifically, discussions of interface metaphors in manuals should be supplemented with explanations of the differences between the real-world reference system and the computer system. Care should be taken to present the metaphor as a simplified model of a more detailed conceptual model of the system [Nielsen 1990c] and not as a direct representation of the system.

Metaphors also present potential problems with respect to internationalization, since not all metaphors are meaningful to all cultures. For example, a Danish interface designer might choose to use the pause signal as a metaphor for delayed system response, drawing upon the common knowledge that radio stations play a special endless tune of the same 13 notes repeated over and over when one show finishes before the scheduled starting time of the next. However, the concept of a pause signal would be quite foreign to users in many other countries, such as the United States, where radio stations fill every available moment with commercials and would never put on a special signal just to fill up time.

5.3 Minimize User Memory Load

Computers are very good at remembering things very precisely, so they should take over the burden of memory from the user as much as possible. In general, people have a much easier time at recognizing something that is shown to them than they have at having to recall the same information from memory without help. This phenomenon is well known to anybody who has learned a foreign language: Your passive vocabulary is always much larger than your active vocabulary. And of course, computers really speak a foreign language as far as the users are concerned.

The computer should therefore display dialogue elements to the users and allow them to choose from items generated by the computer or to edit them. Menus are a typical technology to achieve this goal. It is also much easier for the user to modify information displayed by the computer than to have to generate all of the desired result from scratch. For example, when users want to rename an information object, it is very likely that they will want the new name to be similar to the old one, so the text edit field in which the user is supposed to enter the new name should be prepopulated with the old name, allowing users to make modifications instead of typing everything.

Interfaces based on recognition rely to a great extent on the visibility of the objects of interest to the user. Unfortunately, displaying too many objects and attributes will result in a relative loss of salience for the ones of interest to the user, so care should be taken to match object visibility as much as possible with the user's needs [Gilmore 1991]. As usual we find that "less is more."

Whenever users are asked to provide input, the system should describe the required format and, if possible, provide an example of legal and sensible input, such as a default value. For example, a system asking the user to enter a date could do it as follows:

- `Enter date (DD-Mmm-YY, e.g., 2-Aug-93):`

An even better dialogue design would provide the example in the input field itself as a default value (possibly using today's date or some other reasonable date), thus allowing the user to edit the date rather than having to enter all of it.

There is no need for the user to have to remember or guess at the range of legal input and the unit of measurement that will be used to interpret it. Instead, the system can supply that information as part of the dialogue, such as, for example:

- `Left margin:___10 points [0-128]`

A famous example indicating the need to display measurement units to help the user's memory was the positioning of a space-based mirror by the space shuttle *Discovery* [Neumann 1991]. The mirror was supposed to be aimed at a mountain top in order to reflect a laser beam, and the user had ordered the computer to point the mirror toward a point with an elevation of "10,023 above sea level." The user apparently entered the elevation as if it were measured in feet, whereas, in fact, the system used miles as its measurement unit, causing the mirror to be aimed *away* from the Earth, toward a point 10,000 miles out in space.[5]

To minimize the users' memory load, the system should be based on a small number of pervasive rules that apply throughout the

---

5. With respect to measurement units, other usability principles often lead to a need allow users to select between several alternative units, such as inches, feet, miles, centimeter, meter, and kilometer, depending on their needs.

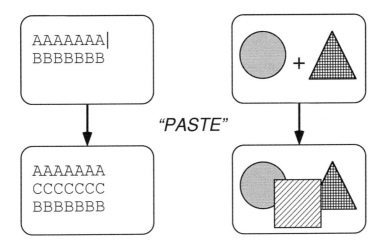

Figure 13 *A generic command: "Paste" can be used to insert a line of c's (text) as well as a striped square (graphics) at the insertion point.*

user interface. If a very large number of rules is needed to determine the behavior of the system, then the user will have to learn and remember all those rules, making them a burden. On the other hand, if the system is not governed by any rules at all, then the user will have to learn every single dialogue element on its own, and it is impossible to predict the behavior of a dialogue element without already knowing (and remembering) how it works.

The use of generic commands [Rosenberg and Moran 1984] is one way to let a few rules govern a complex system. As shown in Figure 13, generic commands make similar things happen in different circumstances, making it sufficient for the user to learn a few commands in order to work with many different types of data. One of the main advantages of generic commands is that they support transfer of learning from one application to the next, since users do not need to relearn those commands they already know [Ziegler *et al.* 1986].

Generic commands need not perform exactly the same function in all circumstances, as long as the user can think of the command as a single unified concept, such as "insert the object from the clip-board" in the case of a `paste` command. As shown by Figure 13, this generic command may actually insert the clipboard *and* move some old objects out of the way, when it operates on text, but perform the insert operation without moving anything when it operates on graphics. The designer of a generic command will need to determine what "naturally" feels like the same command to users, even if some details will differ due to the requirements of the different parts of the system.

5.4   Consistency

Consistency is one of the most basic usability principles. If users know that the same command or the same action will always have the same effect, they will feel more confident in using the system, and they will be encouraged to try out exploratory learning strate-gies because they will already have part of the knowledge needed to operate new parts of the system [Lewis *et al.* 1989].

The same information should be presented in the same location on all screens and dialog boxes and it should be formatted in the same way to facilitate recognition. For example, my heating bill contains a comparison between my current heating use and my use in the same month in the previous year, listed as a table with the current year in the left column and the previous year in the right. To facili-tate my interpretation of these numbers, a footnote on the bill furthermore contains information about the average temperature in each of the two years. Unfortunately, the footnote mentions the previous year before (that is, to the left of) the current year, thus inverting the relation compared to that used in the table. Consis-tency considerations would have implied a design of this printout with the same spatial relation between the two periods for both kinds of information. An order where the previous year was mentioned before the current year might be preferred as being consistent with the way timelines work, but unfortunately one can also argue that the reverse order achieves a better match with the user's task of assessing current heat usage. As is often the case in user interface design, one would have to decide which of these two considerations was most important; once this decision had been made, one should follow it consistently and not mix the two layout rules.

Many aspects of consistency become easier to achieve to the extent that one is following a user interface standard in the design, since the standard will then have specified many details of the dialogue, such as, for example, how to indicate a pop-up menu or which typeface to use in a list of font sizes. See Chapter 8 for a discussion of user interface standards and ways to increase compliance and thereby consistency. Unfortunately, standards compliance is not sufficient to ensure consistency, since the standards leave a fair amount of leeway for the designers. See the discussion of user interface coordination in Section 4.6 (page 90) for ways to promote consistency during interface design.

Consistency is not just a question of screen design, but includes considerations of the task and functionality structure of the system [Kellogg 1987, 1989]. For example, Eberts and MacMillan [1987] found that subjects were more confused when they switched between using a command-line mainframe and a command-line personal computer than when they switched between the command-line personal computer and a graphical personal computer. From a screen design perspective, the two command-line interfaces were very similar, but the underlying operating systems were in fact very different. And the two personal computer interfaces were built on top of systems with the same basic philosophy and features.

A study of a popular spreadsheet program found 10 consistency problems causing common errors for novice users [Doyle 1990]. Seven of these problems were due to inconsistencies between the spreadsheet and the users' task expectations, three were due to inconsistencies between the spreadsheet and other user interfaces, and only two problems were due to inconsistencies within the spreadsheet itself. The spreadsheet's menu navigation method was classified as being inconsistent in all three ways and was therefore counted in all three categories. Of course, other systems may have different distributions of their consistency problems, but it is probably quite representative that the larger scopes of consistency are the most difficult to get right.

5.5 Feedback

The system should continuously inform the user about what it is doing and how it is interpreting the user's input. Feedback should not wait until an error situation has occurred: The system should also provide positive feedback, and it should provide partial feedback as information becomes available. For example, the way to write the German letter ü on many keyboards involves first typing the umlaut, ¨, and then typing the character that is to go under the two dots. Some systems provide no visible feedback as the first part of the character is typed, leading many novice users to conclude that the system does not know how to deal with umlauts. A better design would show the umlaut and then change the cursor in some way to indicate that the system was waiting for the second part of the character.

System feedback should not be expressed in abstract and general terms but should restate and rephrase the user's input to indicate what is being done with it. For example, it is a good idea to give a warning message in case the user is about to perform an irreversible action, such as overwriting a file (see Section 5.9). Assume that the user is about to copy a file to another disk and that the copy operation would overwrite a file with the same name. The worst feedback (except none, of course) would be to state that a file was about to be overwritten, without giving its name. Better feedback would include the name of the file, and even better feedback would include attributes of the two files, such as file type and modification date, to help the user understand whether the copy operation was just replacing an old copy with a newer copy of the same file or whether the file being overwritten was in fact a completely different file that happened to have the same name.

Different types of feedback may need different degrees of persistence in the interface [Nielsen 1987c]. Some feedback is only relevant for the duration of a certain phenomenon, and can thus have low persistence, going away when it is no longer needed. For example a message stating that the printer is out of paper should be removed automatically once the problem has been fixed. Other feedback needs to have medium persistence and stay on the screen until the user explicitly acknowledges it. An example in this category would be a message stating that the user's output had been rerouted to another printer because of some problem with the printer specified by the user. Finally, a few types of feedback may be so important that they require high persistence, remaining a permanent part of the interface. An example might be the indication of remaining free space on a hard disk.

Response Time

Feedback becomes especially important in case the system has long response times for certain operations. The basic advice regarding response times has been about the same for many years [Miller 1968; Card *et al.* 1991]:

- 0.1 second is about the limit for having the user feel that the system is reacting instantaneously, meaning that no special feedback is necessary except to display the result.

- 1.0 second is about the limit for the user's flow of thought to stay uninterrupted, even though the user will notice the delay. Normally, no special feedback is necessary during delays of more than 0.1 but less than 1.0 second, but the user does lose the feeling of operating directly on the data.

- 10 seconds is about the limit for keeping the user's attention focused on the dialogue. For longer delays, users will want to perform other tasks while waiting for the computer to finish, so they should be given feedback indicating when the computer expects to be done. Feedback during the delay is especially important if the response time is likely to be highly variable, since users will then not know what to expect.

Normally, response times should be as fast as possible, but it is also possible for the computer to react so fast that the user cannot keep up with the feedback. For example, a scrolling list may move so fast that the user cannot stop it in time for the desired element to

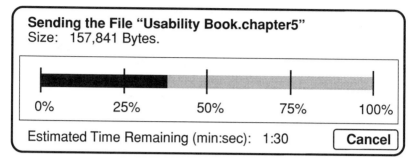

Figure 14 *Percent-done indicator for a hypothetical file-transfer program. The design not only provides feedback expressed in the user's terms (the name of the file) and with respect to the progress of the transfer, it also provides an easy way out (cf. Section 5.6) in case the user gets tired of waiting or discovers that the wrong file is being transferred.*

remain within the available window. The fact that computers can be *too* fast indicates the need for user-interface changes, like animations, to be timed according to a real-time clock rather than being timed as an indirect effect of the computer's execution speed: Even if a faster model computer is substituted, the user interface should still be usable.

In cases where the computer cannot provide fairly immediate response, continuous feedback should be provided to the user in form of a percent-done indicator like the one shown in Figure 14 [Myers 1985]. As a rule of thumb, percent-done progress indicators should be used for operations taking more than about 10 seconds. Progress indicators have three main advantages: They reassure the user that the system has not crashed but is working on his or her problem; they indicate approximately how long the user can be expected to wait, thus allowing the user to do other activities during long waits; and they finally provide something for the user to look at, thus making the wait less painful. This latter advantage should not be underestimated and is one reason for recommending a graphic progress bar instead of just stating the expected remaining time in numbers.

For operations where it is unknown in advance how much work has to be done, it may not be possible to use a percent-done indicator, but it is still possible to provide running progress feedback in terms of the absolute amount of work done. For example, a system searching an unknown number of remote databases could print the name of each database as it is processed. If this is not possible either, a last resort would be to use a less specific progress indicator in the form of a spinning ball, a busy bee flying over the screen, dots printed on a status line, or any such mechanism that at least indicates that the system is working, even if it does not indicate what it is doing.

For reasonably fast operations, taking between 2 and 10 seconds, a true percent-done indicator may be overkill and, in fact, putting one up would violate the principle of display inertia (avoiding flash changes on the screen so rapidly that the user cannot keep pace or feels stressed). One could still give less conspicuous progress feedback. A common solution is to combine a "busy" cursor with a rapidly changing number in small field in the bottom of the screen to indicate how much has been done.

System Failure

Informative feedback should also be given in case of system failure. Many systems are not designed to do so and simply stop responding to the user when they go down. Unfortunately, no feedback is almost the worst possible feedback since it leaves users to guess what it wrong. Systems can be designed for graceful degradation, enabling them to provide some feedback to users even when they are mostly down.

As an example, consider feedback to users of an automated teller machine (ATM). On February 13, 1993, all 1,200 ATMs belonging to a major bank in New York City refused to perform any user transactions for a period of four hours due to a bug in a software upgrade installed at the data center. According to newspaper reports, customers "crisscrossed the city on futile scavenger hunts for an operating cash machine"[6] since they did not know what was going on and hoped that other machines might be working. Since it would be unrealistic to expect a 1,200 node distributed computer system to function perfectly all the time without any software, hardware, or network failures, the user interface at the individual ATMs should be designed to provide information to customers in case of any such downtime. Different messages should be given, depending on whether the error is due to the central system (in which case customers need not waste time finding another machine) or whether the error is local. In order to inform customers correctly, the ATM needs to be able to perform rudimentary diagnostics, and the entire system needs to be built with such diagnostics in mind. Assuming that the system is designed for it, it should be feasible to give users meaningful information about the likely cause and/or location of any system failures.

5.6   Clearly Marked Exits

Users do not like to feel trapped by the computer. In order to increase the user's feeling of being in control of the dialogue, the system should offer the user an easy way out of as many situations as possible. For example, all dialog boxes and system states should have a cancel button or other escape facility to bring the user back to the previous state.

In many cases, exits can be provided in the form of an undo facility that reverts to the previous system state [Abowd and Dix 1992; Yang 1992]. Users quickly learn to rely on the existence of undo, so it should be made pervasively available throughout the system as a generic command that undoes any state changes rather than being restricted to only undoing a special category of user actions. Given that undo and escape facilities are generally available, users will feel encouraged to rely on exploratory learning since they can always try out unknown options, trusting in their ability to get out of any trouble without ill effects. A basic principle for user interface design should be to acknowledge that users will make errors no

---

6. "At a bank, automatic frustration machines," *New York Times* February 14, 1993, p. 45.

matter what else is done to improve the interface, and one should therefore make it as easy as possible to recover from these errors.

As mentioned above, system response times should be as fast as possible. In cases where the computer cannot finish its processing within the 10-second limit for keeping the user's attention, it should always be possible for the user to interrupt the computer and cancel the operation. In general, interfaces should show a high degree of responsiveness [Duis and Johnson 1990], to the extent that paying attention to the user's new actions should get higher priority than finishing the user's old actions. For example, if a graphics program takes a fair amount of time to repaint the screen, it should allow the user to scroll or to change the zoom level even before the screen has been completely redrawn.

The various exit and undo mechanisms should be made visible in the interface and should not depend on the user's ability to remember some special code or obscure combination of keys. Visibility is of course a general user interface design principle, with the possible exception of some dialogue accelerators, but visibility is especially crucial for exit support since users will need these mechanisms in cases where they are in unfamiliar territory and may be afraid to lose data if they do the wrong thing.

5.7 Shortcuts

Even though it should be possible to operate a user interface with the knowledge of just a few general rules, it should also be possible for the experienced user to perform frequently used operations especially fast, using dialogue shortcuts. Typical accelerators include abbreviations, having function keys or command keys that package an entire command in a single keypress, double-clicking on an object to perform the most common operation on it, and having buttons available to access important functions directly from within those parts of the dialogue where they may be most frequently needed. Pen computers, vertual realities, and some mouse interfaces may may also use gestures as accelerators.

A good example of a shortcut to make a frequent operation faster is the use of a structure generator in a hypertext authoring system [Jordan *et al.* 1989]. Since hypertext authors may often want to generate large numbers of similar hypertext structures with a given pattern of typed nodes and links (for example, each of the courses in an online course catalog might have nodes for course content, prerequisites, instructor, textbooks, and location), they can work faster if the system allows them to define templates of these structures and to generate sets of nodes and links based on a template in a single operation. Macro and scripting facilities can be used to achieve similar effects in traditional command languages, and similar facilities are also being introduced to graphical user interfaces.

Type-ahead (typing the next input before the computer is ready to accept it) is not really a shortcut as such since it still requires the user to generate a complete sequence of input, but it can speed up the interaction by allowing the user to get ahead of the computer and not have to pay attention to all the steps in the dialogue. Similarly, in telephone-based interfaces and other speech-based interfaces, users should be allowed to interrupt the voice prompts as soon as they know what to say. Graphical user interfaces can support a feature similar to type-ahead, in what might be called *click-ahead*: Users can click on the spot where the "OK" button will appear to dismiss dialog boxes before they have even appeared, and they can click in partly obscured windows before they have been made active. It is dangerous to allow type-ahead and click-ahead in all circumstances, however. For example, a critical alert message should not go away without having been visible, and the type-ahead buffer should be cleared in case there is an error in the execution of a prior command which would tend to make the rest of the user's input invalid.

Users should be allowed to jump directly to the desired location in large information spaces, such as a file or menu hierarchy. Often, a hypertext-like approach [Nielsen 1990a] can be used with links between information elements that are likely to be used together. In file systems, such links are often called aliases, since they provide a way to name an information object (file) without having to specify the full pathname. Alternatively, popular locations may be given easy-to-remember names that have to be typed in by the user. This approach is popular on many videotex services. Finally, users may be allowed to give their own names to those locations they find especially important. By doing so, users can build up a list of bookmarks that will enable them to return quickly to a small set of locations [Bernstein 1988; Monk 1989]. Of course, following the "minimize-user-memory-load" principle, the user should have easy access to a list of the bookmarks defined by that user [Olsen 1992].

Users should be able to reuse their interaction history [Greenberg 1993]. A study of a command-line system showed that 35% of all commands were identical to one of the five previous commands and that 74% of the commands had been issued at least once before [Greenberg and Whitten 1988]. Thus, a simple menu of the last few things the user had done would make it possible for the user to reissue a large number of commands without having to reenter them. Also, word processors, hypertext systems, and other systems where users navigate large amounts of information should have a backtrack feature or other history mechanisms to allow the user to return directly to prior locations.

Even though command reuse is simpler for command-language interfaces, some direct manipulation interfaces allow users to reissue the last formatting command or repeat the last search command by a simple command-key shortcut. It is also possible to use a kind of comic strip to show previous states of a graphical interface as miniatures [Kurlander and Feiner 1992] using a principle called a visual cache to allow fast direct access to those states [Nielsen 1990g; Wiecha and Henrion 1987].

As a simple example of the use of the user's interaction history to provide shortcuts, some applications keep track of which files users often open in those applications [Barratt 1991]. The applications can then offer users a special menu of the files they are most likely to open next, either because they have been used recently, because they are used a lot in general, or because they are normally used together with other files already opened in a particular session. Statistics on such "working sets" of files that are often used together are slightly harder to get right than statistics on the most recently used files, but they can offer users a convenient shortcut to get at several files in a simpler way than having to find them one at a time in the file system.

System-provided default values constitute a shortcut since it is faster to recognize a default and accept it than having to specify a value or an option. In many cases, users do not even need to see the default value, which can remain hidden on an optional screen that is only accessed in the rare case where it needs to be changed. Defaults also help novice users learn the system since they reduce the number of actions users need to make before using the system, and since the default values give an indication of the kind of values that can legally be specified.

5.8   Good Error Messages

Error situations are critical for usability for two reasons: First, by definition they represent situations where the user is in trouble and potentially will be unable to use the system to achieve the desired goal. Second, they present opportunities for helping the user understand the system better [Frese *et al.* 1991] since the user is usually motivated to pay some attention to the contents of error messages, and since the computer will often have some knowledge of what the problem is.

Error messages should basically follow four simple rules [Shneiderman 1982]:

- They should be phrased in clear language and avoid obscure codes. It should be possible for the user to understand the error message by itself without having to refer to any manuals or code dictionaries. It might be necessary to include internal, system-oriented information or codes to help systems managers track down the problem, but such information should always be given at the end of an otherwise human-readable error message and should be combined with constructive advice, such as "Report this information to your systems manager to get help."

- They should be precise rather than vague or general. For example, instead of saying, "Cannot open this document," the computer should say "Cannot open 'Chapter 5' because the application is not on the disk" (also following the principle about giving feedback by restating the user's input).

- They should constructively help the user solve the problem. For example, the above error message that a document could not be opened could be made more constructive by replacing the words "the application" with the name of the application, indicating to the user what should be done in order to read the document. The message could also offer to try to open the document with some other application that was known to accept data of the given type.

One useful way of generating constructive error messages is by guessing at what the user really meant to say. In the case of textual input, spelling-correction methods have been available for many years [Peterson 1980; Bentley 1985], and these methods can be especially fast and precise when the set of correct user inputs is restricted to a known set of terms such as the names of files and commands [Bickel 1987]. Durham *et al.* [1983] found that even a simple spelling corrector could handle 27% of all user errors in a text-oriented interface, thus confirming the value of this cheap method. The Interlisp programming system even had a feature called DWIM (**D**o **W**hat **I** *Mean*—not what I *say*) [Sandewall 1978; Teitelman 1972], where the computer automatically performed the action it assumed that the user wanted. DWIM is somewhat dangerous, though, unless the computer is absolutely sure.

- Finally, error messages should be polite and should not intimidate the user or put the blame explicitly on the user. Users feel bad enough as it is when they make errors. There is no need for the computer to make the situation even worse by accusing error messages like the classic "ILLEGAL USER ACTION, JOB ABORTED" (in upper case, at that—screaming at the user). Error messages should definitely avoid abusive terms like *fatal, illegal,* and so forth. Often, error messages can be worded such as to suggest that the problem is really the computer's fault—as indeed it is since the interface in principle ought to have been designed to have made the error impossible. For example, the LOGO programming language will give the message *"I don't know how to foo"* if the user calls the undefined procedure *foo*, thus seeming to take a little of the blame [Nicol 1990].

In addition to having good error messages, systems should also provide good error recovery. For example, users should be allowed to undo the effect of erroneous commands, and they should be able to edit and reissue previous commands without having to enter them from scratch.

André Bisseret [1983] from the French INRIA research center tells a story about how he tried to define a user ID, giving rise to the following dialogue:

Computer: `Type user name`
Bisseret: `Bisseret`
Computer: `Error, type user name`

Monsieur Bisseret was *not* pleased to find that the computer considered his name illegal. Unfortunately, the computer only accepted user IDs up to seven characters in length, so it could at least have given a constructive error message by explicitly saying so. But actually, a better redesign would have allowed user names of arbitrary length since doing so would follow the principle of speaking the user's language. There is no need to force users to remember strange contractions of their own and other people's names. Such a redesign would avoid any need to have this error message in the first place since the potential error situation would be designed away. Doing so is also a major dialogue principle, as discussed on page 145.

Multiple-Level Messages

Instead of putting all potentially useful bits of information in all messages, it is possible to use shorter messages that will be faster to read as long as the user is given easy access to a more elaborate message. The most common way to implement multilevel messages is to have only two levels and to supplement the short initial message with a button that can be clicked for more information. In principle, it is also possible to have many levels of detail, with the navigation between the levels based on some kind of hypertext.

In an integrated user-assistance facility based on hypertext, it would also be possible for the user to link from an error message to the location in the help system that gives further assistance on the problem. If the user's difficulty was not the error situation in general but a single incomprehensible word in the message, it would be possible to link from that word to the location in the online manual where it was defined. And if the user wanted further assistance than could be provided by the help system or the manual, it would be possible to link further, to the appropriate location in the tutorial component, to get a computer-aided instruction lesson.

As mentioned above, error messages should normally not reflect mysterious internal states of the computer that are completely incomprehensible to the regular users even though the information may help specialized support staff locate and fix the problem. The notion of multiple-level messages can provide access to such detailed information for those wizard-level users who want it while shielding less-knowledgeable users from being confused and intimidated. Ideally, it should be possible to dig steadily deeper into a set of messages from lower and lower levels of the system [Efe 1987] until the error has been identified.

5.9   Prevent Errors

Even better than having the good error messages recommended in the previous section would be to avoid the error situation in the first place. There are many situations that are known to be error-prone [Norman 1983; Reason 1990; Senders and Moray 1991], and systems can often be designed to avoid putting the user in such situations.

For example, every time the user is asked to spell out something, there is a risk of spelling errors, so selecting a filename from a menu rather than typing it in is a simple way to redesign a system to eliminate an entire category of errors.

User errors can be identified as candidates for elimination through redesign either because of their frequency or because of their serious consequences. These two kinds of information can be gathered either through user testing (see Chapter 6) or by logging errors as they occur during field use of the system (see Section 7.4).

Errors with especially serious consequences can also be reduced in frequency by asking users to reconfirm that they "really, really mean this" before going ahead with the dangerous actions. One should not use confirmation dialogues so often, though, that the user's answer becomes automatic. If a long sequence of actions is performed so frequently that it is experienced as a unit, the users risk making a "capture error" [Norman 1983] if they ever need to deviate from the sequence: Because they are so used to going ahead in a certain way, they may continue and issue the fatal click on the OK button before they have even read the warning message.

Avoid Modes

Modes [Monk 1986] are a frequent source of user error and frustration and should be avoided if possible. The classic example of modes comes from early text editors, which had separate insert and edit modes. When the user was in insert mode, all keyboard input was interpreted as text to go into the file, and when the user was in edit mode, all keyboard input was interpreted as commands. An example from modern word processors is the use of special annotation text that is sometimes visible and sometimes hidden. Modes basically partition the possible user actions such that not all actions are available at all times, which can be frustrating. Also, modes makes it possible for the system to interpret what is seemingly the same user action in different ways depending on the current mode,[7] which will often lead to user errors. One famous user interface designer once had a T-shirt with the caption *"Don't Mode Me In,"* surrounded by a ring of barbed wire [Tesler 1981] to indicate the frustration of being in one mode and wanting to access a feature from some other mode.

146

Unfortunately, modes are almost impossible to avoid totally in an interface of some complexity. For example, most word processors have a word-wrap feature that causes text to move to the next line to prevent overflowing into the margin. In fact, this feature introduces modes into the interface, since the same action (typing) may or may not cause a new-line action to occur, depending on whether an "end-of-line" mode is true. Normally, this mode does not bother users who do not mind whether their writing get split over multiple lines. When users *do* mind, such as when constructing tables, this mode does cause problems, however [Monk 1986].

If modes cannot be avoided totally, one can at least prevent many mode errors by explicitly recognizing the modes in the interface design. By showing states clearly and distinctly to the user, a designer can follow the principle of providing feedback, and thus make it less likely that the user will mistake the current mode. In one experiment, adding different sound effects to each of the modes in a computer game decreased the users' mode errors by 70% [Monk 1986]. Even if sound effects are not appropriate, other means can be used to provide mode feedback such as different colors of windows. In my own case, I often connect from my personal computer to two different mainframes that have identical operating systems and look-and-feel. After several cases of getting confused about which system I was currently dealing with, I changed the definition of the windows used for the terminal sessions to use significantly different typefaces, thus providing me with constant low-key feedback.

In addition to having clear status indicators showing the current mode, the interface should also exhibit clear differences between user actions in different modes to minimize the risk of confusing individual interface elements. Similarly, system feedback should be sufficiently varied to provide additional differentiation between

---

7. Note that modern user interfaces often rely on a kind of mode in the use of window systems: Different user actions in different windows often have different results. This flavor of modes is not as harmful as the traditional modes, because the users do not have to issue special mode-changing commands to move between windows and because the difference between windows will be visually apparent in a well-designed interface [Nielsen 1986].

modes. Mode confusion can also be prevented by the use of so-called spring-loaded modes where the users are only in the mode as long as they actively hold down a button or perform some other action that will automatically take them out of the mode as soon as they let go [Sellen *et al.* 1990].

Even without the added usability problem of modes, one should in general avoid having too-similar commands. In one case, a user had trouble using a certain system and asked for technical support over the telephone. The support person told the user exactly what commands to type, but the user still had problems even after following the instructions to the letter. The support person was unable to diagnose the problem over the phone and finally went to the user's office to make sure that the instructions were actually being carried out. The problem turned out to be that the system required the commands to be typed in lower case and the user had typed them in upper case. This difficulty is known as a "description error," [Norman 1983] since the descriptions of the two situations are almost identical and therefore likely to be confused. In this system, input in the wrong case was simply rejected, but other interfaces may actually act differently on input depending on its case. For example, case-sensitive search is often an option in text editors. Because users can be expected to make description errors very frequently, it is normally preferable to make case-independent search the default and only provide case-sensitive search as an extra feature that has to be explicitly activated by the user.

5.10 Help and Documentation

Even though it is preferable if a system is so easy to use that no further help or documentation is needed to supplement the user interface itself, this goal cannot always be met. Except for systems like automated teller machines where true walk-up-and-use usability is necessary, most user interfaces have sufficiently many features to warrant a manual and possibly a help system. Also, regular users of a system may want documentation to enable them to acquire higher levels of expertise. Even so, the existence of help and documentation does not reduce the usability requirements for the interface itself. "It is all explained in the manual" should never be the system designer's excuse when users complain that an interface is too difficult.

The fundamental truth about documentation is that most users simply *do not* read manuals [Rettig 1991]. Users prefer spending their time on activities that make them feel productive [Carroll and Rosson 1987], so they tend to jump the gun and start using the system without having read all the instructions. If you doubt this common observation and think that your users do read the documentation, try this simple experiment: visit a few users and place a $10 bill somewhere in their manuals. On your next visit, check how many of the bills are still there! (Of course, you can only use this technique once.)

A corollary to this phenomenon is that if users *do* want to read the manual, then they are probably in some kind of panic and will need immediate help. This observation indicates the need for good, task-oriented search and lookup tools for manuals and online documentation. Since many users rarely use the manual before they absolutely have to, they may not have the manual immediately available (it may have been lost or borrowed by another user), which is one reason for the trend toward supplementing printed manuals with online help and online documentation. Also, online information has the potential for getting users the precise information they need faster than a paper book through features like hypertext [Nielsen 1990a] and good search facilities.

As an example, users of the SuperBook® online information browser found information in an online manual in 4.3 minutes compared to 5.6 minutes for users of a printed version of the same manual [Egan *et al.* 1989]. This result was only achieved after usability testing and iterative design of the online interface. Users of the initial design performed the same test tasks in 7.6 minutes, indicating the value of applying usability engineering principles to online documentation as well as to the main system.

SuperBook is a registered trademark of Bellcore.

The main principle to remember about online help and documentation is that these facilities add an extra set of features to a system, thus complicating the interface just by virtue of existing. Even though it is tempting to design extremely advanced and feature-rich help and documentation systems, the need for an extra "help on how to get help" is an obvious symptom of overblown help design. Many users do not progress beyond the first one or two help screens, and they mostly scan the screens for potentially useful information rather than reading long paragraphs of text [Farrand and Wolfe 1992].

In one empirical study of use of online help [Senay and Stabler 1987], 52,576 help sessions on a mainframe system were logged. 23% of all help requests turned out to be erroneous, meaning that the user did not get any help whatsoever, confirming the observation that help is a system in its own right and can present usability problems to the users. Even in the cases where they did succeed in getting some help information, users only rated it as being useful in 35% of the cases. This study confirms the saying, *"help doesn't"* (or at least, it does not always help, so the system had better be usable even without online help).

Online help has the advantage over documentation that it can be context-sensitive. For example, in a graphical user interface, the user might point to elements in a dialog box to have them explained by "balloon help" [Farkas 1993; Sellen and Nicol 1990]. Also, error messages can be linked to online help with further explanation of the error and possible solutions. In any case, one should remember that the user's problem often is related to wanting to do something *else* than what is offered by the current system state, so it should also be possible for the user to ask task-oriented questions.

Of course, one important aspect of help and documentation, whether online or hardcopy, is the quality of the writing, especially including the structuring of the information and the readability of the text [Klare 1984]. In fact, a major in-depth study of online help concluded that "the quality of help texts is far more important than the mechanisms by which those texts are accessed" [Borenstein

1985]. Even so, teaching technical writing is beyond the scope of this book, so this section concentrates on the access mechanisms and the structuring of the information. See, for example, [Horton 1990] for further coverage of technical writing, and see [Mirel 1991] for a survey of research on the usability of printed documentation. See [Borenstein 1985; Duffy *et al.* 1992; Houghton 1984; Kearsley 1988; Lee 1992] for surveys of online help and [Walker 1987] for more information on online documentation. Perhaps most important of all, the information contained in the text should be correct and reflect the version of the system actually being used by the users.

A second corollary to the finding that users normally do not read the manual is that when they do want to read it, they often will not be able to find it. This problem can be overcome by using online documentation, since it normally stays on the computer once it has been installed. Of course, users have been known to remove documentation and help files when they clean up their disks, so even online documentation does not solve the problem completely.

In a field study of how people really use manuals [Comstock and Clemens 1987], the manuals were found to be stored in many strange locations. Some were nicely stored on bookshelves, though they were not organized by subject matter but rather according to their size and the color of the spines—indicating that it would be a good idea to use these visible features of manuals in a manner consistent with the content of the books. Other manuals were in desk/file drawers, in boxes, in briefcases, on the floor, and on top of computers and terminals. Users typically carried the manuals around, used them standing up, and used several manuals at a time.

A Model of Documentation Use

Users go through three stages in interacting with manuals and help systems [Wright 1983, 1991]:

1. *Searching:* Locate information relevant to a specific need.

2. *Understanding* the information.

3. *Applying:* Carry out a procedure as described in the documentation.

Two main search tools are the index and the overview map of the structure of the information space. Overview maps in books are normally in the form of a table of contents, but a diagram may sometimes be helpful too. Indexes are so obviously useful that there should be no need to mention them, except that many manuals are still published without an index. The index to a printed manual should contain not only the system's own terminology but also user-oriented task terminology as well as a large number of synonyms, including the terms commonly used by competing vendors for the same concepts, since some users will have also used those other vendors' systems. Online documentation should also have a rich index with synonyms which can furthermore offer the user full-text search capabilities and hypertext linking between related issues.

To help the user understand the information once it has been found, not only should it be written without undue use of jargon, but it should also be written in a way that corresponds to the tasks users want to do and the sequence in which they should carry out the tasks. If a sequence of steps is given, the steps should be numbered. Also, it is often good to relate the specific information given in the instructions to a conceptual model of the system, for example through the use of a diagram.[8] Since users are likely to have jumped directly into the document without having read the previous sections, each section should be as self-contained as possible. The documentation should also include a variety of examples since it is often easier for users to understand examples than to understand abstract descriptions [LeFevre and Dixon 1986]. Users are often able to modify examples to suit their own needs without having to read much more.

---

8. Illustrations in manuals are very popular with users who in one study rated them the second most important aspect of ease of use (after having well-organized material) [Angiolillo and Roberts 1991]. Thus, even disregarding whatever increased understanding users may derive from them, illustrations serve a purpose by making the documentation more approachable and encouraging the users to read it (or at least to browse it).

After the user has found and understood the information, it comes time to apply it to the system. It is always better for the user to be able to refer to the instructions while carrying them out than to have to remember them, so it should be possible to keep any online help system visible in a separate window while the user returns to the main application. It might even be possible to let the user copy examples directly from the help system to have them executed. To make it simpler for the user to carry out the instructions, they should be stated as much as possible as step-by-step procedures, which, of course, should be given in the sequence in which they should be carried out. Finally, it should be possible for the users to check that they have understood the instructions and carried them out correctly. To a large extent such confirmation is hopefully available directly from whatever feedback the system provides in any case, but the documentation should also mention how the user might check whether the operation has been a success or a failure.

Because of the many uses to which users put documentation, one might need as many as three different levels of documentation:

- Short reference cards and/or job aids [Reitman 1988] for the expert user who just wants to check a fact, and for the novice user who wants to get an overview of the system's capabilities. A similar function may be served by a keyboard template [Nolan 1991] for interfaces that are heavily based on function keys.
- Tutorial and/or introductory manuals for learners.
- Traditional reference manuals for expert users.

For multipart documentation, it is important to make each type of manual as self-contained as possible. Users should not have to combine information from multiple volumes in order to solve typical problems. Also, of course, one should not provide *too* many different types of documentation. Some software packages are released with so many different volumes of documentation that they need a special manual for the use of the manuals. The need for such a meta-manual may serve as an indication that the documentation is on the verge of being excessive.

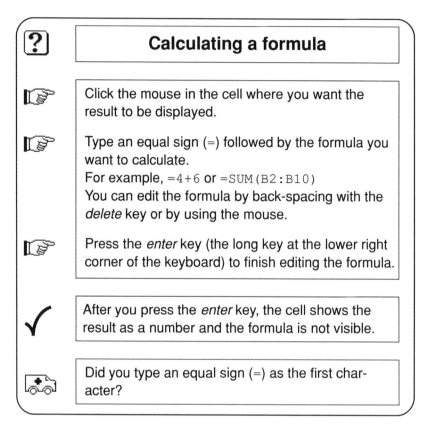

Figure 15 *A hypothetical guided exploration card for a spreadsheet, similar to the cards developed by Carroll* et al. *[1985].*

The Minimal Manual

The minimalist philosophy of documentation [Carroll *et al.* 1987–88] is a kind of reaction against the profusion of documentation users are sometimes given. As an alternative, one can provide a minimal manual that only gives whatever information is absolutely necessary in order for the users to get started using the system with common tasks.

Figure 15 shows an example of a minimalist guided exploration card to help users get started quickly. Even though a minimal manual admittedly cannot contain all the information users might possibly need, experience has shown that users do not read the large manuals anyway, whereas they do benefit from minimal manuals [Carroll 1990a]. A minimal manual should focus on real tasks since users want to get started doing useful work immediately after they start using a system. Also, it should help the user recognize error states and help them recover from the most common errors (the check mark and ambulance in Figure 15).

5.11 Heuristic Evaluation

Heuristic evaluation is done by looking at an interface and trying to come up with an opinion about what is good and bad about the interface. Ideally people would conduct such evaluations according to certain rules, such as those listed in typical guidelines documents. Some collections of usability guidelines have on the order of one thousand rules to follow, however, and are therefore seen as intimidating by developers. Most people probably perform some kind of heuristic evaluation on the basis of their own intuition and common sense instead.

Heuristic evaluation as described here [Nielsen and Molich 1990; Nielsen 1992c, 1994b], however, is a systematic inspection of a user interface design for usability [Mack and Nielsen 1993; Nielsen and Mack 1994]. The goal of heuristic evaluation is to find the usability problems in a user interface design so that they can be attended to as part of an iterative design process. Other usability inspection methods include cognitive walkthroughs [Lewis *et al.* 1990; Wharton *et al.* 1982] and claims analysis [Carroll 1990b; Carroll *et al.* 1991; Kellogg 1990]. Heuristic evaluation involves having a small set of evaluators examine the interface and judge its compliance with recognized usability principles (the "heuristics"). A typical set of heuristics is the principles used as the section headings in this chapter.

In principle, individual evaluators can perform a heuristic evaluation of a user interface on their own, but the experience from

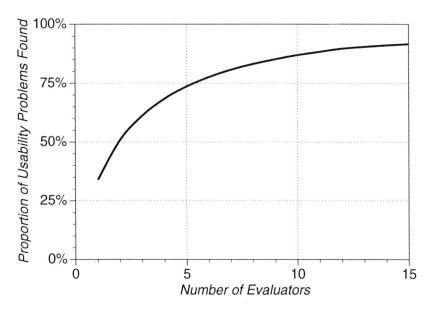

Figure 16 *Usability problems found by heuristic evaluation as a function of the number of evaluators.The figure shows the average results from six studies discussed by Nielsen [1992c].*

several projects indicates that any single evaluator will miss most of the usability problems in an interface. Averaged over six projects [Molich and Nielsen 1990; Nielsen and Molich 1990; Nielsen 1992c, 1994b], single evaluators found only 35% of the usability problems in the interfaces. However, since different evaluators tend to find different problems, it is possible to achieve substantially better performance by aggregating the evaluations from several evaluators. Figure 16 shows the proportion of usability problems found as more and more evaluators are added. The figure clearly shows that there is a nice payoff from using more than one evaluator, and it would seem reasonable to recommend the use of about five evaluators, and certainly at least three. The exact number of evaluators to use would depend on a cost–benefit analysis, and more evaluators should obviously be used in cases where usability is critical or when large payoffs can be expected due to extensive or mission-critical use of a system.

Heuristic evaluation is performed by having each individual evaluator inspect the interface alone. Only after all evaluations have been completed are the evaluators allowed to communicate and have their findings aggregated. This procedure is important in order to ensure independent and unbiased evaluations from each evaluator. The results of the evaluation can be recorded either as written reports from each evaluator or by having an observer present during the evaluation sessions and having the evaluators vocalize their comments as they go through the interface. Written reports have the advantage of presenting a formal record of the evaluation, but require an additional effort from the evaluators and also need to be read and aggregated by an evaluation manager. Using an observer adds to the overhead of each evaluation session but reduces the workload on the evaluators and provides the opportunity for having the result of the evaluation available fairly soon after the last evaluation session since the observer only needs to understand and organize his or her own notes and not a set of reports written by others. Furthermore, the observer can assist the evaluators in operating the interface in case of problems with, e.g., an unstable prototype, and help if the evaluators have limited domain expertise and need to have certain aspects of the interface explained.

In a user test situation, such as those discussed in Chapter 6, the observer (normally called the "experimenter") has the responsibility of interpreting the user's actions in order to infer how these actions are related to the usability issues in the design of the interface. This makes it possible to conduct user testing even if the users do not know anything about user interface design. In contrast, the responsibility for analyzing the user interface is placed with the evaluator in a heuristic evaluation session, so a possible observer only needs to record the evaluator's comments about the interface, and does not need to interpret the evaluator's actions.

Two further differences between heuristic evaluation sessions and traditional user testing are the willingness of the observer to answer questions from the evaluators during the session and the extent to which the evaluators can be provided with hints on using the interface. For traditional user testing, one normally wants to discover the mistakes users make when using the interface, and the experimenters are therefore reluctant to provide more help than absolutely necessary. Also, users are requested to discover the answers to their questions by using the system rather than having them answered by the experimenter. For the heuristic evaluation of a domain-specific application, it would be unreasonable to refuse to answer the evaluators' questions about the domain, especially if non-domain experts are serving as the evaluators. On the contrary, answering the evaluators' questions will enable them to better assess the usability of the user interface with respect to the characteristics of the domain. Similarly, when evaluators have problems using the interface, they can be given hints on how to proceed in order not to waste precious evaluation time struggling with the mechanics of the interface. It is important to note, however, that the evaluators should not be given help until they are clearly in trouble and have commented on the usability problem in question.

Typically, a heuristic evaluation session for an individual evaluator lasts one or two hours. Longer evaluation sessions might be necessary for larger or very complicated interfaces with a substantial number of dialogue elements, but it is likely that it would be better to split up the evaluation in several smaller sessions, each concentrating on a part of the interface.

During the evaluation session, the evaluator goes through the interface several times and inspects the various dialogue elements and compares them with a list of recognized usability principles. These heuristics are general rules that seem to describe common properties of usable interfaces. In addition to the checklist of general heuristics to be considered for all dialogue elements, the evaluator obviously is also allowed to consider any additional usability principles or results that come to mind that may be relevant for any specific dialogue element.

In principle, the evaluators decide on their own how they want to proceed with evaluating the interface. A general recommendation would be that they go through the interface at least twice, however. The first pass would be intended to get a feel for the flow of the interaction and the general scope of the system. The second pass then allows the evaluator to focus on specific interface elements while knowing how they fit the larger whole.

Since the evaluators are not *using* the system as such (to perform a real task), it is possible to perform heuristic evaluation of user interfaces that exist on paper only and have not yet been implemented [Nielsen 1990d]. This makes heuristic evaluation suitable for use early in the usability engineering lifecycle. See Exercise 8 on page 273 for an example of a heuristic evaluation of a paper mock-up interface.

If the system is intended as a walk-up-and-use interface for the general population or if the evaluators are domain experts, it will be possible to let the evaluators use the system without further assistance. If the system is domain-dependent and the evaluators are fairly naive with respect to the domain of the system, it will be necessary to assist the evaluators to enable them to be able to use the interface. One approach that has been applied successfully is to supply the evaluators with a typical usage scenario [Carroll and Rosson 1990; Clarke 1991; Nielsen 1990d], listing the various steps a user would take to perform a few realistic tasks. Such a scenario should be constructed on the basis of a task analysis of the actual users and their work in order to be as representative as possible of the eventual use of the system.

The output from using the heuristic evaluation method is a list of usability problems in the interface, annotated with references to those usability principles that were violated by the design in each case in the opinion of the evaluator. Heuristic evaluation does not provide a systematic way to generate fixes to the usability problems or a way to assess the probable quality of any redesigns. However, because heuristic evaluation aims at explaining each observed usability problem with reference to established usability principles, it will often be fairly easy to generate a revised design according to the guidelines provided by the dialogue principle that was violated. Also, many usability problems have fairly obvious fixes as soon as they have been identified.

For example, if the problem is that the user cannot copy information from one window to another, then the solution is obviously to include such a copy feature. Similarly, if the problem is the use of inconsistent typography in the form of upper- and lower case formats and fonts, the solution is obviously to pick a single typographical format for the entire interface. Even so, even for these simple examples the designer has no information to help design the exact changes to the interface (for example, how to enable the user to make the copies or which of the two font formats to standardize).

One possibility for extending the heuristic evaluation method to provide some design advice is to conduct a debriefing session after the last evaluation session [Nielsen 1994b]. The participants in the debriefing should include the evaluators, any observer used during the evaluation sessions, and representatives of the design team. The debriefing session would mostly be conducted in a brainstorming mode and would focus on discussions of possible redesigns to address the major usability problems and general problematic aspects of the design. A debriefing is also a good opportunity for discussing the positive aspects of the design, since heuristic evaluation does not otherwise address this important issue.

Heuristic evaluation is explicitly intended as a "discount usability engineering" method [Nielsen 1989b, 1990a]. Independent research [Jeffries *et al.* 1991] has indeed confirmed that heuristic evaluation is a very efficient usability engineering method, and one recent case study found a benefit–cost ratio for a heuristic evaluation project of 48, with the cost of using the method being about $10,500 and the expected benefits being about $500,000 [Nielsen 1994c]. As a discount usability engineering method, heuristic evaluation is not guaranteed to provide "perfect" results or to find every last usability problem in an interface.

Effect of Evaluator Expertise

As always in computing [Egan 1988], there are major individual differences between the performance of evaluators in heuristic evaluation. In eight case studies, the Q_3/Q_1 ratio between the number of usability problems found by the top and bottom quartile (best 25% versus worst 25%) of the evaluators ranged from 1.4 to 2.2 with a mean of 1.7. These numbers represent cases where evaluators with essentially the same background and qualifications were compared. There are thus major benefits to be gained if one could identify people who are good at doing heuristic evaluation as the evaluators. In one case study [Nielsen and Molich 1990], 34 evaluators with the same background evaluated 2 different user interfaces, and the correlation between the number of usability problems found by individual evaluators in the two systems was $r = .57$. This definitely indicates better than random consistency in the evaluators' ability to find usability problems ($p < .01$), but at the same time also indicates substantial unexplained variability in performance from one evaluation to the next. Even though it might be possible to establish a group of "good" evaluators over time by selecting people who exhibit good performance in several evaluations, this is thus a slow process and will sacrifice performance on the first several evaluation studies.

In a case study [Nielsen 1992c], the same user interface was subjected to heuristic evaluation by three groups of evaluators: usability "novices" with knowledge about computers in general but no special usability expertise, "single experts" who were usability specialists but not specialized in the domain of the interface, and "double experts" with expertise in both usability in general and the kind of interface being evaluated.[9] The performance of the novice evaluators was fairly poor, with each of them finding an average of 22% of the usability problems in the interface. The single experts found 41% of the problems each, making them 1.8 times as good as the novices, and the double experts found 60% each, making them 2.7 times as good as the novices and 1.5 times as good as the single experts. These results shows that there are systematic group differences in evaluator performance in addition

---

9. Logically, the users themselves might have been a fourth group. However, it is much better to use available users for user testing, since users are normally not very good at analyzing systems according to abstract principles. In contrast, users are perfectly suited to *using* the system, and one can then observe what actually happens instead of asking the users to guess what might happen.

to the individual differences. Even though heuristic evaluation can be performed by people with little or no usability expertise (which is an advantage from a discount usability engineering perspective), it is preferable to use usability specialists as the evaluators, and optimal performance requires double specialists.

If a sufficient number of usability specialists is not available, one can consider using technical writers from the documentation and help groups for heuristic evaluation. The writers have to understand the system anyway, and they have a natural tendency to knowing when something will be difficult to explain (which probably would mean that it would be hard to use, too).

Another way of utilizing different kinds of expertise is the *pluralistic usability walkthrough* technique [Bias 1991], where the heuristic evaluation is performed by representative users, product developers, and usability specialists. Users bring their subject matter expertise to bear on the evaluation, so this variant of heuristic evaluation is especially appropriate when only "single expert" usability specialists without knowledge of the application domain are available. Randolph Bias [1991] advocates having the various evaluators perform the initial evaluation on an individual basis before the group discussion. Instead of the more traditional approach where each evaluator evaluates the complete interface before discussing it, he advocates evaluating a single screen design at a time, having the full group discuss each screen before the evaluators move on to the next screen. This technique may be most appropriate for the evaluation of traditional character-based, full-screen interfaces that are clearly divided into distinct screens for each of the users' sub-tasks, though many graphical user interfaces also have distinct dialog boxes that can be inspected one at a time. During the group discussions, Bias recommends letting the users present their evaluation results first, in order not to have the computer specialists dominate the discussion.

One benefit of the pluralistic walkthrough method is that the dual presence of users and designers allow for preliminary collection of user input early in the stages of a design. At this stage, manuals, help systems, and other documentation may not yet be available, and users might not be able to use the system unaided. In a pluralistic walkthrough session, the system designers can serve as "living manuals," allowing the users to ask the questions they would normally seek answered in the manual.

Chapter 6   *Usability Testing*

User testing with real users is the most fundamental usability method and is in some sense irreplaceable, since it provides direct information about how people use computers and what their exact problems are with the concrete interface being tested. Even so, the methods discussed in other chapters of this book can serve as good supplements to gather additional information or to gain usability insights at a lower cost.[1]

There are several methodological pitfalls in usability testing [Holleran 1991; Landauer 1988b], and as in all kinds of testing one needs to pay attention to the issues of reliability and validity. Reliability is the question of whether one would get the same result if the test were to be repeated, and validity is the question of whether the result actually reflects the usability issues one wants to test.

---

1. There is an association of usability professionals that publishes a newsletter on practical issues related to usability testing and meets at regular intervals to discuss issues related to usability. For further information about the Usability Professionals' Association, contact its office: Usability Professionals' Association, 10875 Plano Road, Suite 115, Dallas, TX 75238, USA. Tel. +1-214-349-8841, fax +1-214-349-7946.

Reliability

Reliability of usability tests is a problem because of the huge individual differences between test users. It is not uncommon to find that the best user is 10 times as fast as the slowest user, and the best 25% of the users are normally about twice as fast as the slowest 25% of the users [Egan 1988]. Because of this well-established phenomenon, one cannot conclude much from, say, observing that User A using Interface X could perform a certain task 40% faster than User B using Interface Y; it could very well be the case that User B just happened to be slower in general than User A. If the test was repeated with Users C and D, the result could easily be the opposite. For usability engineering purposes, one often needs to make decisions on the basis of fairly unreliable data, and one should certainly do so since *some* data is better than *no* data. For example, if a company had to choose between Interfaces X and Y as just discussed, it should obviously choose Interface X since it has at least a little bit of evidence in its favor. If several users have been tested, one could use standard statistical tests[2] to estimate the significance of the difference between the systems [Brigham 1989]. Assume, for example, that the statistics package states that the difference between the systems is significant at the level $p = .20$. This means that there is a 20% chance that Y was actually the best interface, but again one should obviously choose X since the odds are 4 to 1 that it is best.

Standard statistical tests can also be used to estimate the confidence intervals of test results and thus indicate the reliability of the size of the effects. For example, a statistical claim that the 95% confidence interval for the time needed to perform a certain test task is 4.5 ± 0.2 minutes means that there is a 95% probability that the true value is between 4.3 and 4.7 (and thus a 5% probability that it is really smaller than 4.3 or larger than 4.7). Such confidence intervals are important if the choice between two options is dependent not

---

2. Statistics is of course a topic worthy of several full books in its own right. See, for example, [Pedhazur and Schmelkin 1991] for basic methods, and [Lehmann and D'Abrera 1975] for more specialized statistical tests. An introduction to the use of statistics in the user interface field is given in Section 42.5 of [Landauer 1988b].

just on which one is best but also on how *much* better it is [Landauer 1988a, 1988b]. For example, a usability problem that is very expensive to fix should only be fixed if one has a reasonably tight confidence interval showing that the problem is indeed sufficiently bothersome to the users to justify the cost.

In a survey of 36 published usability studies, I found that the mean standard deviation was 33% for measures of expert-user performance (measured in 17 studies), 46% for measures of novice-user learning (measured in 12 studies), and 59% for error rates (measured in 13 studies). In all cases, the standard deviations are expressed as percent of the measured mean value of the usability attribute in question. These numbers can be used to derive early approximations of the number of test users needed to achieve a desired confidence interval. Of course, since standard deviations vary a great deal between studies, any particular usability test might well have a higher or lower standard deviation than the values given here, and one should perform further statistical tests on the actual data measured in the study.

Anyway, the results show that error rates tend to have the highest variability, meaning that they will generally require more test users to achieve the same level of confidence as can be achieved with fewer test users for measures of learnability and even fewer for measures of expert user performance. Figure 17 shows the confidence intervals for several possible desired levels of confidence from 50% to 90% in steps of 10%, as well as for 95%, assuming that the underlying usability measures follow a normal distribution. A confidence level of 95% is often used for research studies, but for practical development purposes, it may be enough to aim for an 80% level of confidence (the third curve from the top in each of the three nomographs).

The values on the *y*-axis should be interpreted as follows: The confidence interval (corresponding to the confidence level of one of the curves) is plus or minus that many percent of the measured mean value of the usability attribute. For example, assume that we are interested in measuring expert-user performance well enough that there is a 90% chance that the true value is no more than 15%

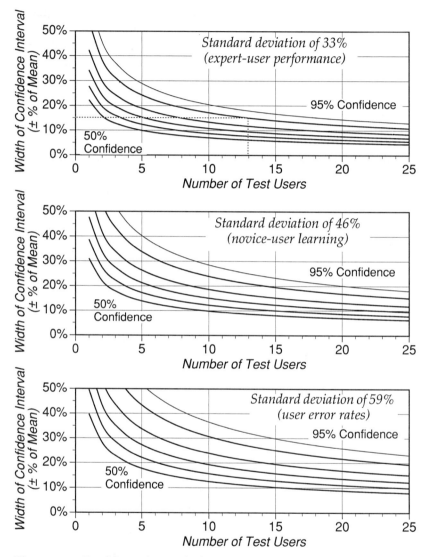

Figure 17 *Confidence intervals for usability testing from 1 to 25 users. Graphs for three different typical levels of standard deviations of the mean measured value. In each graph, the bottom curve is the 50% confidence level, followed by curves for 60%, 70%, 80%, 90%, and 95% (the top curve). The stippled lines in the top graph are discussed in the text.*

different from the mean value measured in our usability test. To find the necessary number of test users, we would start at the 15% mark on the y-axis in the top diagram in Figure 17 (corresponding to the desired length of the interval) and find the corresponding point on the 90% confidence level curve. We would then drop a line from that point to the x-axis to find the necessary number of test users (about 13). The diagram also shows that 5 test users would give us only a 70% probability of getting within ±15% of the true mean and that our 90% confidence interval would be ±24%. This level of accuracy might be enough for many projects.

Validity

Validity is a question of whether the usability test in fact measures something of relevance to usability of real products in real use outside the laboratory. Whereas reliability can be addressed with statistical tests, a high level of validity requires methodological understanding of the test method one is using as well as some common sense.

Typical validity problems involve using the wrong users or giving them the wrong tasks or not including time constraints and social influences. For example, a management information system might be tested with business school students as test users, but it is likely that the results would have been somewhat different if it had been tested with real managers. Even so, at least the business school students are people who likely will *become* managers, so they are probably more valid test users than, say, chemistry students. Similarly, results from testing a hypertext system with a toy task involving a few pages of text may not always be relevant for the use of the system in an application with hundreds of megabytes of information.

Confounding effects may also lower the validity of a usability test. For example, assume that you want to investigate whether it would be worthwhile to move from a character-based user interface to a graphical user interface for a certain application. You test this by comparing two versions of the system: one running on a 24×80 alphanumeric screen and one running on a 1024×1024 pixel graphics display. At a first glance, this may seem a reasonable test to answer the question, but more careful consideration shows that the comparison between the two screens is as much a comparison between large and small screens as it is between character-based and graphical user interfaces.

6.1   Test Goals and Test Plans

Before any testing is conducted, one should clarify the purpose of the test since it will have significant impact on the kind of testing to be done. A major distinction is whether the test is intended as a formative or summative evaluation of the user interface. *Formative evaluation* is done in order to help improve the interface as part of an iterative design process. The main goal of formative evaluation is thus to learn which detailed aspects of the interface are good and bad, and how the design can be improved. A typical method to use for formative evaluation is a thinking-aloud test. In contrast, *summative evaluation* aims at assessing the overall quality of an interface, for example, for use in deciding between two alternatives or as a part of competitive analysis to learn how good the competition really is.[3] A typical method to use for summative evaluation is a measurement test.

Test Plans

A test plan should be written down before the start of the test and should address the following issues:

- The goal of the test: What do you want to achieve?
- Where and when will the test take place?
- How long is each test session expected to take?
- What computer support will be needed for the test?
- What software needs to be ready for the test?
- What should the state of the system be at the start of the test?

---

3. Remember, by the way, that manual or paper-based solutions that do not involve computers at all are also in the running and should be studied as well.

- What should the system/network load and response times be? If possible, the system should not be unrealistically slow (see the discussion of prototyping in Section 4.8), but neither should it be unrealistically fast because it is run on a system or network with no other users. One may have to artificially slow down the system to simulate realistic response times.
- Who will serve as experimenters for the test?
- Who are the test users going to be, and how are you going to get hold of them?
- How many test users are needed?
- What test tasks will the users be asked to perform?
- What criteria will be used to determine when the users have finished each of the test tasks correctly?
- What user aids (manuals, online help, etc.) will be made available to the test users?
- To what extent will the experimenter be allowed to help the users during the test?
- What data is going to be collected, and how will it be analyzed once it has been collected?
- What will the criterion be for pronouncing the interface a success? Often, this will be the "planned" level for the previously specified usability goals (see page 80), but it could also be a looser criterion such as "no new usability problems found with severity higher than 3."

Test Budget

The test plan should also include a budget for the test. Some costs will be out-of-pocket, meaning that they have to be paid cash. Other costs are in the nature of using company staff and resources that are already paid for. Such indirect costs may or may not be formally charged to the usability budget for the specific project, depending on how the company's accounting mechanisms are set up, but they should be included in the usability manager's internal budget for the test in any case. Typical cost elements of a user test budget are

- Usability specialists to plan, run, and analyze the test: out-of-pocket expense if consultants are used

- Administrative assistants to schedule test users, enter data, etc.
- Software developers to modify the code to include data collection or other desired test customization
- The test users' time: out-of-pocket expense if outside people are hired for the test
- Computers used during testing and during analysis
- The usability laboratory or other room used for the test
- Videotapes and other consumables: out-of-pocket expense

The cost estimates for the various staff members should be based on their loaded salary and not on their nominal salary. A loaded salary is the total cost to the company of having a person employed and includes elements like benefits, vacation pay, employment taxes or fees, and general corporate overhead.

The test budget should be split into fixed and variable costs, where fixed costs are those required to plan and set up the test no matter how many test users are run, and variable costs are the additional costs needed for each test user. Splitting the cost estimates in this way allows for better planning of the number of test users to include for each test. Obviously, both fixed and variable costs vary immensely between projects, depending on multiple factors such as the size of the interface and the salary level of the intended users. Based on several published budgets, estimates for a representative, medium-sized usability test can be derived, with fixed costs of $3,000 and variable costs of $1,000 per test user [Nielsen and Landauer 1993]. Note that any specific project is likely to have different costs than these estimates.

Given estimates for fixed and variable costs, it then becomes possible to calculate the optimal number of test users if further assumptions are made about the financial impact of finding usability problems and the probability of finding each problem with a single test user. Unfortunately, these latter two numbers are much harder to estimate than the costs of testing, but any given organization should be able to build up a database of typical values over time. Again based on values from published studies, a representative value of finding a usability problem in a medium-sized project can be taken as $15,000.

Nielsen and Landauer [1993] showed that the following formula gives a good approximation of the finding of usability problems:

Usability_Problems_Found(i) = $N(1 - (1 - \lambda)^i)$,

where i is the number of test users, N is the total number of usability problems in the interface, and λ is the probability for finding any single problem with any single test user. The values of N and λ vary considerably between projects and should be estimated by curve-fitting as data becomes available for each project. It is also recommended that you keep track of these numbers for your own projects such that you can estimate "common" values of these parameters for use in the planning of future tests.

For several projects we studied, the mean number of problems in the interface, N, was 41 and the mean probability for finding any problem with a single user, λ, was 31% [Nielsen and Landauer 1993]. The following discussion uses these mean values to illustrate the use of the mathematical model in the budgeting of usability activities. Of course, one should really use the particular N and λ values that have been measured or estimated for the particular project one wants to analyze.

Given the assumptions mentioned above, Figure 18 shows how the pay-off ratio between the benefits and the costs changed in our average example with various numbers of test users. The highest ratio was achieved with three test users, where the projected benefits were $413,000, and the costs were $6,000. However, in principle, one should keep testing as long as the benefit from one additional test user is greater than the cost of running that user. Under the above model, this would imply running 15 test users at a cost of $18,000 to get benefits worth $613,000. If the recommendation in Section 4.10 to use iterative design is followed, it will be better to conduct more, smaller, tests (one for each iteration) than to spend everything on a single test.

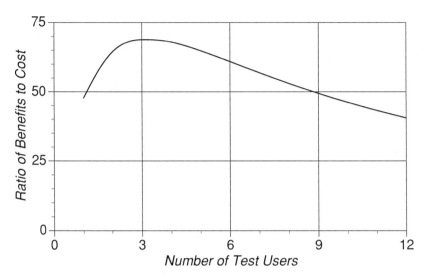

Figure 18 *The pay-off ratio (how much larger the benefits are than the costs) for user tests with various numbers of test users under the assumptions for a "typical" medium-sized project described in the text.*

Pilot Tests

No usability testing should be performed without first having tried out the test procedure on a few pilot subjects. Often, one or two pilot subjects will be enough, but more may be needed for large tests or when the initial pilot tests show severe deficiencies in the test plan. The first few pilot subjects may be chosen for convenience among people who are easily available to the experimenter even if they are not representative of the actual users, since some mistakes in the experimental design can be found even with subjects such as one's colleagues. Even so, at least one pilot subject should be taken from the same pool as the other test users.

During pilot testing, one will typically find that the instructions for some of the test tasks are incomprehensible to the users or that they misinterpret them. Similarly, any questionnaires used for subjective satisfaction rating or other debriefing will often need to be changed based on pilot testing. Also, one very often finds a mismatch between the test tasks and the time planned for each test session. Most commonly, the tasks are more difficult than one expected, but of course it may also be the case that some tasks are too easy. Depending on the circumstances of the individual project, one will either have to revise the tasks or make more time available for each test session.

Pilot testing can also be used to refine the experimental procedure and to clarify the definitions of various things that are to be measured. For example, it is often difficult to decide exactly what constitutes a user error or exactly when the user can be said to have completed a given test task, and the pilot test may reveal inconsistencies or weaknesses in the definitions contained in the test plan.

6.2   Getting Test Users

The main rule regarding test users is that they should be as representative as possible of the intended users of the system. If the test plan calls for a "discount usability" approach with very few test users, one should not choose users from outlier groups but should take additional care to involve average users. If more test users are to be used, one should select users from several different subpopulations to cover the main different categories of expected users.

The main exception from the rule that test users should be representative of the end users is testing with sales people. For many products, sales staff is used to give demonstrations to prospective customers, and the ease with which they can give these demos may be a major selling point. Often, sales people handle multiple products and do not get extensive experience from actual use of any individual product. The experience of demonstrating a user interface is very different from that of actually using it for a real task, and even though most usability efforts should aim at making the system easier to use for the users, it may increase sales significantly if "demoability" is also considered as a usability attribute.

Sometimes, the exact individuals who will be using a system can be identified. This is typically the case for systems that are being developed internally in a company for use in a given department of that company. In this case, representative users are easy to find, even though it may present some difficulties to get them to spend time on user testing instead of doing their primary job. Internal test users are often recruited through the users' management who agrees to provide a certain number of people. Unfortunately, managers often tend to select their most able staff members for such tests (either to make their department look good or because these staff members have the most interest in new technology), so one should explicitly ask managers to choose a broad sample with respect to salient user characteristics such as experience and seniority.

In other cases, the system is targeted at a certain type of users, such as lawyers, the secretaries in a dental clinic, or warehouse managers in small manufacturing companies. These user groups can be more or less homogeneous, and it may be desirable to involve test users from several different customer locations. Sometimes, existing customers are willing to help out with the test since it will get them an early look at new software as well as improving the quality of the resulting product, which they will be using. In other cases, no existing customers are available, and it may be more difficult to gain access to representative users. Sometimes, test users can be recruited from temporary employment agencies, or it may be possible to get students in the domain of interest from a local university or trade school. It may also be possible to enter a classified advertisement under job openings in order to recruit users who are currently unemployed. Of course, it will be necessary to pay all users recruited with these latter methods.

Yet other software is intended for the general population, and one can in principle use anybody as test users, again using employment agencies, students, or classified advertising to recruit test users. Especially when testing students, one should consider whether the system is also intended to be used by older users, since they may have somewhat different characteristics [Czaja et al. 1989; Nielsen and Schaefer 1993] and may therefore need to be included as an additional test group. A good source of older test users is retirees, who may also serve as a pool of talent with specific domain expertise.

Novice versus Expert Users

One of the main distinctions between categories of users is that between novice and expert users (see also Section 2.5, *Categories of Users and Individual User Differences*, on page 43 for further dimensions of interest). Almost all user interfaces need to be tested with novice users, and many systems should also be tested with expert users. Typically, these two groups should be tested in separate tests with some of the same and some different test tasks.

Sometimes, one will have to train the users with respect to those aspects of a user interface that are unfamiliar to them but are not relevant for the main usability test. This is typically necessary during the transition from one interface generation to the next, where users will have experience with the old interaction techniques but will be completely baffled by the new ones unless they are given some training. For example, a company that is moving from character-based interfaces to graphical user interfaces will have many users who have never used a mouse before, and these users will have to be trained in the use of the mouse before it is relevant to use them as test users of a mouse-based system. Using a mouse is known to be hard for the first several hours, and it is almost impossible to use a mouse correctly the first few minutes. If users are not trained in the use of the mouse and other standard interaction techniques before they are asked to test a new interface, the test will be completely dominated by the effects of the users' struggle with the interaction devices and techniques, and no information will be gained as to the usability of the dialogue.

One example of the potentially devastating effect of not training users before a test was a study of the use of a single window versus multiple windows for an electronic book [Tombaugh *et al.* 1987]. When novice users without any specific training were used as test subjects, the single-window interface was best for reading the electronic book. The time needed to answer questions about the text was 85 seconds when using the multiwindow interface and 72 seconds when using the single-window interface. In a second test, the test users were first given 30 minutes' training in the use of a mouse to control multiple windows, and the time to answer the questions about the text was now 66 seconds for the single-window interface and only 56 seconds for the multiwindow interface. Thus, both interfaces benefited from having more experienced users, but the most interesting result is that the overall conclusion with respect to determining the "winner" of the test came out the opposite. The single-window solution would be best for a "walk-up-and-use" system for users without prior mouse experience. On the other hand, the multiwindow solution would be best in the more common case where the electronic book was to be used in an office or school environment where people would be using the same computer extensively. For such environments, the wrong conclusion would have been drawn if a test with untrained users had been the only one.

Between-Subjects versus Within-Subjects Testing

Often, usability testing is conducted in order to compare the usability of two or more systems. If so, there are two basic ways of employing the test users: *between-subject testing* and *within-subject testing*.

Between-subject testing is in some sense the simplest and most valid since it involves using different test users for the different systems. Thus, each test user only participates in a single test session. The problem with between-subject designs is the huge individual variation in user skills referred to on page 166. Therefore, it can be necessary to run a very large number of test users in each condition in order to smooth over random differences between test users in each of the groups.

Between-subject testing also risks a bias due to the assignment of test users to the various groups. For example, one might decide to test 20 users, call for volunteers, and assign the first 10 users to one system and the next 10 to the other. Even though this approach may seem reasonable, it in fact introduces a bias, since users who volunteer early are likely to be different from users who volunteer late. For example, early volunteers may be more conscientious in reading announcements, or they may be more interested in new technology, and thus more likely to be super-users. There are two methodologically sound ways to assign test users to groups: The simplest and best is random assignment, which minimizes the risk of any bias but requires a large number of test users because of individual variability. The second method is matched assignment, which involves making sure that each group has equally many users from each of those categories that have been defined as being of interest to the test. For example, users from different departments might be considered different categories, as may old versus young users, men versus women, and users with different computer experience or different educational backgrounds.

Alternatively, one may conduct the test as a within-subject design, meaning that all the test users get to use all the systems that are being tested. This method automatically controls for individual variability since any user who is particularly fast or talented will presumably be about equally superior in each test condition. Within-subject testing does have the major disadvantage that the test users cannot be considered as novice users anymore when they approach the other systems after having learned how to use the first system. Often, some transfer of skill will take place between systems, and the users will be better at using the second system than they were at using the first. In order to control for this effect, users are normally divided into groups, with one group using one system first and the other group using the other system first. The issues discussed above regarding the assignment of users to groups also apply to this aspect of within-subject testing.

6.3   Choosing Experimenters

No matter what test method is chosen, somebody has to serve as the experimenter and be in charge of running the test. In general, it is of course preferable to use good experimenters who have previous experience in using whatever method is chosen. For example, a study where 20 different groups of experimenters tested the same interface, there was a correlation of $r = .76$ between the rated quality of the methodology used by a group and the number of usability problems they discovered in the interface [Nielsen 1992a]. When running 3 test subjects, experimenters using very good methodology found about 5–6 of the 8 usability problems in the interface, and experimenters using very poor methodology only found about 2–3 of the problems.

This result does not mean that one should abandon user testing if no experienced usability specialist is available to serve as the experimenter. First, it is obviously better to find a few usability problems than not to find any, and second, even inexperienced experimenters can use a decent (if not perfect) methodology if they are careful. It is possible for computer scientists to learn user test methods and apply them with good results [Nielsen 1992a; Wright and Monk 1991].

In addition to knowledge of the test method, the experimenter must have extensive knowledge of the application and its user interface. System knowledge is necessary for the experimenter to understand what the users are doing as they perform tasks with the system, and to make reasonable inferences about the users' probable intentions at various stages of the dialogue. Often, users' actions will go by too fast for experimenters, who are trying to understand what the system is doing at the same time as they are analyzing the users.

The experimenter does not necessarily need to know how the system is implemented, even though such knowledge can come in handy during tests of preliminary prototypes with a tendency to crash. If the experimenter does not know how to handle system crashes, it is a good idea to arrange to have a programmer with the necessary skills stand by in a nearby office.

One way to get experimenters with a high degree of system knowledge is to use the system's designers themselves as evaluators [Wright and Monk 1991]. In addition to the practical advantages, there are also motivational reasons for doing so, since the experience of seeing users struggle with their system always has a very powerful impact on designers [Jørgensen 1989]. There are some problems with having people run tests of their own systems, though, including a possible lack of objectivity that may lead them to help the users too much (see also the footnote on page 204). A common weakness is the tendency for a designer to explain away user problems rather than acknowledging them as real issues. To avoid these problems, developers can serve as one *part* of the usability testing team while usability specialists handle relations with the users [Ehrlich *et al.* 1994].

6.4 Ethical Aspects of Tests with Human Subjects

Users are human, too. Therefore, one cannot subject them to the kind of "destructive testing" that is popular in the components industry. Instead, tests should be conducted with deep respect for the users' emotions and well-being [Allen 1984; American Psychological Association 1982].

At first, it might seem that usability testing does not represent the same potential dangers to the users as would, say, participation in a test of a new drug. Even though it is true that usability test subjects are not normally bodily harmed, even by irate developers resenting the users' mistreatment of their beloved software, test participation can still be quite a distressful experience for the users [Schrier 1992]. Users feel a tremendous pressure to perform, even when they are told that the purpose of the study is to test the system and not the user. Also, users will inevitably make errors and be slow at learning the system (especially during tests of early designs with many severe usability problems), and they can easily get to feel inadequate or stupid as they experience these difficulties. Knowing that they are observed, and possibly recorded, makes the feeling of performing inadequately even more unpleasant to the users. Test users have been known to break down and cry during usability testing, even though this only happens in a small minority of cases.

At first, one might think that highly educated and intelligent users would have enough self-confidence to make fear of inadequacy less of a problem. On the contrary, high-level managers and highly specialized professionals are often especially concerned about exhibiting ignorance during a test. Therefore, experimenters should be especially careful to acknowledge the professional skills of such users up front and emphasize the need to involve people with these users' particular knowledge in the test.

The experimenter has a responsibility to make the users feel as comfortable as possible during and after the test. Specifically, the experimenter must never laugh at the users or in any way indicate that they are slow at discovering how to operate the system. During the introduction to the test, the experimenter should make clear that it is the system that is being tested and not the user. To emphasize this point, test users should never be referred to as "subjects," "guinea pigs," or other such terms. I personally prefer the term "test user," but some usability specialists like to use terms such as "usability evaluator" or "participant," which emphasize even more that it is the system that is being tested. Since the term "evaluator" technically speaking refers to an inspection-oriented role where usability specialists judge a system instead of *using* it to perform a task, I normally do not use this term myself when referring to test users.

The users should be told that no information about the performance of any individual users will be revealed and specifically that their manager will not be informed about their performance. The test itself should be conducted in a relaxed atmosphere, and the experimenter should take the necessary time for small talk to calm down the user before the start of the experiment, as well as during any breaks. It might also be a good idea to serve coffee, soft drinks, or other refreshments—especially if the test takes more than an hour or so. Furthermore, to bolster the users' confidence and make them at ease, the very first test task should be so easy that they are virtually guaranteed an early success experience.

The experimenter should ensure that the test room, test computer, and test software are ready before the test user arrives in order to avoid the confusion that would otherwise arise due to last-minute adjustments. Also, of course, copies of the test tasks, any questionnaires, and other test materials should be checked before the arrival of the user such that they are ready to be handed out at the appropriate time. The test session should be conducted without disruptions: typically, one should place a sign saying, *"User test in progress—Do not disturb"* outside the (closed) door and disable any telephone sets in the test room.

The test results should be kept confidential, and reports from the test should be written in such a way that individual test users cannot be identified. For example, users can be referred to by numbers (User1, User2, etc.) and not by names or even initials.[4] The test should be conducted with as few observers as possible, since the size of the "audience" also has a detrimental effect on the test user: It is less embarrassing to make a fool of yourself in front of 1 person than in front of 10. And remember that users *will* think that they are making fools of themselves as they struggle with the interface and overlook "obvious" options, even if they only make the same mistakes as everybody else. For similar reasons, videotapes of a user test session should not be shown publicly without explicit permission from the user. Also, the users' manager should never be allowed to observe the test for any reason and should not be given performance data for individual users.

During testing, the experimenter should normally not interfere with the user but should let the user discover the solutions to the problems on his or her own. Not only does this lead to more valid and interesting test results,[5] it also prevents the users from feeling that they are so stupid that the experimenter had to solve the problems for them. On the other hand, the experimenter should not let a user struggle endlessly with a task if the user is clearly bogged down and getting desperate. In such cases, the experimenter can

---

4. Ensuring anonymity requires a fair amount of thought. For example, a report of a test with users drawn from a department with only one female staff member referred to all users as "he," even when describing observations of the woman since her anonymity would otherwise have been compromised.

5. It is a common mistake to help users too early. Since users normally do not get help when they have to learn a computer system on their own, there is highly relevant information to be gained from seeing what further difficulties users get into as they try to solve the problem on their own.

Before the test:
Have everything ready before the user shows up.
Emphasize that it is the *system* that is being tested, not the user.
Acknowledge that the software is new and untested, and may have problems.
Let users know that they can stop at any time.
Explain any recording, keystroke logging, or other monitoring that is used.
Tell the user that the test results will be kept completely confidential.
Make sure that you have answered all the user's questions before proceeding.

During the test:
Try to give the user an early success experience.
Hand out the test tasks one at a time.
Keep a relaxed atmosphere in the test room, serve coffee and/or have breaks.
Avoid disruptions: Close the door and post a sign on it. Disable telephone.
Never indicate in any way that the user is making mistakes or is too slow.
Minimize the number of observers at the test.
Do not allow the user's management to observe the test.
If necessary, have the experimenter stop the test if it becomes too unpleasant.

After the test:
End by stating that the user has helped you find areas of improvement.
Never report results in such a way that individual users can be identified.
Only show videotapes outside the usability group with the user's permission.

Table 9 *Main ethical considerations for user testing.*

gently provide a hint or two to the user in order to get on with the test. Also, the experimenter may have to terminate the test if the user is clearly unhappy and unable to do anything with the system. Such action should be reserved for the most desperate cases only. Furthermore, test users should be informed before the start of the test that they can always stop the test at any time, and any such requests should obviously be honored.

After the test, the user should be debriefed and allowed to make comments about the system. After the administration of the questionnaire (if used), any deception employed in the experiment should be disclosed in order not to have the user leave the test with an erroneous understanding of the system. An example of a deception that should be disclosed is the use of the Wizard of Oz method (see page 96) to simulate nonexisting computer capabilities. Also, the experimenter can answer any additional user questions that could not be answered for fear of causing bias until after the user had filled in the questionnaire. The experimenter should end the debriefing by thanking the user for participating in the test and explicitly state that the test helped to identify areas of possible improvement in the product.[6] This part of the debriefing helps users recover their self-respect after the many errors they probably felt they made during the test itself. Also, the experimenter should endeavor to end the session on a positive and relaxed note, repeating that the results are going to be kept confidential and also engaging in some general conversation and small talk as the user is being escorted out of the building or laboratory area.

Table 9 summarizes the most important ethical considerations for user testing. In addition to following the rules outlined here, it is a good idea for the experimenters to have tried the role of test subjects themselves a few times, so that they know from personal experience how stupid and vulnerable subjects may feel.

6.5   Test Tasks

The basic rule for test tasks is that they should be chosen to be as representative as possible of the uses to which the system will eventually be put in the field. Also, the tasks should provide reasonable coverage of the most important parts of the user interface. The test tasks can be designed based on a task analysis or based on a product identity statement listing the intended uses for the product. Information from logging frequencies of use of commands in running systems (see page 217) and other ways of learning how users actually use systems, such as field observation, can also be used to construct more representative sets of test tasks for user testing of similar systems [Gaylin 1986].

---

6. However, it may also be necessary to mention that the development team will not necessarily be able to correct all identified problems. Users can get very disappointed if they find that the system is released with one of "their" problems still in the interface in spite of a promise to correct it.

The tasks need to be small enough to be completed within the time limits of the user test, but they should not be so small that they become trivial. The test tasks should specify precisely what result the user is being asked to produce, since the process of using a computer to achieve a goal is considerably different from just playing around. For example, a test task for a spreadsheet could be to enter sales figures for six regions for each of four quarters, with some sample numbers given in the task description. A second test task could then be to obtain totals and percentages, and a third might be to construct a bar chart showing trends across regions. Test tasks should normally be given to the users in writing. Not only does this ensure that all users get the tasks described the same way, but having written tasks also allows the user to refer to the task description during the experiment instead of having to remember all the details of the task. After the user has been given the task and has had a chance to read it, the experimenter should allow the user to ask questions about the task description, in order to minimize the risk that the user has misinterpreted the task. Normally, task descriptions are handed to the user on a piece of paper, but they can also be shown in a window on the computer. This latter approach is usually chosen in computer-paced tests where users have to perform a very large number of tasks.

Test tasks should never be frivolous, humorous, or offensive, such as testing a paint program by asking the user to draw a mustache on a scanned photo of the President. First, there is no guarantee that everybody will find the same thing funny, and second, the nonserious nature of such tasks distracts from the test of the system and may even demean the users. Instead, all test tasks should be business-oriented (except, of course, for tests of entertainment software and such) and as realistic as possible. To increase both the users' understanding of the tasks and their sense of being realistic usage of the software, the tasks can be related to an overall scenario. For example, the scenario for the spreadsheet example mentioned above could be that the user had just been hired as sales manager for a company and had been asked to give a presentation the next day.

The test tasks can also be used to increase the user's confidence. The very first test task should always be extremely simple in order to guarantee the user an early success experience to boost morale. Similarly, the last test task should be designed to make users feel that they have accomplished something. For example, a test of a word processor could end with having the user print out a document. Since users will feel inadequate if they do not complete all the given tasks, one should never give the users a complete listing of all the test tasks in advance. Rather, the tasks should be given to the users one at a time such that it is always possible to stop the test without letting the user feel incompetent.

6.6 Stages of a Test

A usability test typically has four stages:

1. Preparation
2. Introduction
3. The test itself
4. Debriefing

Preparation

In preparation for the experiment, the experimenter should make sure that the test room is ready for the experiment, that the computer system is in the start state that was specified in the test plan, and that all test materials, instructions, and questionnaires are available. For example, all files needed for the test tasks should be restored to their original content, and any files created during earlier tests should be moved to another computer or at least another directory. In order to minimize the user's discomfort and confusion, this preparation should be completed before the arrival of the user. Also, any screen savers should be switched off, as should any other system components, such as email notifiers, that might otherwise interrupt the experiment.

Introduction

During the introduction, the experimenter welcomes the test user and gives a brief explanation of the purpose of the test. The experimenter may also explain the computer setup to users if it is likely to be unfamiliar to them. The experimenter then proceeds with introducing the test procedure. Especially for inexperienced experimenters, it may be a good idea to have a checklist at hand with the most important points to be covered, but care should be taken not to make the introduction seem mechanical, as could easily be the case if the experimenter were to simply read from the checklist.

Typical elements to cover in a test introduction include the following:

- The purpose of the test is to evaluate the software and not the user.

- Unless the experimenter is actually the system designer, the experimenter should mention that he or she has no personal stake in the system being evaluated, so that the test user can speak freely without being afraid of hurting the experimenter's feelings. If the experimenter *did* design the system, this fact is probably better left unsaid in order to avoid the opposite effect.

- The test results will be used to improve the user interface, so the system that will eventually be released will likely be different from the one seen in the test.

- A reminder that the system is confidential and should not be discussed with others. Even if the system is not confidential, it may still be a good idea to ask the test user to refrain from discussing it with colleagues who may be participating in future tests, in order not to bias them.

- A statement that participation in the test is voluntary and that the user may stop at any time.[7]

---

7. Even though this may not need to be mentioned explicitly in the experimenter's introduction, users who do elect to stop the experiment should still get whatever payment was promised for the time they have spent, even if they did not complete the experiment, and even if the data from their participation cannot be used.

- A reassurance that the results of the test will be kept confidential and not shown to anybody in a form where the individual test user can be identified.
- An explanation of any video or audio recording that may be taking place. In cases where the video record will not be showing the user's face anyway, but only the screen and keyboard and the user's back, it is a good idea to mention this explicitly to alleviate the user's worries about being recorded.
- An explanation that the user is welcome to ask questions since we want to know what they find unclear in the interface, but that the experimenter will not answer most questions during the test itself, since the goal of the test is to see whether the system can be used without outside help.
- Any specific instructions for the kind of experiment that is being conducted, such as instructions to think out loud or to work as fast as possible while minimizing mistakes.
- An invitation to the user to ask any clarifying questions before the start of the experiment.

Many people have the test users sign an informed consent form that repeats the most important instructions and experimental conditions and states that they have understood them. I do not like these forms since they can increase the user's anxiety level by making the test seem more foreboding than it really is. Sometimes, consent forms may be required for legal reasons, and they should certainly be used in cases where videotapes or other records or results from the test will be shown to others. In any case, it is recommended to keep any such forms short, to the point, and written in everyday language rather than legalese, so that the users do not fear that they are being entrapped to sign away more rights than they actually are.

During the introduction phase, the experimenter should also ensure that the physical set-up of the computer is ergonomically suited for the individual test user. A common problem is the position of the mouse for left-handed users, but it may also be necessary to adjust the chair or other parts of the room such that the user feels comfortable. If the actual computer model is unfamiliar to the user, it may be a good idea to let the user practice using some other software before the start of the test itself, to avoid contaminating the test results with the user's initial adjustments to the hardware.

After the introduction, the user is given any written instructions for the test, including the first test task, and asked to read them. The experimenter should explicitly ask the test user whether he or she has any questions regarding the experimental procedure, the test instructions, or the tasks before the start of the test.

Running the Test

During the test itself, the experimenter should normally refrain from interacting with the user, and should certainly not express any personal opinions or indicate whether the user is doing well or poorly. The experimenter may make uncommitted sounds like "uh-huh" to acknowledge comments from the user and to keep the user going, but again, care should be taken not to let the tone of such sounds indicate whether the user is on the right track or has just made a ridiculous comment. Also, the experimenter should refrain from helping the test user, even if the user gets into quite severe difficulties.

The main exception from the rule that users should not be helped is when the user is clearly stuck and is getting unhappy with the situation. The experimenter may also decide to help a user who is encountering a problem that has been observed several times before with previous test users. The experimenter should only do so if it is clear beyond any doubt from the previous tests what the problem is and what different kinds of subsequent problems users may encounter as a result of the problem in question. It is tempting to help too early and too much, so experimenters should exercise caution in deciding when to help. Also, of course, no help can be given during experiments aiming to time users' performance on a task.

In case several people are observing the experiment, it is important to have appointed one of them as the official experimenter in advance and only have that one person provide instructions and speak during the experiment. In order not to confuse the user, all other observers should keep completely quiet, even if they do not agree with the way the experimenter is running the experiment. If they absolutely need to make comments, they can do so by unobtrusively passing the experimenter a note or talking with the experimenter during a break.

Debriefing

After the test, the user is debriefed and is asked to fill in any subjective satisfaction questionnaires. In order to avoid any bias from comments by the experimenter, questionnaires should be administered *before* any other discussion of the system. During debriefing, users are asked for any comments they might have about the system and for any suggestions they may have for improvement. Such suggestions may not always lead to specific design changes, and one will often find that different users make completely contradictory suggestions, but this type of user suggestion can serve as a rich source of additional ideas to consider in the redesign.

The experimenter can also use the debriefing to ask users for further comments about events during the test that were hard for the experimenter to understand. Even though users may not always remember why they did certain things, they are sometimes able to clarify some of their presumptions and goals.

Finally, as soon as possible after the user has left, the experimenter should check that all results from the test have been labelled with the test user's number, including any files recorded by the computer, all questionnaires and other forms, as well as the experimenter's own notes. Also, the experimenter should write up a brief report on the experiment as soon as possible, while the events are still fresh in the experimenter's mind and the notes still make sense. A full report on the complete sequence of experiments may be written later, but the work of writing such a report is made considerably simpler by having well-organized notes and preliminary reports from the individual tests.

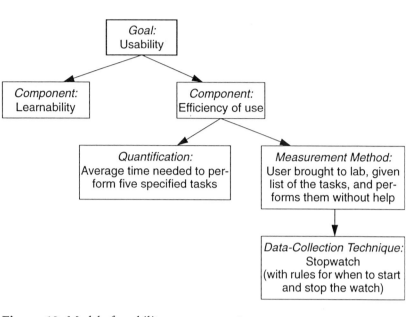

Figure 19 *Model of usability measurement*

6.7   Performance Measurement

Measurement studies form the basis of much traditional research on human factors and are also important in the usability engineering lifecycle for assessing whether usability goals have been met (see page 79) and for comparing competing products. User performance is almost always measured by having a group of test users perform a predefined set of test tasks while collecting time and error data.

A major pitfall with respect to measurement is the potential for measuring something that is poorly related to the property one is really interested in assessing. Figure 19 shows a simple model relating the true goal of a measurement study (the usability of the system) to the actual data-collection activities that may sometimes erroneously be thought of as the core of measurement. As indicated by the model, one starts out by making clear the goal of the exercise. Here, we will assume that "usability" as an abstract concept is the goal, but it could also be, e.g., improved customer perceptions of the quality of a company's user interfaces.

Goals are typically quite abstract, so one then breaks them down into components like the usability attributes discussed further in Section 2.2. Figure 19 shows two such components, learnability and efficiency of use. As further discussed in Section 4.3, one then needs to balance the various components of the goal and decide on their relative importance. Once the components of the goal have been defined, it becomes necessary to quantify them precisely. For example, the component "efficiency of use" can be quantified as the average time it takes users to perform a certain number of specified tasks. Even if these tasks are chosen to be representative of the users' normal task mix, it is important to keep in mind that the test tasks are only that: test tasks and not all possible tasks. In interpreting the results from the measurement study, it is necessary to keep in mind the difference between the principled component that one is aiming for, that is, efficiency of use in general, and the specific quantification which is used as a proxy for that component (i.e., the test tasks). As an obvious example, an iterative design process should not aim at improving efficiency of use for a system just by optimizing the interface for the execution of the five test tasks and nothing else (unless the tasks truly represent all of what the user ever will do with the system).

Given the quantification of a component, one needs to define a method for measuring the users' performance. Two obvious alternatives come to mind for the example in Figure 19: either bring some test users into the laboratory and give them a list of the test tasks to perform, or observe a group of users at work in their own environment and measure them whenever a task like the specified test tasks occurs. Finally, one needs to define the actual activities that are to be carried out to collect the data from the study. Some alternatives for the present example could be to have the computer measure the time from start to end of each task, to have an experimenter measure it by a stopwatch, and to have users report the time themselves in a diary. In either case it is important to have a clear definition of when a task starts and when it stops.

Typical quantifiable usability measurements include

- The time users take to complete a specific task.
- The number of tasks (or the proportion of a larger task) of various kinds that can be completed within a given time limit.
- The ratio between successful interactions and errors.
- The time spent recovering from errors.
- The number of user errors.
- The number of immediately subsequent erroneous actions.
- The number of commands or other features that were utilized by the user (either the absolute number of commands issued or the number of *different* commands and features used).
- The number of commands or other features that were never used by the user.
- The number of system features the user can remember during a debriefing after the test.
- The frequency of use of the manuals and/or the help system, and the time spent using these system elements.
- How frequently the manual and/or help system solved the user's problem.
- The proportion of user statements during the test that were positive versus critical toward the system.
- The number of times the user expresses clear frustration (or clear joy).
- The proportion of users who say that they would prefer using the system over some specified competitor.
- The number of times the user had to work around an unsolvable problem.
- The proportion of users using efficient working strategies compared to the users who use inefficient strategies (in case there are multiple ways of performing the tasks).
- The amount of "dead" time when the user is not interacting with the system. The system can be instrumented to distinguish between two kinds of dead time: response-time delays where the user is waiting for the system, and thinking-time delays where the system is waiting for the user. These two kinds of dead time should obviously be approached in different ways.

- The number of times the user is sidetracked from focusing on the real task.

Of course, only a subset of these measurements would be collected during any particular measurement study.

6.8   Thinking Aloud

Thinking aloud may be the single most valuable usability engineering method. Basically, a thinking-aloud test involves having a test subject use the system while continuously thinking out loud [Lewis 1982]. By verbalizing their thoughts, the test users enable us to understand how they view the computer system, and this again makes it easy to identify the users' major misconceptions. One gets a very direct understanding of what parts of the dialogue cause the most problems, because the thinking-aloud method shows how users interpret each individual interface item.

The thinking-aloud method has traditionally been used as a psychological research method [Ericsson and Simon 1984], but it is increasingly being used for the practical evaluation of human–computer interfaces [Denning *et al.* 1990]. The main disadvantage of the method is that is does not lend itself very well to most types of performance measurement. On the contrary, its strength is the wealth of qualitative data it can collect from a fairly small number of users. Also, the users' comments often contain vivid and explicit quotes that can be used to make the test report more readable and memorable.

At the same time, thinking aloud may also give a false impression of the cause of usability problems if too much weight is given to the users' own "theories" of what caused trouble and what would help. For example, users may be observed to overlook a certain field in a dialog box during the first part of a test. After they finally find the field, they may claim that they would have seen it immediately if it had been in some other part of the dialog box. It is important not to rely on such statements. Instead, the experimenter should make notes of what the users were *doing* during the part of the experiment where they overlooked the critical field. Data showing where users actually looked has much higher validity than the users' claim that they would have seen the field if it had been somewhere else. The strength of the thinking-aloud method is to show what the users are doing and why they are doing it *while* they are doing it in order to avoid later rationalizations.

Thinking out loud seems very unnatural to most people, and some test users have great difficulties in keeping up a steady stream of utterances as they use a system.[8] Not only can the unnaturalness of the thinking aloud situation make the test harder to conduct, but it can also impact the results. First, the need to verbalize can slow users down, thus making any performance measurements less representative of the users' regular working speed. Second, users' problem solving behavior can be influenced by the very fact that they are verbalizing their thoughts. The users might notice inconsistencies in their own models of the system, or they may concentrate more on critical task components [Bainbridge 1979], and these changes may cause them to learn some user interfaces faster or differently than they otherwise would have done. For example, Berry and Broadbent [1990] provided users with written instructions on how to perform a certain task and found that users performed 9% faster if they were asked to think aloud while doing the task. Berry and Broadbent argue that the verbalization reinforced those aspects of the instructions which the users needed for the task, thus helping them become more efficient. In another study [Wright and Converse 1992], users who were thinking aloud while performing various file system operations were found to make only about 20% of the errors made by users who were working silently. Furthermore, the users in the thinking-aloud study finished their tasks about twice as fast as the users in the silent condition.

---

8. Verbalization seems to come the hardest to expert users who may perform many operations so quickly that they have nothing to say. They may not even consciously know what they are doing in cases where they have completely automated certain common procedures.

The experimenter will often need to continuously prompt the user to think out loud by asking questions like, "What are you thinking now?" and "What do you think this message means?" (*after* the user has noticed the message and is clearly spending time looking at it and thinking about it). If the user asks a question like, "Can I do such-and-such?" the experimenter should not answer, but instead keep the user talking with a counter-question like, "What do you think will happen if you do it?" If the user acts surprised after a system action but does not otherwise say anything, the experimenter may prompt the user with a question like, "Is that what you expected would happen?" Of course, following the general principle of not interfering in the user's use of the system, the experimenter should *not* use prompts like, "What do you think the message on the bottom of the screen means?" if the user has not noticed that message yet.

Since thinking aloud seems strange to many people, it may help to give the test users a role model by letting them observe a short thinking-aloud test before the start of their own experiment. One possibility is for the experimenter to enact a small test, where the experimenter performs some everyday task like looking up a term in a dictionary while thinking out loud. Alternatively, users can be shown a short video of a test that was made with the sole purpose of instructing users. Showing users how a test videotape looks may also help alleviate their own fears of any videotaping that will be done during the test.

Users will often make comments regarding aspects of the user interface which they like or do not like. To some extent, it is one of the great advantages of the thinking-aloud method that one can collect such informal comments about small irritants that would not show up in other forms of testing. They may not impact measurable usability, but they might as well be fixed. Unfortunately, users will often disagree about such irritants, so one should take care not to change an interface just because of a comment by a single user. Also, user comments will often be inappropriate when seen in a larger interface design perspective, so it is the responsibility of the experimenter to interpret the user's comments and not just accept them indiscriminately. For example, users who are using a mouse for the first time will often direct a large proportion of their comments toward aspects of moving the mouse and pointing and clicking, which might be interesting for a designer of more intuitive input hardware but are of limited use to a software designer. In such a test, the experimenter would need to abstract from the users' mouse problems and try to identify the underlying usability problems in the dialogue and estimate how the users would have used the interface if they had been better at using the pointing device.

Constructive Interaction

A variation of the thinking-aloud method is called *constructive interaction* and involves having two test users use a system together [O'Malley *et al.* 1984]. This method is sometimes also called *codiscovery learning* [Kennedy 1989]. The main advantage of constructive interaction is that the test situation is much more natural than standard thinking-aloud tests with single users, since people are used to verbalizing when they are trying to solve a problem together. Therefore, users may make more comments when engaged in constructive interaction than when simply thinking aloud for the benefit of an experimenter [Hackman and Biers 1992]. The method does have the disadvantage that the users may have different strategies for learning and using computers. Therefore, the test session may switch back and forth between disparate ways of using the interface, and one may also occasionally find that the two test users simply cannot work together.

Constructive interaction is especially suited for usability testing of user interfaces for children since it may be difficult to get them to follow the instructions for a standard thinking-aloud test.

Constructive interaction is most suited for projects where it is easy to get large numbers of users into the lab, and where these users are comparatively cheap, since it requires the use of twice as many test users as single-user thinking aloud.

Retrospective Testing

If a videotape has been made of a user test session, it becomes possible to collect additional information by having the user review the recording [Hewett and Scott 1987]. This method is sometimes called *retrospective testing*. The user's comments while reviewing the tape are sometimes more extensive than comments made under the (at least perceived) duress of working on the test task, and it is of course possible for the experimenter to stop the tape and question the user in more detail without fearing to interfere with the test, which has essentially already been completed.

Retrospective testing is especially valuable in cases where representative test users are difficult to get hold of, since it becomes possible to gain more information from each test user. The obvious downside is that each test takes at least two times as long, so the method is not suited if the users are highly paid or perform critical work from which they cannot be spared for long. Unfortunately, those users who are difficult to get to participate in user testing are often exactly those who are also very expensive, but there are still some cases where retrospective testing is beneficial.

Coaching Method

The coaching method [Mack and Burdett 1992] is somewhat different from other usability test methods in having an explicit interaction between the test subject and the experimenter (or "coach"). In most other methods, the experimenter tries to interfere as little as possible with the subject's use of the computer, but the coaching method actually involves steering the user in the right direction while using the system.

During a coaching study, the test user is allowed to ask any system-related question of an expert coach who will answer to the best of his or her ability.[9] Usually, the experimenter or a research assistant serves as the coach. One variant of the method involves a separate coach chosen from a population of expert users. Having an independent coach lets the experimenter study how the coach answers the user's questions. This variant can be used to analyze the expert coach's model of the interface. Normally, though, coaching focuses on the novice user and is aimed at discovering the information needs of such users in order to provide better training and documentation, as well as possibly redesigning the interface to avoid the need for the questions.

The coaching method has proven helpful in getting Japanese users to externalize their problems while using computers [Kato 1986]. Other, more traditional methods are sometimes difficult to use in Japan, where cultural norms make some people reluctant to verbalize disagreement with an interface design.

The coaching situation is more natural than the thinking-aloud situation. It also has an advantage in cases where test users are hard to come by because the intended user population is small, specialized, and highly paid. Coaching provides the test users with tangible benefits in return for participating in the test by giving them instruction on a one-to-one basis by a highly skilled coach.

Finally, the coaching method may be used in cases where one wants to conduct tests with expert users without having any experts available. Coaching can bring novice users up to speed fairly rapidly and can then be followed by more traditional tests of the users' performance once they have reached the desired level of expertise.

6.9   Usability Laboratories

Many user tests take place in specially equipped usability laboratories [Nielsen 1994a]. Figure 20 shows a possible floor plan for such a laboratory. I should stress, however, that special laboratories are a convenience but not an absolute necessity for usability testing. It is

---

9. One variant of the coaching method would be to restrict the answers to certain predetermined information. In an extensive series of experiments, one could then vary the rules for the coach's answers in order to learn what types of answers helped users the most. Unfortunately, this variant requires extremely skilled and careful coaches since they need to compose answers on the fly to unpredictable user questions.

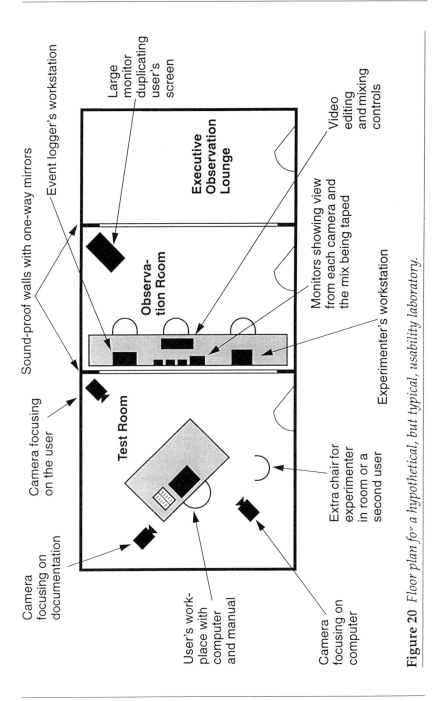

Figure 20 *Floor plan for a hypothetical, but typical, usability laboratory.*

possible to convert a regular office temporarily into a usability laboratory, and it is possible to perform usability testing with no more equipment than a notepad.

In September 1993, I surveyed thirteen usability laboratories from a variety of companies [Nielsen 1994a]. The median floor space of the laboratories was 63 m^2 (678 square feet), and the median size of the test rooms was 13 m^2 (144 square feet). The smallest laboratory was 35 m^2 (377 square feet) with only 9 m^2 (97 square feet) for the test user. The largest laboratory was 237 m^2 and had 7 rooms, allowing a variety of tests to take place simultaneously [Lund 1994]. The largest single test room was 40 m^2 (430 square feet) and was found in a telephone company with a need to test groupware interfaces with many users.

Having a permanent usability laboratory decreases the overhead of usability testing (once it is set up, that is!) and may thus encourage increased usability testing in an organization. Having a special room and special equipment dedicated to usability testing means that there will be fewer scheduling problems associated with each test and also makes it possible to run tests without disturbing other groups.

Usability laboratories typically have sound-proof, one-way mirrors[10] separating the observation room from the test room to allow the experimenters, other usability specialists, and the developers to discuss user actions without disturbing the user. Users are not so stupid that they do not know that there are observers behind a wall with a large mirror in a test room, so one might as well briefly show the users the observation room before the start of the test. Knowing who and what are behind the mirror is much less stressful for the users than having to imagine it. People usually come to ignore unseen observers during the test, even though they know they are there.

Having an executive observation lounge behind the main observation room again allows a third group of observers (e.g., the devel-

---

10. One-way mirrors were found in 92% of the labs in my survey.

opment team) to discuss the test without disturbing the primary experimenters and the usability specialists in the observation room.

Typically, a usability laboratory is equipped with several video cameras under remote control from the observation room.[11] These cameras can be used to show an overview of the test situation and to focus in on the user's face, the keyboard, the manual and the documentation, and the screen. A producer in the observation room then typically mixes the signal from these cameras to a single video stream that is recorded, and possibly timestamped for later synchronization with an observation log entered into a computer during the experiment. Such synchronization makes it possible to later find the video segment corresponding to a certain interesting user event without having to review the entire videotape.

More rarely, usability laboratories include other equipment to monitor users and study their detailed behavior. For example, an eyetracker can be used to collect data on what parts of the screens the user looks at [Benel *et al.* 1991].

To Videotape or Not

Having videotapes of a user test is essential for many research purposes where one needs to study the interaction in minute detail [Mackay and Tatar 1989]. For practical usability engineering purposes, however, there is normally no need to review a user test on videotape since one is mostly interested in finding the major "usability catastrophes" anyway. These usability problems tend to be so glaring that they are obvious the first time they are observed and therefore do not require repeated perusal of a record of the test session. This is especially true considering estimates that the time needed to analyze a videotape is between 3 and 10 times the duration of the original user test. In most cases, this extra time is better spent running more test subjects or testing more iterations of the design.

---

11. The average number of cameras in each test room was 2.2 in my survey, with 2 cameras being the typical number and a few labs using 1 or 3.

Videotape does have several uses in usability engineering, however. For example, a complete record of a series of user tests is a way to perform formal impact analysis of usability problems [Good *et al.* 1986]. Impact analysis involves first finding the usability problems and then going back to the videotapes to investigate exactly how many users had each usability problem and how much they were delayed by each problem. Since these estimates can only be made *after* one knows what usability problems to look for, an impact analysis requires a videotape or other detailed record of the test sessions. Alternatively, one can run more tests and count the known problems as they occur. Impact analyses can then be used to prioritize the fixing of the usability problems in a redesign such that the most effort is spent on those problems that are faced by many users and impact them severely.

Videotape also serves as an essential communications medium in many organizations where it may otherwise be difficult for human factors professionals to persuade developers and managers that a certain usability problem is in fact a problem. Seeing a video of a user struggling with the problem often convinces these people. This goal can also be achieved by simpler means, however, since it is normally even more effective to have the doubter observe a user test in person.[12]

A final argument in favor of videotaping and equipment-extensive usability laboratories is the need to impress upper management and research funding agencies with the unique aspects of usability work. Some usability specialists feel that simpler techniques may not be sufficiently impressive to outsiders, whereas having an

---

12. Doing so requires strict adherence to the "shut-up" rule: The developers should be advised in advance that they are not supposed to interfere with the user during the experiment. Doing so can be extremely hard for a person who normally has quite strong defensive feelings toward the design. Developers have been known to forcibly interrupt a test user's "maltreatment" of their beloved system and shout, "Why don't you press *that* function key!" This, of course, totally destroys the test. Randy Pausch from the University of Virginia allows developers to be present during user testing but requires them to preface any interruption with the phrase, "I am sorry that I am such a poor programmer that I made the system this difficult to use."

expensive laboratory will result in increased funding and respect due to its "advertising value" [Lindgaard 1991].

Cameraless Videotaping

The main aspects of a test session can be captured on videotape without the use of cameras. Many computers provide a video output that either is directly compatible with video recording or can be made so fairly cheaply by a scan converter.[13] This video signal can be fed directly into the "video in" jack of the video recorder and will thus allow the recording of the exact image the user sees on the monitor. This technique will normally result in better image quality than filming the monitor with a camera, but the video resolution will still be poorer than that of most computer monitors. Furthermore, an audio signal can be fed into the video recorder's "audio in" jack from a microphone, thus creating a composite recording of the screen and the user's comments [Connally and Tullis 1986].

Cameraless videotaping has the obvious disadvantages of not including the user in the picture and not making it possible for a camera operator to zoom in on interesting parts of the screen or the manual page being studied in vain by the user. Unless a high-definition television standard is used, one will also suffer a loss of resolution since current television standards use a poorer quality signal than that used by almost all computer monitors. These limitations may make the resulting videotape less appealing and convincing in some cases. At the same time, cameraless videotaping is considerably cheaper because neither cameras nor operators are needed, and the users are normally less intimidated by a microphone than by a camera.

Portable Usability Laboratories

In addition to permanent usability laboratories, it is possible to use portable usability laboratories for more flexible testing and for field studies. With a portable usability laboratory, any office can be

---

13. Scan converters were used by 46% of the labs in my survey.

rapidly converted to a test room, and user testing can be conducted where the users are rather than having to bring the users to a fixed location.

A true discount portable usability laboratory need consist of no more than a notepad and possibly a laptop computer to run the software that is being tested. Normally, a portable usability laboratory will include slightly more equipment, however. Typical equipment includes a camcorder (possibly just home video equipment, but preferably of professional quality since the filming of user interfaces requires as high resolution as possible) and a lavaliere microphone (two microphones are preferred so that the experimenter can also get one). The regular directional microphone built into many camcorders is normally not sufficient because of the noise of the computer. Also, a tripod helps steady the image and carry the camera during the hour-long test sessions.

Usability Kiosks

A final approach to the collection of usability data is the *usability kiosk*, which really is a self-served usability laboratory for use as part of a hallway methodology [Gould *et al.* 1987]. In general, the hallway method involves putting a user interface on display in a heavily trafficked area such as outside a company cafeteria in order to collect comments from users and other passersby. A usability kiosk can conduct automated usability testing with self-selected users in such a setting by providing access to a computer running a test interface, suggesting various test tasks to the users, and recording their task times and any comments they might have.

Chapter 7

Usability Assessment Methods beyond Testing

Even though usability testing forms the cornerstone of most recommended usability engineering practice, there are several other usability methods that can and should be used to gather supplementary data. I have already discussed heuristic evaluation in Chapter 5 (page 155) as a method where usability specialists, or even the developers themselves, apply their knowledge of established usability principles to find usability problems without the need to involve users.

7.1   Observation

Simply visiting the users to observe them work is an extremely important usability method with applications both for task analysis and for information about the true field usability of installed systems [Diaper 1989b]. Observation is really the simplest of all usability methods since it involves visiting one or more users and then doing as little as possible in order not to interfere with their work. Of course, the observer can take notes (unobtrusively), and it may even be possible to use videotaping in some environments, though most computer customers do not like to have outsiders come in and videotape their business.

When conducting an observation, the observer should stay quiet most of the time. The goal is to become virtually invisible to the users so that they will perform their work and use the system in the same way they normally do. Every now and then, it may become necessary to interrupt a user to ask for an explanation of some activity that is impossible for the observer to understand, but such questions to the users should be kept to a minimum. It is normally better to make a note of the strange user action and see if the observer can understand it if it occurs again later. If not, then the user can be questioned during a debriefing session at the end of the visit.

Since the observer will normally be a representative from the development group, the computer vendor, or from corporate head-quarters, users will naturally have many questions to ask of the observer, and they may request help in getting the system to do certain tasks. During the beginning of the visit, the observer should decline any such requests for assistance, giving the explanation that he or she is there to observe how the users work when they do not have a systems expert around. Toward the end of the visit, it may be reasonable for the observer to step out of the role and help the users, both to pay them back for participating in the study and to learn more about the things the users want done and why they could not do them themselves.

One advantage of observing users doing their own tasks is that one often finds that they use the software in unexpected ways that one would (by definition) not have sought to test in a planned labora-tory experiment. For example, users have often been found to use their word processor to edit electronic forms. They will have a template stored in a file that they will open up, fill in, and save under a new name, leaving the template file unchanged. A common user error in these cases is to save the revised document without changing its name, thus overwriting the template, because the word processor had no concept of templates and thus offered them no protection. Based on such observations, some word processors have been released in revised versions to handle templates as a special file category.

7.2   Questionnaires and Interviews

Many aspects of usability can best be studied by simply asking the users. This is especially true for issues relating to the users' subjective satisfaction and possible anxieties, which are hard to measure objectively.[1] Questionnaires and interviews are also useful methods for studying how users use systems and what features they particularly like or dislike.

From a usability perspective, questionnaires and interviews are indirect methods, since they do not study the user interface itself but only users' opinions about the user interface.[2] One cannot always take user statements at face value. Data about people's actual behavior should have precedence over people's claims of what they *think* they do. In a classic study, Root and Draper [1983] asked users whether they knew various commands. Later in the questionnaire, users were also asked to provide free-form comments on the commands, and 26% of the users commented on the command zap even though they had previously stated that they did not know it. The study also found that users gave more useful answers if they had been using the system shortly before answering the questionnaire. Finally, the most striking result was a comparison of the results from questionnaires administered before and after the introduction of some new features to the system. The correlation between users' predictions of whether they would like the new features and their ratings of the features after having tried them was only 0.28, indicating that one should not always interpret the results literally when asking users about user interface elements they have not tried.

In another example, users of a mobile telephone system were given a questionnaire with questions about the difficulty of the instructions [Karis and Zeigler 1989]. The results showed that 24 of the 25

---

1. As mentioned on page 34, some physiological measures can be used to measure stress objectively, but such methods are rarely used in software development projects.

2. Of course, questionnaires and interviews *are* direct methods when it comes to measuring user satisfaction.

respondents stated that the instructions were "about average" or "simple" to understand, indicating that the instructions were satisfactory. When the same subjects were given a test, however, their average performance was only 50% correct, leading to the more accurate conclusion that the instructions were far from adequate. In other words, the users *thought* that they had understood the instructions, whereas in fact they had not.

Questionnaires and interviews are very similar methods since both involve asking users a set of questions and recording their answers. Questionnaires are printed on paper or presented interactively on a computer and can be administered without the need to have any other people present beside the user answering the questions. In contrast, interviews involve having an interviewer read the questions to the respondent, and the answers are recorded by the interviewer instead of being filled in by the respondent. Interviews thus require much more usability staff time, but they do have the advantage of being more flexible, since the interviewer can explain difficult questions in more depth and can rephrase a question if the respondent's answer indicates that the question was misunderstood. Also, interviews can be more free-form than questionnaires, with the interviewer opportunistically asking follow-up questions that were not in the script. Of course, any such free-form elements in interviews will make them harder to analyze quantitatively, and questionnaires are normally better if one is just looking for hard numbers. A further difference is that interviews generate immediate results, starting after the first customer visit, whereas questionnaires are subject to mailing, response, and coding delays.

Questionnaires are usually administered by mail, and the response rate can be increased substantially by including a prepaid and pre-addressed reply envelope. One study had a response rate of 26% when no reply envelope was enclosed, and 90% when a prepaid reply envelope was supplied [Armstrong and Lusk 1988]. For questionnaires that are sent to a business address, the existence of a pre-addressed reply envelope is more of a factor than whether the postage has been prepaid [Armstrong and Lusk 1988].

In principle, it is possible to distribute a questionnaire to the entire user population. Questionnaires are probably the only usability method that makes such extensive coverage feasible, with the ensuing possibility for discovering differences between various user categories as well as the specific needs of various small groups of users. In practice, one will often limit a questionnaire to a randomly selected sample of between fifty and a thousand users, depending on how detailed data is needed.

Interviews may be conducted over the telephone but normally involve having the interviewer travel to the user's location. Interviews are therefore subject to scheduling constraints, but they do have the advantage of getting fairly high response rates. Once a user has agreed to schedule an interview, it is normally also possible for the interviewer to complete it.

Interviews are well suited to exploratory studies where one does not know yet what one is looking for, since the interviewer can adjust the interview to the situation. Interviews typically include many open-ended questions where users are encouraged to explain themselves in depth, often leading to colorful quotes that can be used to enliven reports and presentations to management. In order to ensure unbiased responses, the interviewer should stay neutral during the interview and not agree or disagree with user statements. Nor should the interviewer try to explain to the user why the system behaved in a certain way, even if the user complains heavily about it. Questions should be phrased in an open and neutral way, and should encourage the user to reply with full sentences rather than just with a "yes" or a "no." For example, instead of asking, "Did you like this new feature?" and "Did you use it?" one could ask, "What do you think of this new feature?" and "What have you used this new feature for so far?"

Both in interviews and in questionnaires with open questions it is often fruitful to ask users to recall critical incidents in their use of the system. Critical incidents are occasions where the system was particularly poor or surprisingly good, and knowing the detailed circumstances of such incidents can often help avoid worst-case incidents in the future and help make the benefits of best-case incidents available to other users also.

During an interview, the interviewer can continuously evaluate the user's replies, making it possible to rephrase questions that seem to have been misunderstood. In contrast, questionnaires have to stand on their own. It is therefore essential that all questionnaires be subjected to pilot testing and iterative design before they are distributed to the users in large numbers. Essentially, a questionnaire is a user interface in its own right, and one should use usability engineering principles to ensure that the respondents will interpret it correctly. Also, questionnaires that irritate the users by being too long, too hard to understand, or too unprofessional will often get a low response rate.

Even though it may require a fair amount of work to revise the questions until they are easy to understand and easy to answer, once a final questionnaire design exists, it is easy to collect data from a large number of users. It is also possible to reuse the same questionnaire at later occasions to check on the evolution in user attitudes or to compare the replies from users of different systems.

Questionnaires may contain open questions where the users are asked to write in their own reply in natural language, but users often do not bother to do so, or they may write cryptic statements that are hard to interpret. Therefore, questionnaires normally rely heavily on closed questions, where the users have to supply a single fact (such as number of hours worked with the system per week), go through a checklist (such as indicating which types of tasks each user performs with the system), or state their opinion on a rating scale. Checklists may have room for write-in options, but one should try to make the preprinted list of options as complete as possible, as many users will only consider the options that are explicitly listed, making the results from write-in options less representative of all the users. In one study where users were first observed using a system and then given a questionnaire about it, the replies to a checklist of features were 85% accurate (when compared with the experimenters' observations of the respondents' actual use of the system) which is pretty good, but the replies given to an open question that did not list the features were only 48% accurate [Edgerton *et al.* 1993]. Checklists can be made more usable by including recognizable dialogue elements, such as the precise names of commands or features as well as icons and dialog box layouts.

Rating scales are often used to ask users how well they liked various aspects of the system or how useful they find different features. See Table 4 (page 36) and Table 3 (page 35) for examples of semantic differential and Likert scale questions that can be included in questionnaires. To ensure ease-of-use of the questionnaire, only a small number of different types of questions should be mixed in the same questionnaire. Also, the rating scales for replies should be the same throughout a questionnaire.

Questionnaires to measure user satisfaction can be quite sophisticated such as the QUIS (Questionnaire for User Interface Satisfaction) method [Chin *et al.* 1988], which has users rate 27 system attributes on 10-point scales, followed by a factor analysis. Normally, however, it is recommended to use shorter questionnaires[3] in order to maximize the response rate. Questionnaires that are kept to a single page (or at least the two sides of a single sheet of paper) stand a much better chance of being filled out by busy users than longer questionnaires that seem to be much more of a burden. It is true for all usability methods that one should know in advance what one wants to do with the data that is collected, but this rule is especially important for questionnaires: Only ask a question if you want to know the answer (that is, if the replies will make any difference to your project). To assess whether you really need to ask a question, try a thought experiment where you imagine two drastically different reply statistics and consider how you would change the project in either case.

---

3. A factor analysis of an 18-question subjective satisfaction questionnaire found that 87% of the total variance in the responses was accounted for by three underlying factors: system usefulness, information quality, and interface quality [Lewis 1992]. It should be possible to assess these three factors with a reasonably small number of questions.

A common aspect of both questionnaires and interviews is that one cannot necessarily trust all the users' answers. People have a tendency to give the replies they think they *ought* to give, especially to sensitive questions where certain answers may be embarrassing or may be deemed socially unacceptable. Thus, one should always consider the possibility that the situation is somewhat different from that indicated by the users in the case of such sensitive questions. As an example of a potentially sensitive question, users might be asked how much time they spent searching for the answer in the manual before calling a help-line with a problem. Since the users know that they "ought" to have tried to solve the problem themselves, it is likely that their replies will tend to overestimate the amount of time spent reading the manual. Response bias in favor of socially acceptable answers is more pronounced for interviews conducted in person and less pronounced for questionnaires administered by a computer where people seem to be less anxious to avoid embarrassment.

7.3   Focus Groups

Focus groups [Caplan 1990; Goldman and McDonald 1987; Greenbaum 1988, 1993; O'Donnell *et al.* 1991] are a somewhat informal technique that can be used to assess user needs and feelings both before the interface has been designed and after it has been in use for some time. In a focus group, about six to nine users are brought together to discuss new concepts and identify issues over a period of about two hours. Each group is run by a moderator who is responsible for maintaining the focus of the group on whatever issues are of interest. From the users' perspective, a focus-group session should feel free-flowing and relatively unstructured, but in reality, the moderator has to follow a preplanned script for what issues to bring up. Focus groups often bring out users' spontaneous reactions and ideas through the interaction between the participants and have the major advantage of allowing observation of some group dynamics and organizational issues.

McClelland and Brigham [1990] present an example of the use of focus groups in the design of an advanced telecommunications system for office and home workers. First, a "user needs workshop" was held where six communications users discussed their communications needs and problems with respect to current tools and practices. Then, six experts spent two days in a design workshop, outlining five different design directions and usage scenarios to address the user needs identified in the initial focus group. Finally, the focus group with the six users was reconvened to discuss these proposals for a future system.

To prepare for a focus group, the moderator needs to prepare a list of the issues to be discussed and set goals for the kinds of information that are to be gathered. During the group session, the moderator has the difficult job of keeping the discussion on track without inhibiting the free flow of ideas and comments. Also, the moderator needs to ensure that all members of the group get to contribute to the discussion and guard against having the opinions of any single participant dominate unduly. After the session, data analysis can be as simple as having the moderator write a short report summing up the prevailing mood in the group, illustrated with a few colorful quotes. More detailed analyses can also be performed but are difficult and often time-consuming because of the unstructured nature of focus groups.

Focus groups are fairly demanding in terms of the number of representative users needed. Because of the need to keep the discussion flowing and have a variety of perspectives represented, a focus group cannot be run with much fewer than six users. Furthermore, it is normally preferable to run more than one focus group since the outcome of any single focus group session may not be representative and since some discussions may have been sidetracked so that too much time is spent on minor peculiarities of the system.

As with all methods that are based on asking users what they want instead of measuring or observing how they actually use things, focus groups involve the risk that the users may think they want one thing even though they in fact need another. This problem can be minimized by exposing the users to as concrete examples of possible of the technology being discussed in the focus group. As an example of this phenomenon, Greif [1992] reports on focus groups conducted to assess the potential of a version management facility in a new version of the Lotus 1-2-3 spreadsheet. Initially, the new features were presented to users as a way to allow multiple spreadsheet users to compare and contrast alternative view of budgets and other sets of numbers across computer networks. The focus group users were sceptical about these ideas and expressed distrust in networks and a nervousness about what other people would do to their spreadsheets. Only after having seen a prototype and scenarios of the use of version management for extensive "what-if" analyses did the focus group participants change from being sceptical to having a strong feeling that they would like to get the new features.

One cheap way of approximating the focus-group approach without the expense of gathering all these users is to rely on computer conferencing and various forms of electronic networks. For example, Yang [1990] started a project on undo facilities by posting a question to the British academic network asking users what undo facilities they used and how they liked them. If questions are posted to a computer conference group with an interest in the issues, considerable discussion can often result. A disadvantage is that online discussions are difficult (or impossible) to keep confidential unless they take place on an in-house computer facility.

Two sources of bias are that computer conference subscribers tend to be people with above average interest in computers, and that the participants in any particular online discussion group tend to be users with above average involvement in the topic of that group. Therefore, discussions in an online forum will probably not reflect the concerns of true novice users, but they may on the other hand be a good way of getting in touch with "power users." On the one hand, one should remember that bulletin board postings are probably not representative of the majority of users. On the other hand, advanced users (or "lead users" [von Hippel 1988]) sometimes face needs that will later be general in the marketplace, but they face them long before average users encounter these needs. Thus, addressing the power users' needs may sometimes (but not always) be a way of getting a head start on future usability work.

7.4   Logging Actual Use

Logging involves having the computer automatically collect statistics about the detailed use of the system. Normally, logging is used as a way to collect information about field use of a system after release, but logging can also be used as a supplementary method during user testing to collect more detailed data.

Logging the users' actual use of the system is particularly useful because it shows how users perform their actual work and because it is easy to automatically collect data from a large number of users working under different circumstances. Typically, an interface log will contain statistics about the frequency with which each user has used each feature in the program and the frequency with which various events of interest (such as error messages) have occurred.

Statistics showing the frequency of use of commands and other system features can be used to optimize frequently used features. Features that are not used or that are used very rarely should be investigated to see whether it is possible to improve them or make them more accessible to the users. It may also be possible to completely remove such features from the system.

For example, Bradford *et al.* [1990] logged and analyzed 6,112 erroneous commands issued by users of a line-oriented operating system. Thirty percent of the errors were simple spelling errors, indicating the potential for a spelling corrector to help the users of the system. Fully 48% of the errors were mode errors where users issued commands that were inappropriate for the current state of the system. This category of problem would probably be difficult to correct in a maintenance release, but knowing about the mode problem would be of great help in designing the next major change of the system.

Statistics showing the frequency of various error situations can be used to improve the usability of future releases of the system. If certain errors occur very frequently, one should consider whether it would be possible to redesign the system to avoid these error situations, or at least make them less likely to occur. Also, frequent error messages are certainly candidates for concentrated usability efforts to make them more understandable and constructive.

For example, Mosteller and Rooney (as reported by Chapanis [1991]) logged 3,000 error messages received by programmers at a mainframe facility. About 85% of the events were accounted for by nine common error messages that were then studied in depth. One particularly poorly worded error message ("Symbol not defined in procedure") accounted for 9.8% of the total and was often encountered repeatedly by the same programmer because it was difficult to correct the underlying error without any additional information. Mosteller and Rooney improved the wording of this one error message and later found that it only accounted for 1.7% of the errors logged after the change, thus indicating that the programmers were able to avoid repeating the error with the new error message.

In a study of the use of online help, Senay and Stabler [1987] logged 52,576 help sessions and found that the 10% of the help screens that were accessed the most accounted for 92% of the requests. Obviously, this result could be used to focus the attention of the technical writers on improving those screens before other, less frequently accessed screens.

Logging is usually achieved either by instrumenting low-level parts of the system software, such as keyboard and mouse drivers, or by modifying the software of interest. The latter approach is much preferred, since it makes it easier to log events of interest. If the only available data is raw input and output, it becomes much harder to analyze the higher-level events of interest for system usability, such as feature use or error situations. Ideally, instrumentation might be possible on an intermediate level if the system is implemented through a user interface management system (UIMS) which handles input and output while knowing about the underlying system features being accessed [Olsen and Halversen 1988]. Once a system has been instrumented for logging it is an easy matter to keep collecting data over extended periods of time. If the statistical analysis of the data is also automated, it becomes possible to use logging as a method to alert the usability staff to any changes in user needs that are shown by changes in the way they use the system.

If the instrumented system runs on a mainframe or on workstations with a shared file space, it is easy to collect logging data by simply copying the log files from each user at regular intervals. Unfortunately, much modern software runs on personal computers that may not even be connected through a network. It may be necessary to collect logs by going around to the users and copying floppies, but in some cases, it may be possible to collect log data through electronic mail—either automatically or by asking the users to periodically run a small script that sends off the log file.

Logging a user's use of a system raises some privacy concerns that can normally be addressed by explaining to users that only summary statistics are being collected and that results will only be reported in a form where the individual users cannot be identified. In any case, basic ethics dictates that users should be informed when interaction logging is going on and that they should be able to disable the log if they so desire. Except for these privacy concerns, logging has the major advantage compared with practically all other usability methods of not interfering with the users in any way. Basically, users can ignore the log and use the system in exactly the way they would anyway.

In addition to statistical use of logging data, it is also possible to log complete transcripts of user sessions either for use in later playback [Neal and Simons 1983, 1984] or for analysis of patterns of use, such as what commands are issued next after an error situation [Siochi and Ehrich 1991]. Transcript logging raises even more sensitive privacy issues than statistical logging of event frequencies, since it is possible to reconstruct exactly what the user was doing. Indeed, it may be the purpose of the transcript log to do exactly that. Therefore, it should always be possible for users to turn off

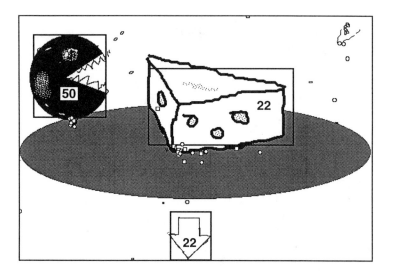

Figure 21 *Sample display of logging data from a study of a graphical user interface for children. The rectangles denote hypertext anchors in the form of buttons and were not visible to the users. The numbers on each anchor indicate the number of clicks on that anchor, and the other marks indicate clicks outside the anchor regions. A few marks inside the anchor rectangles indicate cases where a user pressed down the mouse button outside the bounds of an anchor, moved the mouse cursor inside the anchor, and then released the mouse button.*

transcript logging when they perform sensitive tasks, and the logging data should be safeguarded against unauthorized access. Furthermore, one should not show playbacks of user sessions to managers or others who are not involved in the usability study. In general, the ethical principles for use of video recordings of user testing (see page 181) should also apply to computerized playbacks of user sessions.

A final use of logging data is to study the users' detailed use of a user interface to find usability problems that may not be apparent when observing users. For example, Figure 21 shows results from a study of a nonverbal hypermedia interface designed for children [Nielsen and Lyngbæk 1990]. We logged the location of the users' clicks on the screen and later displayed the aggregated data from 23 children on screens like the one shown here. Not only did the statistics show what graphics were most popular with the children, but the detailed analysis of clicks outside the intended hypertext anchors revealed some usability problems. As seen in Figure 21, the active rectangles did not cover the graphics completely in all cases, and users made several clicks (without effect) just on the border of the anchors. Since the cursor was a hand pointing upward (☝), users tended to place it just below the object of interest, meaning that they often missed their target without knowing why. This example also shows that statistics from logging may be more vivid when displayed in integration with the user interface than when reported as stand-alone tables.

Combining Logging with Follow-Up Interviews

A major problem with logging data is that it only shows what the users did but not why they did it. It is possible to combine logging with other methods such as interviews, where users are shown data about their own use of the system and asked to elaborate on whatever interesting phenomena may be evident in the data. For example, a user who had not been using a certain feature in a system might be asked *why* he or she had not used the feature.

Confronting users with statistics of their system use should be done with great sensitivity in order to avoid any hint of a "big brother is watching" atmosphere.

7.5   User Feedback

For installed systems, the users themselves can form a major source of usability information if one is willing to listen to their feedback. User feedback has several advantages:

- It is initiated by the users, so it shows their immediate and pressing concerns.
- It is an ongoing process, so feedback will be received without any special efforts to collect it.

- It will quickly show any changes in the users' needs, circumstances, or opinions, since new feedback will be received whenever such changes occur.

Of course, one will tend to hear mostly from dissatisfied users and from the most vocal ones, so user feedback may not always be representative of the majority of users. Also, many complaints will be idiosyncratic, based on erroneous analyses, or a desire for known features from systems that are actually worse. Therefore, it is recommended to supplement the feedback initiated by the users themselves with methods where a representative set of users are actively sought out and observed or questioned.

Mainframe or tightly networked systems can directly include a "useless" or "gripe" command that will allow users to vent their frustration by sending a complaint to the development team immediately after they encounter a part of the system that does not address their needs. Such a command would take a snapshot of the system state and the user's prior actions and forward this information together with any free-form comments added by the user to explain the problem. It is important for the command to collect as much information as possible automatically in order to minimize the user's overhead in describing the situation.

Even without a special command to collect complaints automatically, feedback can be collected by giving users access to special electronic mail addresses, network newsgroups, or bulletin boards where they can post complaints, praise, and suggestions for future system changes. Customer support help lines can also serve double duty as a way to collect statistics about frequent user problems. Of course, non-electronic methods like modification request forms and reply cards bound into the manuals can also be used to collect user feedback. No matter what method is used, it is important not just to record the users' immediate complaints but also to classify the problems and determine patterns and likely root causes.

Finally, many software companies use *beta testing*, where a forthcoming product is released to a small number of selected customers for their comments. Beta testing can provide user feedback that arrives in time to improve the first full release of the product, so it is highly recommended not just to view beta testing as a debugging method to find programming errors but also to set up a systematic method for collecting and analyzing user comments regarding mismatches between the software and their needs. Of course, just as beta testing should not be the only method used for debugging, it should not be the only method for usability engineering, since beta feedback will arrive too late to do as much good as results from earlier usability engineering methods.

No matter what methods are used to collect user feedback, it is important that those users who go to the trouble to comment on the system are made to feel that their feedback is taken seriously. Reply cards and other user comments should not just be piled up in a corner until it comes time for the next release; they should be acknowledged immediately after receipt. If possible, the acknowledgment should not be a form letter but should explicitly address the concerns raised by the user—even if only to say that the problem would seem unsolvable with current technology. The need for such ongoing commitment to reply to individual user comments is one of the major disadvantages of the user-feedback method. On the other hand, if users feel that they are talking to a black hole, they will soon stop providing feedback, and this valuable source of field information will be lost.

7.6   Choosing Usability Methods

Table 10 shows a summary of the methods covered in Chapters 5, 6, and 7. For reasons of space, the table is necessarily simplified, but it still provides a good, quick overview of the methods. It is apparent from the table that the methods are intended to supplement each other, since they address different parts of the usability engineering lifecycle (see Chapter 4), and since their advantages and disadvantages can partly make up for each other. It is therefore highly recommended not to rely on a single usability method to the exclusion of others.

Method Name	Lifecycle Stage	Users Needed	Main Advantage	Main Disadvantage
Heuristic evaluation	Early design, "inner cycle" of iterative design	None	Finds individual usability problems. Can address expert user issues.	Does not involve real users, so does not find "surprises" relating to their needs.
Performance measures	Competitive analysis, final testing	At least 10	Hard numbers. Results easy to compare.	Does not find individual usability problems.
Thinking aloud	Iterative design, formative evaluation	3–5	Pinpoints user misconceptions. Cheap test.	Unnatural for users. Hard for expert users to verbalize.
Observation	Task analysis, follow-up studies	3 or more	Ecological validity; reveals users' real tasks. Suggests functions and features.	Appointments hard to set up. No experimenter control.
Questionnaires	Task analysis, follow-up studies	At least 30	Finds subjective user preferences. Easy to repeat.	Pilot work needed (to prevent misunderstandings).
Interviews	Task analysis	5	Flexible, in-depth attitude and experience probing.	Time consuming. Hard to analyze and compare.
Focus groups	Task analysis, user involvement	6–9 per group	Spontaneous reactions and group dynamics.	Hard to analyze. Low validity
Logging actual use	Final testing, follow-up studies	At least 20	Finds highly used (or unused) features. Can run continuously.	Analysis programs needed for huge mass of data. Violation of users' privacy.
User feedback	Follow-up studies	Hundreds	Tracks changes in user requirements and views.	Special organization needed to handle replies.

Table 10 *Summary of the usability methods covered in Chapters 5–7.*

Also, the table indicates that the choice of method may be partly dependent on the number of users that are available for usability activities. If very few users are available, emphasis should be placed on heuristic evaluation, thinking aloud, and observation. If more users are available, performance measurement and focus groups become feasible, and if a large number of users are available, questionnaires, interaction logging, and systematic collection of spontaneous user feedback can be considered. Of course, variations of the methods may call for fewer or more users. For example, the collaborative interaction variation (page 198) requires twice as many users as regular thinking aloud, but offers the advantage of a more natural working situation for the test users.

The experience of the available usability staff may also impact the choice of methods. The two simplest methods to use are probably thinking aloud and observation since they leave most of the "work" to the users, while leaving the usability person to shut up and observe. By participating in a number of observations and thinking aloud studies, a usability professional can build up an understanding of usability principles that will significantly improve that person's performance as a heuristic evaluator. Also, increased understanding of usability helps design valid measurement and logging studies and provides the background to design questionnaires and interviews that probe important usability issues. Finally, focus group moderators need to be able to react to group dynamics in real time.

Combining Usability Methods

There are many possible ways of combining the various usability methods, and each new project may need a slightly different combination, depending on its exact characteristics. A combination that is often useful is that of heuristic evaluation and thinking aloud or other forms of user testing. Typically, one would first perform a heuristic evaluation to clean up the interface and remove as many "obvious" usability problems as possible. After a redesign of the interface, it would be subjected to user testing both to check the outcome of the iterative design step and to find remaining usability problems that were not picked up by the heuristic evaluation.

There are two major reasons for alternating between heuristic evaluation and user testing as suggested here. First, a heuristic evaluation pass can eliminate a number of usability problems without the need to "waste users," who sometimes can be difficult to find and schedule in large numbers. Second, these two categories of usability assessment methods have been shown to find fairly distinct sets of usability problems, meaning that they supplement each other rather than leading to repetitive findings [Desurvire *et al.* 1992; Jeffries *et al.* 1991; Karat *et al.* 1992].

As another example, consider a video telephone system for interconnecting offices [Cool *et al.* 1992]. Such a system has the potential for changing the way people work and interact, but these changes will become clear only after an extended usage period. Also, as with many computer-supported cooperative work applications, video telephones require a critical mass of users for the test to be realistic: If most of the people you want to call do not have a video connection, you will not rely on the system. Thus, on the one hand field testing is necessary to learn about changes in the users' long-term behavior, but on the other hand such studies will be very expensive. Therefore, one will want to supplement them with heuristic evaluation and laboratory-based user testing such that the larger field population does not have to suffer from glaring usability problems that could have been found much more cheaply. Iterative design of such a system will be a combination of a few, longer-lasting "outer iterations" with field testing and a larger number of more rapid "inner iterations" that are used to polish the interface before it released to the field users.

Similarly, interviews and questionnaires may be combined by using open interviews with a small number of users for exploratory analysis to define specific issues that are to be covered in closed questionnaires mailed to a large number of users.

Chapter 8   *Interface Standards*

User interface standards have become the object of increasingly intense activities in recent years [Abernethy 1988; Holdaway and Bevan 1989], including work in the International Standards Organization (ISO) [Brooke *et al.* 1990] and the European Union [Stewart 1990]. Work is also going on in national standards organizations [Dzida 1989] and in several major computer companies [Berry 1988; Good 1989; Tognazzini 1989; Wolf 1989]. These activities are part of a general current interest in information processing standards [Berg and Schumny 1990] but are also based on the widely held feeling that consistency is one of the most important usability considerations [Nielsen 1989c]. Even though consistency is obviously not the only usability factor [Grudin 1989], there are still good reasons to strive to obtain it in balance with other usability considerations [Nielsen 1990e] in a usability engineering process, and such additional considerations are indeed also included in many current standards activities.

User Benefits from Consistency and Standards

Consistency normally enhances the users' possibility for transfer of skill from one system to another. By doing so, interface standards lead to ease of learning and ease of use, thus lowering training costs. In several studies, consistency reduced training time to between 25–50% of that needed for inconsistent interfaces [Polson

1988]. Consistency improves the users' productivity by leading to higher throughput and fewer errors because the users can predict what the system will do in any given situation and because they can rely on a few rules to govern use of the system. The smaller number of errors and shorter learning time again lead to improved user satisfaction with the system and fewer frustrations with systems which the user cannot use. Finally, consistency strengthens users' expectations with respect to being able to use new software, leading to feelings of mastery and self-confidence.

Relying on a single interface standard will lead to reduced requirements for user support because users will not request help as frequently when all software is consistent. And the support that has to be offered anyway will be less expensive because support personnel will not have to learn so many different interfaces themselves.

For a user interface standard to increase usability in the resulting products, two conditions have to be met: The standard must specify a usable interface, and the standard must be usable by developers so that they actually build the interface according to the specifications. As reported by Potter *et al.* [1990], a user interface may have usability problems even when an interface standard is followed without violations, but luckily, most interface standards seem to specify reasonable interfaces.

Vendor Benefits from Consistency and Standards

If a vendor company has defined an architecture for consistent interfaces, then that definition can form a coherent basis for company expansion. Because every deviation from this basis will stand out and be the subject for investigation and in-depth discussions, the architecture can retard spurious innovation so that company products evolve in a controlled manner. Having a standard interface will reduce development costs, both with respect to designers (who will not have to design every aspect of the interface) and with respect to programmers (who may reuse code that implements standard aspects of the interface). In interviews with developers in a company having a user interface standard, one major reason mentioned for wanting a formal standard was that it helped minimize wasted time during project meetings. Prior to the introduction of the standard, a lot of time was spent arguing about minor interface-design details whereas now it was possible to close such discussions rapidly by referring to the standard, thus making it possible to concentrate on higher-level matters [Thovtrup and Nielsen 1991]. In the same way, consistency can lead to reduced maintenance costs, first because the initial interface implementation will be built on a solid foundation, and second because all systems following a given standard will evolve together, again leading to reuse of any design and code changes.

Because of the ease of use and learning mentioned above, consistent software can be expected to lead to increased software consumption and thus to larger sales. For a given vendor that has a special interface architecture, that interface style will lead to better product positioning in the marketplace (the notion of product families) and to the development of a new market segment consisting of those users who have already bought some of the vendor's products and who are likely to buy additional products from the same vendor to insure consistency with the interfaces they already know.

Consistent software has the potential for leading to more aesthetic user interfaces because the different aspects of the interface comply with a single underlying norm and because (presumably) a significant human factors effort has been invested in the design of the interface architecture. Designers may then build on this foundation and could be expected to produce more creative designs when they are allowed to focus on designing those aspects of a product which are unique to that product rather than having to reinvent every interaction technique needed for a complete interface. And finally, consistent software simply fulfills a market demand since compliance with user interface conventions will in itself lead to better reviews of software in the trade press. In many cases, consistency of the user interface is one of the checklist items covered in magazine reviews of software packages.

The Dangers of Standards

Even though a finished standard will save development costs for the individual product, arriving at a good standard is a costly process in itself, and the time and money needed to develop the standard must be invested up front before it can be used, thus possibly leading to delay for the products that are to be based on the standard. There may also be a conflict between taking the time required to develop a good common user interface versus the pressure to get the first product out the door. Rosenberg [1989] estimates that it takes about five products to break even. Having a standard also implies an overhead in the software lifecycle to ensure conformance and some need for evaluating whether new user interfaces are in fact consistent. It may even be necessary to have some kind of enforcement in place. It is difficult to assess conformance with a standard in an area as fuzzy as user interfaces, so one may have to conduct experiments to get empirical verification of consistency.

A defined common user interface risks being a lowest common denominator to the extent that one wants to incorporate a large installed base of perhaps somewhat primitive interfaces. In any case, the common user interface might be stifling for innovation in new products and introduce resistance to change even where change is needed. The very idea of consistency also implies reduced flexibility in the design of individual products so that they may not be able to be as tailored to application-specific requirements or contexts. In addition, a standard may not just prevent enhancements, but it could even enforce bad design if it includes poor rules.

From an organizational perspective, having a corporate standard might lessen motivation among developers if they feel that they do not share ownership of the user interface. And the very fact that one has a formalized program for consistency could mean that standards compliance could distract from other design issues, perhaps to the extent that developers feel that they do not need to take other human factors considerations into account as long as they follow the standard. By the same token, too much focus on a common user interface could promote "foolish" consistency in cases where good design would deviate from the standard.

Some of the disadvantages of user interface standards can be avoided by having a formal program in place from the start to amend the chosen common user interface according to new needs and new technologies. If one does not let a standard evolve, then either new products will become steadily more obsolete or developers will utilize new technologies and interaction principles without regard to commonality, leading to an erosion of consistency.

8.1 National, International and Vendor Standards

The three main types of standards are national and international standards, industry standards, and in-house standards. Even though a few national [DIN 1988] and international standards have been passed, and more are under way, it is likely that this potentially most-restrictive form of standard will actually have the least importance due to the slow-moving nature of international standards bodies as compared with the changing nature of the computer field. Luckily, many of the participants in the various international standards groups have recognized the potential disaster in legislating a standard that would restrict developments in user interfaces to the current state of the art. Therefore, most standard proposals tend to specify broad principles or performance levels to be achieved rather than specifying exactly how the interface should look.

See the regular column "The Standards Factor" in the ACM *SIGCHI Bulletin* for progress reports on the standards activities in ISO (International Standards Organization), ANSI (American National Standards Institute), and several other standards bodies.

International standards may gain special prominence in the years to come because of the European Union directive (discussed on page 10) stating that as of 1993, "Software must be easy to use" and "The principles of software ergonomics must be applied." These phrases are obviously not very precise, so it is likely that the member countries will require supplementary regulations in order to implement the directive. These supplementary regulations may very well turn out to be references to ISO standards, which again may mean that ISO compliance could become desired (or even mandatory) for software used in Europe.

For practical development purposes, the industry standards promoted by various operating system and window system vendors may be more important than the international standards. These industry standards tend to specify the look and feel of user interfaces in great detail. Unfortunately, these standards are mutually conflicting with respect to many of these details even though they mostly follow the same overall interaction style.

Because of the differences between the various industry standards, developers should take great care when moving between platforms not to subject their designs to interface contamination, where details from other standards creep across platforms. Similarly, designers who have been using a different standard in the past should be given explicit training in the differences between standards when transferring to designing for another platform [Nielsen *et al.* 1992].

Vendor standards are currently focused on the lower levels of dialogue design, with most emphasis on alphabetical and lexical issues such as what should happen when the user presses down the mouse button and how a hierarchical pop-up menu should look. They provide less guidance at the syntax level, though they still often provide some broad principles for issues like the layout of dialog boxes. Typically, it is possible to design quite different-looking interfaces for the same application under any given vendor standard. This may be an advantage from the perspective of software developers, but it does indicate the need to supplement the chosen vendor standard with a more detailed in-house standard.

In contrast to their extensive coverage of low-level issues, vendor standards typically do not address the semantic and task levels of dialogue design (except for a few rules like the use of undo, which is not even always specified in sufficient detail for all applications). Because of this emphasis on the lower levels of the dialogue, vendor standards cannot guarantee usability of the overall interface, leaving a need for designers to rely on other usability engineering methods.

Most parts of the main international standard in the user interface area, ISO 9241, had not been released in final form as of this writing. From the drafts it seems that it will contain considerably more emphasis on the semantic and task levels of dialogue design, which will make it hard to verify whether a given interface is standards-compliant. Also, it remains to be seen whether developers will be able to follow these more loosely specified rules.

8.2   Producing Usable In-House Standards

With respect to both international standards and industry standards set by major vendors, most developers will have to accept the standards as they are given to them. For standards that are developed locally within an organization, however, it is possible to aim for a high degree of usability of the standard itself. The goals should be to produce a standard that the developers can actually understand and apply and to maximize the compliance of the resulting products. The latter goal may be difficult to measure until it is too late, but the understandability of the document can be assessed and improved with standard usability engineering methods.

Two approaches that have proven successful for the usability testing of standards are to ask some designers to design a small toy interface using the standard, and to show them another small interface with a number of standards violations and ask them to list the violations [Thovtrup and Nielsen 1991]. The designers' use of the standards document can be observed during these tests, and one can even ask them to think aloud (see Section 6.8) to assess the ease of use of the document. The resulting toy designs can be checked for conformance, and the designers' lists of violations in the test interface can be compared with the true solutions to see which violations were overlooked and which legal design elements were spuriously claimed to be violations. These results can be used to assess whether the standard can be applied in practice and is likely to lead to consistent interfaces.

Not much research is available on this topic yet, but existing evidence does indicate the potential for "meta-usability problems" (usability problems in a usability document). Mosier and Smith [1986] reported that only 58% of the users of a large collection of interface guidelines found the information they were looking for (an additional 36% "sometimes found it"). de Souza and Bevan [1990] had three designers design an interface using a draft of the ISO standard for menu interfaces and reported that the designers violated 11% of the rules and had difficulties in interpreting 30% of the rules. The draft standard was improved after the experiment, so the main lesson from this study is the need for usability testing of usability standards.

Similarly, Thovtrup and Nielsen [1991] reported that the compliance of student projects with a very simple standard was measured at no more than 71% and that 3 real products from a major software house violated between 7 and 12 of the rules in that company's standard. In other words, user interface standards are difficult to follow, so just releasing a document to a company's various product teams is not likely to be enough to guarantee compliant and consistent interfaces.

Experience shows that the body text of a standards document is the least important element in communicating a standard [Tetzlaff and Schwartz 1991; Thovtrup and Nielsen 1991]. Developers pay considerably more attention to the examples in a standard and to any lists and checklists, such as lists of approved terms or recommended function-key assignments. Two lessons from this observation are to include plenty of examples in a standard and to take extreme care that the examples are very well designed and completely compliant with the standard. Also, the examples should not include design elements that are not part of the standard (at least not without explaining that any such elements are optional), since designers will pick up such elements from the examples in the belief that they are part of the standard.

In addition to printed examples, standards can be communicated by the distribution of exemplary applications: a small number of applications developed to instantiate the common user interface that one would like other applications to follow. When designing new applications, designers tend to emulate the way existing applications do things, so it is important to provide good role models. Examples can also be communicated by animations or other hypermedia techniques, as was done on the Apple CD-ROM *Making It Macintosh* [Alben *et al.* 1994] with about 100 animated illustrations and explanations of approved interaction techniques.

Standards compliance is also an organizational issue. Developers need to feel that consistency is part of the corporate image. They can also be made aware of the need for consistency through "art exhibits" of consistent interfaces [Good 1989], internal computerized bulletin boards with interface discussions and standards interpretations, and by "evangelists" spreading the word to developers and to the users (to build pressure on the developers). Different groups of developers may interpret the same standard differently, leading to inconsistencies across products unless steps are taken to increase cross-group communication.

One method for cross-group communication is called *consistency inspection* [Wixon *et al.* 1994]. Consistency inspection is a usability inspection method aimed at finding inconsistencies among a set of user interface designs. Each interface is inspected one at a time by a team of evaluators consisting of one representative from each of the development groups. Step by step, elements of each interface are reviewed and notes are made of any inconsistencies with the way any of the other systems do things. Some inconsistencies are easy to resolve during the inspection session, either with reference to the user interface standard or because the nature of the designs make one of the solutions clearly better than the other. Other inconsistencies are harder to resolve and should be left for future discussion, user testing, or additional design work.

A variant of the consistency inspection is the *synergy review* which takes place earlier in the lifecycle before the interface has been fully designed. In the same way as with a consistency inspection, the participants in a synergy review are drawn from multiple projects, and they also review the interfaces one at a time. However, since the interfaces have not been fully designed yet, the synergy review focuses on finding potential similarities and overlaps between the interfaces as conceived in the early stages of design and not on an inspection of design details. The outcome of a synergy review is a list of interface elements and features that are likely to be shared by two or more of the projects. For example, multiple interfaces being developed by a given company might have a need to allow the user to choose elements from a long list or to monitor changes in the state of a number of processes. Such common design elements are prime candidates for coordination between projects, and having discovered them up front not only helps ensure consistency but also minimizes duplicate efforts and promotes sharing of design ideas, test results, and possibly even user interface implementation code.

Chapter 9

International User Interfaces

International user interfaces are those that are intended for use in more than one country. Designing international user interfaces may or may not involve language translation, but it should certainly involve consideration of the special needs of other countries and cultures. Increasing technological sophistication in many countries of the world and the resulting larger world trade imply greater need to pay attention to international aspects of user interfaces. A growing number of American companies have reached a situation where most of their sales are outside the U.S. (in 1991 four of the five largest U.S. computer companies derived more than 50% of their sales from abroad [Russo and Boor 1993]). Companies in smaller countries often have a very large, or even dominating, proportion of their sales outside their own country.

Viewed from the vendor perspective, this large number of international sales means that software sales will increasingly depend on the international usability of products and not just their domestic usability. And seen from the users' perspective, more than half of the world's software users will soon be using interfaces that were originally designed in a foreign country. Usability for this large number of users will depend upon increased awareness of the issues in designing user interfaces for international use [Nielsen 1990f].

As the European Union (previously named the European Community) is establishing the so-called Single Market, international software is becoming even more important in that part of the world with the growth of cross-frontier trade and with more companies becoming multinational. It is important to realize, however, that the Single Market is not a "single" market in the sense that all Europeans can now be treated the same. The language differences have not gone away and the cultural differences between the regions will also remain. So the European Single Market has actually increased the need to pay attention to the issues discussed in this chapter.

In an unpublished study from 1990, Tim Frank Andersen from the Technical University of Denmark analyzed software reviews from various personal computer magazines published in Denmark, the U.K., and the U.S. The American software reviews contained practically no discussion of international usability issues (0.06 comments per review). In contrast, the average British review contained 0.41 comments on international usability issues, and the average Danish review contained 0.80 such comments. These numbers clearly indicate the difference in importance of international issues in these countries: Most software is currently designed directly for the American market and therefore normally needs no further modifications to support local needs. The U.K. has almost the same language as the U.S., and can therefore often use American software with little modification. In contrast, Denmark has a different language, including the special characters æ, ø, and å, leading to greater needs for local customization. One would of course expect even greater emphasis on international usability issues in countries with more elaborate special needs such as the extensive character sets used in many Asian countries [Sukaviriya and Moran 1990].[1]

---

1. A case study of the transfer of a Japanese software package to the Ivory Coast also emphasized the need to consider the different infrastructures and user attitudes in different cultures [Tousséa-Oulaï and Ura 1991].

International usage issues thus play a major role in smaller and non-English speaking countries, even though they may be invisible to users and developers based in the United States [Sprung 1990].[2]

9.1 International Graphical Interfaces

At first sight, it might seem that the current trend toward graphical interfaces and the use of icons instead of words might solve the international use problem. This is not so, however, as icons and color connotations are not necessarily universal. For example, a mailbox icon is often used in electronic mail applications, but mailboxes actually look very different in different countries. I certainly remember being very insecure about whether I was using an "official" mailbox the first time I mailed a postcard in Brussels.

Icons can be classified in three categories according to their graphic design[3] [Lodding 1983; Rogers 1989]:

1. *Resemblance icons:* Depicting a physical object which the icon is intended to represent. Using a picture of an envelope to represent a file of electronic mail would be a resemblance icon.

2. *Reference icons:* Depicting some object which by reference or analogy might represent the concept the icon is intended to represent. For example, using a picture of a clamp to represent a file-compression utility (because it squeezes) would be a reference icon. It would be hard to come up with a good resemblance icon for file compression except through use of a before–

---

2. English-speaking readers wanting to get a feel for mistranslated user interfaces can find an annotated example in [Nielsen 1990h]. See also the example in Exercise 13 on page 276.

3. Icons and other graphic interface elements can also be classified in three categories according to the role they play when being used: *signals* (information sensed at the skill-based level, such as braking when you see a red traffic light), *signs* (information derived from rule-based behavior, such as adjusting your speed based on whatever the latest speed limit posting read), and *symbols* (information deduced by knowledge-based reasoning, such as puzzling out the meaning of unfamiliar icons in a foreign airport) [Rasmussen 1983]. These two classifications are different taxonomies of graphic design and usage circumstances, even though they use some of the same terms.

after combination of a large and a small document, but icons showing state changes are notoriously hard to understand. Reference icons are sometimes also called symbolic icons or index icons.

3. *Arbitrary icons:* Arbitrary shapes that only have meaning by convention. Traffic signs are often arbitrary icons and may form a good source of computer icons because of their fairly standardized international use. For example, a warning triangle might be used as the icon for a warning message. Obviously, arbitrary icons are the hardest for users to learn, unless they are so widely used that the convention becomes second nature. For example, it is doubtful that many people worry that the shape "?" is completely arbitrary as an indicator of a question.

The mailbox problem is due to different countries having different designs of the physical object depicted by the icon. Even so, resemblance icons will often be reasonably recognizable in many countries, at least if they depict fairly common objects. Pictures of uncommon objects may be harder to recognize, as shown by the test in Hungary of proposed international icons for sports. Only 9% of Hungarians correctly interpreted the icon showing a squash player, because most Hungarians have never seen a game of squash [Brugger 1990].

Reference and arbitrary icons will often do considerably worse than resemblance icons in internationalization. Even in cases where an arbitrary icon has a wide international following, it may be unknown in some countries, as indicated by the 13% recognition rate in Japan of a first-aid icon based on the Red Cross logo [Brugger 1990]. Varying national conventions may reduce the usability of designs that are intended to be reference icons. For example, a picture of a (dining) table can be used as a reference icon to represent a table of numbers that can be popped up in a hypertext system. The analogy between tables as furniture and tables as typographical objects only holds if the user speaks certain languages, however. In many other languages, completely different words are used for the two concepts (for example, *bord* and *tabel* in Danish), and the table icon would be reduced to the status of an

☒ **Font Substitution?**   ☑ **Font Substitution?**

Figure 22 *Two possible checkbox designs for a graphical interface. The left example would be interpreted by many Japanese as meaning that fonts should* ***not*** *be substituted.*

arbitrary icon for users speaking those languages. In general, interface puns[4] are dangerous, though they can be hard to resist.

A further problem with internationalization of graphical interfaces is the total lack of tradition for involving graphic designers in the translation process. Translating the word "mailbox" to "postkasse" or some other appropriate term can be done easily by string substitution if the application is constructed according to the resource-separation principle discussed on page 251, but redesigning a mailbox icon requires graphic design talent.

Even noniconic graphics can lead to problems as illustrated in Figure 22. Since an X-mark is normally used in Japan to signify that something is *not* wanted, the leftmost dialogue element would often be misinterpreted in Japan.

As a further example, the use of *italic typefaces* to add emphasis to text in a graphical interface may not be appropriate when the text is in kanji. Instead, some word processors sold in Japan have added an amikake formatting feature, where a | shaded box | is placed over text for highlighting.

Gestural Interfaces

Just as icons are not necessarily universal, gestures like those used in pen-based computers and some virtual reality systems may need scrutiny for international usability. As an example, proof-readers' marks are often used for editing in pen interfaces, even though they have their roots in typographical traditions that may differ between countries. For example, the American mark for

---

4. Visual puns can be funny and engaging in certain applications such as entertainment and education. See Figures 4.15 and 4.16 in [Nielsen 1990a] for a good example of a visual pun in a nonverbal hypermedia system for children.

inserting a blank space is #, whereas the corresponding Danish sign is ⌐. Even vocabulary differences may cause changes in gestural systems, as shown by the need for twice as many words in the German version of the Newton handwriting recognizer as the English version because of the long German words [Flohr 1994].

9.2 International Usability Engineering

Basically, an international interface is a *new* interface and should in principle be subjected to exactly the same usability engineering process as any other interface. This is true whether the interface is translated or used in its original version by users from another culture. Of course, it is often possible (and necessary) to make do with less than a full-blown usability effort and still ensure international usability, assuming that the original version of the interface has been developed according to good usability methodology.

As always, the main usability engineering activities are early focus on users and their tasks and empirical user testing with users from the foreign country. Furthermore, any translation should be performed by a translator with knowledge of the usability principles for interactive systems since it is not enough to be good at traditional, static translation.

For example, graphics programs often have a special drawing grid that may be activated to restrict the pen from moving freely. An English version of one such program used a menu with the commands Turn Grid On and Turn Grid Off to switch between the two drawing modes. The Danish version, however, used the commands Med net ("use grid") and Uden net ("without grid"), respectively. Several test subjects were observed to have problems with these commands: Novice users did not realize that these two commands toggle the same option because they look sufficiently different to a user quickly scanning the menu, where only one of the commands is displayed at any given time. The English version starts with the same two words for both commands, thus improving the likelihood that a novice user will recognize them when scanning the menu. Also, the English commands have more active connotations, implying in what direction the drawing mode will change if a command is selected. The Danish versions are more passive, which led some users to think that the command displayed in the menu was indicating the *current* drawing state rather than being the name of the opposite drawing state (which one can *change* to).

Each of the translated menu items was perfectly adequate when seen by itself as a static interface element. But when they were used as part of an interaction (inherently dynamic), several users erroneously reversed their meaning. Even experienced users sometimes made this mistake. This example shows the need for attention to the principles of dialogue design even during a translation: Details do matter! The example also shows the need for empirical testing with real users since the problem only occurs for novices.

Since the translation is embedded in an interactive environment, one can help the translators avoid many usability problems by providing them with the rationale for the original interface design.[5] If translators know why a certain word was chosen in an interface, they can better choose a translation that has the same connotations. Knowledge of the intention of the original wording would have avoided the problem in the Russian section of a multilanguage phrase book for tourists which translated the phrase, "There's a bug in my hotel room," to "There's a listening device in my hotel room."[6] As a more computer-related example, if the name File was chosen as a menu title to be consistent with an industry standard, it would be best to translate it to whatever term is used in the translated standard rather than another word that may seem more appropriate at first sight. The design rationale should include the main conclusions from the user tests of the original interface to reduce the risk that a translator will introduce known usability problems.

---

5. See page 108 for further discussion of design rationales.
6. *New York Times*, May 12, 1991, p. A28.

While observing a word processor user in France, I found that she consistently confused the two search commands in the system. One command searched the current document for the next occurrence of some specified text, and the other command searched the file system for files containing some specified text. In the English version of this menu-based word processor, the first command was called simply `Find`, whereas the second was called `Find File`. In the French version, *both* commands were called `Rechercher` (which means "find"), with the only distinction being that the document-specific command was in the edit menu and the file system command was in the file menu. The user, however, did not pay much attention to the menu headings but just grabbed the first `Rechercher` command she happened to come by, thus often getting the wrong one and being very confused by the result. This problem might well have been avoided if the translator had been given access to a design rationale outlining the usability considerations behind the original choice of the command name `Find File`.

Similarly, it is a good idea to develop glossaries with translations of each of the important terms relating to your application for each of the languages you plan to translate to. Many of the terms in such a glossary can be reused from existing user interface standards, and it is a good idea to look at the multilanguage lists of common terms found as appendices to some of the major vendor standards, even if your design does not otherwise follow these standards. You do not want your users to be talking about the translated equivalent of "viewport" if all other users in their country use a term corresponding to "window" for the same concept. In addition to using generic user interface terminology like "window," "scroll bar," etc., most systems probably also have application-specific terms that need to be translated by specialists in the appropriate domain in order to build an application-specific glossary. Having such glossaries ensures consistency in translations of different elements of the total interface (screen designs, manuals, instructional materials, etc.), even if they are translated by different translators. Without a glossary, even a single translator may have difficulties due to the verbal disagreement phenomenon (there are so many different terms for any given concept, that two different people will normally pick two different terms when asked) [Furnas *et al.* 1987].

Many interfaces are used in other countries without translation. This can be either because those other countries are too small or poor to support a translation effort or because the software is too specialized to have more than a few users in each country. Use of untranslated software can also be caused by a desire for internal standards in a multinational company or by the presence of foreigners in the country where the software originates. Therefore, it is desirable to design interfaces and documentation such that they have as high an international usability as possible, even if they are not translated. Doing so will also make the job of any translator easier.

International usability of written materials obviously rests on the avoidance of complicated language in terms of vocabulary and sentence construction [Kincaid *et al.* 1990]. Whether you talk about the English bull in a china shop or the Danish elephant in a glass shop may not matter all that much, but many idioms can be very difficult to translate and understand and should be avoided in writing manuals.[7] To stay with animal examples, what do I mean when I say that "there is no cow on the ice?"[8] Similarly, manuals and tutorials should not use examples that are overly dependent on local culture, including sports like baseball or cricket which are only popular in some countries.

To ensure optimal translations, at least one translator on the team should be a resident native of the target country, since expatriates lose touch with details of the language after a few years abroad. As

---

7. Further translation difficulties may arise from using derivative words with expanded meanings. Doing so seems to be especially easy and common in English—or at least in the style of English where "all nouns can be verbed." For example, the title `Goodies` for a menu with utility features in a program may seem appropriate and perhaps slightly chic to American users. This menu title can lead to problems, however, if a literal translation is chosen that makes the user think of candy.

8. No cow on the ice = no serious difficulties to overcome (Danish idiom). To appreciate the meaning, consider what you would do if you were a farmer and one of your cows *had* walked out on the ice.

an admittedly extreme example, a propaganda leaflet dropped in millions of copies by U.S. peacekeeping forces when they entered Somalia in December 1992 included a picture of an American soldier shaking hands with a Somali man. The intended caption was "United Nations," but because of a mix-up in the vowels, it actually read "Slave Nation." This problem occurred because the only available translator with military clearance had emigrated from Somalia many years earlier.[9]

A software design may have to be customized even if a full translation is not performed. The need for such customization becomes more apparent in computer-supported cooperative work (CSCW) [Ishii 1990] and other forms of software that are more dependent on cultural and organizational norms than traditional productivity software for individual use.

As a concrete example of the need for customization, software with a search function may assume that individuals can be located by first searching for their family name and then picking the desired person from a menu. First, it is of course necessary to realize that the family name is actually the first name in many cultures, so simplistically hardwiring the search to look for last names will not do.[10] Second, some countries have a much smaller variability in family names than, say, the U.S. For example, the two most common Danish family names (Jensen and Nielsen) are each shared by 6% of the population, and the five most common family names account for 24% of all Danes [Søndergaard 1987]. A search for employees named Jensen or Nielsen in a Danish company would generate many screenfulls of people[11] (including many with the same first name), so the search interface would have to be

---

9. *New York Times*, December 27, 1992, p. 10.

10. There are even further variations on this theme to be considered. In Iceland, names are similar to the European naming system with the "first" name first, but telephone directories and other listings are sorted by first name since the last name is not really a family name in the normal sense but rather a patronymic. The main lesson is the need to avoid any hardwiring of assumptions.

11. See [Nielsen 1990f] for a further discussion of the international naming problem.

modified to be of any use. Such individual circumstances for various countries will be much easier to take into account if they are known before the initial implementation of the software.

Finally, care should be taken not to limit software design by arbitrary assumptions that happen to cause no problems in the country where the software is developed. In one case, an American air traffic control system could not be used in London because it did not distinguish between positive and negative longitudes (most countries are located in a single hemisphere, after all), causing the system to fold its model of the airspace around London at the Greenwich 0° line [Lamb 1988].

To ensure that the recommended early focus on users and their tasks also includes international users, it is necessary to facilitate communication between the development organization and the company's international division or sales staff. International representatives should be involved throughout the early product planning stages and should be encouraged to comment on the special needs of their various markets.

9.3   Guidelines for Internationalization

Several practical considerations need to be embedded deeply in any implementation to ensure that the resulting code will be useful overseas instead of breaking because of some implicit assumption.[12] This section lists some of the most common mistakes and advises how to avoid them. See [del Galdo 1990] for a more detailed list of internationalization guidelines.

---

12. The Localization Industry Standards Association (LISA) is an association of companies interested in the localization, documentation, and translation of their products. Address for further information: 9B chemin Castan, CH-1224 Chene-Bougeries, Switzerland, +41 22 349 2222, fax +41 22 349 8977, email Anobile.LISA@applelink.apple.com or manobile@divsun.unige.ch.

Characters

Many countries have character sets that extend beyond the A–Z alphabet used in English and the original ASCII character set. The most obvious guideline is to accommodate whatever is the local character set, and a further guideline is to treat additional local characters as "first class citizens" and allow them to be used in variable names, filenames, etc., on an equal footing with the A–Z characters.

Many countries (especially in Asia) have very large character sets that cannot be encoded in the 256 different values of an 8-bit byte [Lunde 1993]. Often, 16 (or more) bits are used to represent each character, and the software needs to be able to handle that. Many other countries (including most European countries) have character sets that extend the original 7-bit ASCII code with a few additional characters but still fit within an 8-bit byte. Software will break in these countries if it routinely strips away the eighth bit in character codes on the assumption that ASCII codes only have seven bits.

Handling of character sets becomes even more complicated if several languages need to be represented in the same document [Becker 1984] or on the same computer, which is a common need for many users, including most multinational companies. Two current approaches to truly international character sets are the Unicode two-byte standard and the ISO 10646 four-byte standard [Sheldon 1991].[13]

Even assuming that an extended character set is accepted, true localized handling of different character sets requires that one abandons any simplistic reliance on the numeric values of the character codes. For example, a translation from lowercase to upper-

---

13. The main difference between Unicode and ISO 10646 is the treatment of Japanese, Chinese, and Korean ideograms (kanji, etc.). ISO 10646 and Unicode 1.1 are identical in two-byte format, cramming all the ideograms into a single Han set, eliminating duplicate characters. ISO 10646 has, in its definition, the flexibility to eventually allow full character sets for each language, using UCS-4 (four-byte format). Further information is available by anonymous FTP from the host `unicode.org` on the Internet.

case characters cannot be done simply by adding 26 to the numeric value of the character, since one would want, for example, æ to be mapped to Æ even though these two characters may not be 26 positions apart in the character encoding. Similarly, sorting has to take special characters into account, such as ä, å, æ, é, è, ô, ö, ø, ñ, ç, ü, and ß (a German character that should be sorted as if it were two characters (ss)[14]).

In some countries, ö is sorted as an o, and in other countries, it is sorted as a separate letter toward the end of the alphabet. Inconsistencies like this indicate the need for separate sorting functions for each country. Also, some languages have slight differences, depending on whether the items being sorted are names or regular words. Unfortunately, even within the same country, collation tables used by different vendors sometimes have tiny differences, and may not always correspond exactly to national standards. Thus, a set of words may be alphabetized differently, depending on what platform the software is running on, even if the software follows the appropriate localization rules and collation tables. Following the appropriate national standards for each country is probably the best solution for applications that are intended to be used across multiple platforms. See [Canadian Standards Association 1992] for an example of a well-planned sorting standard that considers multilingual texts.

Kanji character sorting is even more difficult. For example, names are phonetically sorted in Goju-on (AIUEO) order. To do this, one has to estimate how a character is read (pronounced) in each particular name. Many systems use a name dictionary for this purpose, but a single dictionary entry for each name is not always sufficient. In some cases, the reading of a name depends on the district where the person came from or the history of his or her family.

---

14. The reverse problem also exists. In Danish, the two-character sequence aa is mostly sorted as if it were the single character å. To make things really difficult, the exact sorting depends on how the word is pronounced. In Spanish, "ch" is considered a single character (sorted between "cz" and "d"), as is "ll."

Numbers and Currency

Different notations are used for numbers in different countries. The main difference is probably the character used for the decimal "point," which is a period in some countries and a comma in others. Typically, the character that is not used as a decimal separator is then used as a thousands separator, though white space is sometimes used instead for the thousands separator. Also, some countries use special symbols ($, £, ƒ, etc.) to indicate their currency and others use abbreviations (DM, kr., etc.). These symbols and abbreviations go before the number in some countries and after in others. Thus, ten thousand currency units can be written as

- $10,000.00 (in the United States)
- 10.000,00 kr. (in Denmark)

Furthermore, even though it seems that most countries use two decimals in their currencies, a few countries use three, and some countries only have full currency units and use no decimals.

Time and Measurement Units

User interfaces need to handle different measurement systems, with the most important being the SI system (Système International) of metric units and the American system of inches, feet, miles, Fahrenheit, etc. The time of day is sometimes written in a 24-hour notation (e.g., 22:00) and sometimes in a 12-hour notation (e.g., 10:00 PM).

Different notations are also in use for writing dates, with the most common probably being

- D/M/Y (for example, 5/10/93 for October 5, 1993)
- D/M-Y (for example, 5/10-93)
- M/D/Y (for example, 10/5/93 or 10/05/93)
- Y.M.D (for example, 1993.10.05)
- Y-M-D (for example, 1993-10-05)

These notations can certainly be confusing: Is 10/5/93 the tenth of May or October fifth? To avoid misunderstandings, it is highly recommended to write out the name of the month with letters in international communications rather than giving its number. For use within a single country, numeric representations may be preferred because of their compactness and because they allow easy estimates of time intervals. In either case, software should allow for local date formats and for use of the local names of months and the days of the week.

In addition to the specification of dates and months, the use of week numbers is very common in Europe. For example, one may list a meeting as taking place during Week 25 (the 25th week of the year). Finally, it should of course be noted that some countries use other calendars than the Gregorian, so one might also have to cope with transformations between completely different date systems. For example, in Japan dates are sometimes given with reference to the year of the Emperor's reign (but it would be a cultural blunder to include a feature to update these dates after the death of the current emperor).

Don't Despair

The singlemost important advice for the design of international user interfaces is actually that one should not give up just because it turns out to be impossible to follow all the guidelines in a given project. It is better to provide *some* flexibility than to hardwire everything with local conventions, even if full flexibility and support for all the world's cultures cannot be achieved. Likewise, the inclusion of a few foreign users during user testing is still much better than to proceed on the basis of information from domestic users only, even if full tests cannot be conducted in all potential user countries.

9.4   Resource Separation

One of the major ways to achieve improved international usability in practice is to separate the interface and the system's functionality in the implementation [Edmonds 1991]. In traditional ways of writing software, the user interface specification was deeply intertwined with the rest of the code, normally to the extent that the character strings that were to be issued as prompts and error messages were part of procedure calls in those parts of the code that needed the prompts and messages. Obviously, the translation of such software is quite difficult and requires access to, and perusal of, the source code.

Newer systems have started to store the specification of the user interface in separate resources that are integrated with the rest of the code when the application is run. For example, when all text strings that are to be seen by the user are stored in one location, it becomes a simple matter to translate them. Often, system messages need to include references to user data that is not known until run time, but such references can be inserted as parameters in the message text. It is important to have the capability to switch the order in which the parameters are displayed at run time in case a different word order is required by some language. For example, the string "Copy file <#1> to disk <#2>?" could be stored in the resource database and would generate the text " `Copy file Chapter 9 to disk Backup`?" when the question is actually asked. Other languages may require phrasing like "Copy to disk *Backup* from the file *Chapter 9*?"

Similarly, the specification of window and dialog box layouts for graphical user interfaces can be stored in resource databases. The layout specification would include information on the size of the window and the relative location of each element, including text strings, user-input fields, and icons. The icons would be stored elsewhere in the resource database so that they could be edited to conform to local graphics conventions. Using a special direct manipulation screen layout editor, it then becomes possible for the translator to rearrange dialogue elements to suit the local language as well as resize text fields to make room for additional or longer words in languages like German.[15]

---

15. In case resizing is not possible, a general guideline for the design of the original text fields is to leave room for about 30% extra characters in the translated versions.

In addition to the resource databases, version control tools are needed to help translate interface upgrades. Many interface elements will remain the same, and so should their translations (for the sake of cross-version consistency). Other interface elements will change, and even unchanged strings may require retranslation if they are used in new contexts. Also, a translation tool is needed to show the translator the various resources in the context in which they will be used.

In some systems, many local conventions such as the sorting sequence for characters, the proper way of writing dates, the names of months, etc., are stored in a central resource base that can be used by any application. If individual applications integrate such system-wide resources with their own, they can achieve a fairly high degree of localization without any further work at all, since the interface will "magically" take on considerably local character just by virtue of using the resource stored in the local system.

9.5   Multilocale Interfaces

Localization based on system-wide resources and translation of application-specific resources is sufficient to support use of an interface for a single, specific culture. Thus, if you are a German living in Germany who only communicates with other Germans in German, then your problems should be solved if all your software vendors had done a proper job of localizing their systems to German. Even though many users would find this form of single-locale support sufficient, there are also many users who need multilocalized interfaces. Examples would include anybody who moves to or visits a foreign country as well as anybody who communicates or exchanges data with people in other countries.

Ideally, each running interface and each datafile should be associated with a locale that identifies the proper localization needed to communicate with the current user. If a new user starts using the system, or if the data is transferred to another country, it should be possible to select a new locale and have the interface and data interpretation change appropriately. For example, assume that you have a database with prices for certain goods set by a vendor located in the U.S. One such price might be $1,498.95, and it should be represented as such if the locale is set to "USA." If the file with this price list was sent by electronic mail to a customer in Germany, the locale would change and the price should be displayed as $1.498,95 (but *not* as DM 1.498,95).[16]

Thus, even though the value of the system attribute "local currency symbol" would change from $ to DM as the locale changed from USA to Germany, the system should not compromise data integrity by changing the measurement unit for data that had already been entered. Of course, the system *should* take care of the changing decimal point and thousands separator. Similarly, the database commands, error messages, and such should change from English to German as the locale changed. If the German user had a French visitor, it should be possible for the visitor to temporarily set the locale to France and operate the system in French.

---

16. However, even a correct conversion into local notation may be risky. For example, if the price had been $1,498 (without a decimal point), a German rendering as $1.498 might be mistaken for a per-piece price of about one and a half dollar, if the German user knew something about American notation and was cued into a "non-German info interpretation" mode by the dollar sign. One solution to this particular problem would be to always display the decimal point, but the general issue is harder: It will be necessary to communicate to users whether information has been localized or not.

Chapter 10   *Future Developments*

You will often read about new methods that are supposed to be available "Real Soon Now" for the improvement of usability without any of the fear and loathing some people associate with the usability methods described in this book. As a matter of fact, I can confidently predict that you will discover such a method within a few months of reading my book, since there are always new, supposedly revolutionary, methods being proposed.

Unfortunately, there is no "silver bullet" that will magically solve the usability problem (the way silver bullets were supposed to be the way to kill werewolves). If you have just a few years of experience in the software engineering field, you will no doubt remember many claims of silver bullet innovations to address the general problem of software construction. Some of these innovations actually turned out to improve the software engineering lifecycle, and others proved more ephemeral. None of them made the fundamental problems go away [Brooks 1987]. *Plus ça change, plus c'est la même chose* (the more it changes, the more it's the same thing).

The same level of healthy skepticism that software engineering practitioners have acquired over the years should be retained for judging claims of usability engineering silver bullets. The fundamental problems of usability engineering are to learn the characteristics of the actual users and their tasks, to generate creative design solutions that map between computer capabilities and these users and their tasks, and to test the solutions against the infinite potential for mismatches among the interface, users, and their tasks. Everything comes back to the two phenomena of individual humans and real-world tasks [Nielsen 1989d], both of which exhibit a discouraging tendency to defy predefined restrictions.

Because of this fundamental reality of usability engineering, the basic need for the methods described in this book will remain, no matter what improvements and refinements are discovered in the future. Most usability specialists are actually fairly much in agreement about the fundamentals of usability engineering, even though they may differ when it comes to detailed recommendations [Mulligan *et al.* 1992]. Of course, improvements are likely to happen, and I am myself actively working to invent some of them. The reader should just be warned against the seductive euphoria that one can easily get from reading about new methods.

One problem with many reports on supposed advances in usability engineering is that they confound the effect of the proposed method on its own with the effect of its use as part of an experiment. Often, such advances are invented by some of the world's leading usability experts who are highly motivated themselves when using their own newest method, as well as being highly motivating of the other project participants. In many cases, the good results reported may be as much due to general skills and abilities of these experts and the high level of excitement on the project as to any inherent value of the proposed method or tool.

10.1 Theoretical Solutions

A Holy Grail for many usability scientists is the invention of analytic methods that would allow designers to predict the usability of a user interface before it has even been tested. Not only would such a method save us from user testing, it would allow for precise estimates of the trade-offs between different design solutions without having to build them. The only thing that would be better would be a generative theory of usability that could design the user interface itself based on a description of the usability goals to be achieved. The most famous analytic method is known as GOMS (for goals, operators, methods, and selection rules) [Card *et al.* 1983].

The basic GOMS method is fairly simple: It involves listing possible user *goals* and subgoals (e.g., changing a word in a text document); the *operators* users have available as motor, perceptual, or cognitive primitives (e.g., click the mouse, look at the menubar, remember a name); the *methods* users compose out of sequences of these operators to achieve the goals or subgoals (e.g., selection is done by moving the cursor to point to the word and then double-clicking the mouse); and the *selection rules* necessary to decide what to do next if the user has several goals pending or if there are several methods that will accomplish a given goal (e.g., the word can be removed by selecting it and issuing a cut command or by backspacing over it). It will be apparent that a model of a user interface of any realistic scale will be very big. Each operation and selection rule is modeled as taking a certain amount of time to carry out, such as the "mental operator" (e.g., to remember a name) that is estimated at 1.35 seconds, and the analyst can then finally calculate the time needed to perform various tasks by adding up the time for all the individual steps.

The basic GOMS model has several weaknesses [Carroll and Campbell 1986], the most important of which is its limitation to error-free performance by expert users. In real life, even expert users make large numbers of errors, and the performance of novice and casual users is of paramount importance for most applications of usability engineering. Modifications to the model are dealing with some of these weaknesses [Olson and Olson 1990], but it still cannot be said to completely account for all the phenomena of human–computer interaction.

Several research studies have shown benefits of using GOMS to analyze user interfaces, and there are even some practical case studies where GOMS has been useful in the real world [Gray *et al.* 1992]. One study compared various ways of estimating the time needed by users to perform database queries on telephone

	Dialog Box 1 Query	Dialog Box 2 Queries	Pop-Up Menu 1 Query	Pop-Up Menu 2 Queries
GOMS analysis	16.6	22.6	5.8	11.2
User testing	15.4	25.5	4.3	6.5

Table 11 *Time in seconds to look up one or two telephone numbers: GOMS predictions versus measured results from user testing.*

numbers, using either a dialog box or a pop-up menu interface [Nielsen and Phillips 1993]. As can be seen from Table 11, the GOMS predictions were very close to the actual times painstakingly measured by having 20 test users perform hundreds of boring tasks. The main deviation between the predictions and the measurements is the time needed for two queries with the pop-up menu. Use of the pop-up interface involved clicking on the telephone number and selecting the database from the menu. Looking up two telephone numbers involved doing exactly the same sequence for both numbers, making it natural to model a two-number query as taking twice as long as a single-number query. In reality, the second query is much faster than the first because users can automatically repeat a set sequence of actions without having to put it together first. This phenomenon is known in the research literature as one of the many suggested modifications of GOMS [Olson and Nilsen 1987–1988], but this modification was not known to the analysts in our study. Unfortunately, due to this need to know a large variety of research results and modifications, GOMS and similar approaches are still seen as intimidating by most practitioners [Bellotti 1988] and they are not used much yet.

An alternative theoretical approach to the improvement of user interfaces is the development of better notations for the formal specifications of dialogues. The assumption is that better descriptions of exactly what will happen in a dialogue are necessary to gain an understanding of the dialogue and to be able to communicate designs to developers, to readers of standards documents, and to a user interface management system that might automatically implement the design without further work on the part of the developer. Current practice is based on very loose specifications of user interface designs, and designers often find that their intentions have not been completely realized when they see the way the developers interpreted the design documents.

Multiple approaches to formal specification of user interfaces have been suggested, including many based on specification techniques for traditional software engineering extended to accommodate the special needs of highly dynamic, interactive systems. Examples include state-transition diagrams [Wellner 1989], BNF [Reisner 1981], Petri nets [Stotts and Furuta 1989], production systems [Olsen 1990], logic programming [Roach and Nickson 1983], and temporal logic [Johnson 1991]. New notations have also been developed specifically for the specification of user interfaces, such as the User Action Notation, UAN [Hartson *et al.* 1990]. In spite of this extensive research activity, almost no user interfaces are currently subjected to formal specification.

Some researchers claim that a task analysis based on observation and natural language description will inherently be vague. To allow for more precise descriptions as well as possibly deeper insights through detailed analysis, several notations and methods for formal task analysis techniques have been proposed [Diaper 1989a; Diaper and Johnson 1989]. Again, these techniques make sense in principle, but seem to be too difficult for most developers to learn and apply to practical projects. The Task–Action Grammar (TAG) [Payne and Green 1986, 1989; Schiele and Green 1990] is a formal modelling technique somewhat in between the interface specification languages and the task analysis languages and is intended to model the mapping in a system between the users' task and the user interface. Several case studies have found the TAG model useful for the analysis of small user interfaces, but it does not seem to have seen much use in practice.

Speech input/output 33%
Individualized interaction. 19%
Increased use of graphics, mice, icons, etc. 16%
Dialogues developed by the users themselves 12%
Other new I/O-media than speech 12%
Increased computer knowledge in the general population. 12%
Task-oriented solutions. 12%
System adapts to the user's level 12%
A few, "standard" user interfaces. 9%
Increased awareness of usability issues. 9%
Natural language. 7%
AI-techniques (in addition to speech and natural language) 7%
Self-explanatory systems without manuals 7%
"The past will survive," COBOL systems still in use, etc. 7%
Computer support for cooperative work 7%

Table 12 *Fifty-seven Danish computer professionals participating in a user interface seminar in October 1986 answered the question: "It is likely that the situation will be different in the year 2000 concerning usability of computer systems. Please list one or a few of the most important changes compared with the situation today." The table shows my classification of the top answers (in percent of the 57 responses).*

10.2 *Technological Solutions*

It is tempting to believe that new interaction techniques will be so easy to use that they will solve the usability problem just by virtue of being applied in an interface. For example, the ability to speak to a computer is viewed by many as the way to achieve a break-through in usability.[1] In 1986, I asked a group of computer professionals with interests in user interface issues to predict the major changes in the year 2000. As shown in Table 12, the overwhelming

---

1. Speech input often represents future computer technology in science fiction films—possibly because spoken dialogues are easier for the audience to comprehend. One memorable scene in a *Star Trek* film had the chief engineer subjected to time travel back to our present, where he tried to use one of the currently popular personal computers equipped with a mouse. He promptly picked up the mouse and used it as a microphone to give voice input to the computer. See Mantei [1990] for amusing examples of how real users react the first time they see a computer mouse.

"winner" was speech.[2] Other technologies such as flat screens and portable computers came far down the list, being suggested by only 4% of the respondents, even though they currently seem much more likely to succeed by the year 2000.

Current speech technology is certainly still too unreliable to form the foundation of future interface developments. From the perspective of this book, however, the main point is that even when perfect speech recognition is achieved some day, there will still be a need for usability engineering efforts to ensure the quality of the resulting dialogues. Just consider the number of times you have misinterpreted spoken instructions when speaking with fellow humans.

User interface management systems,[3] normally referred to as UIMS [Hartson and Hix 1989; Hix 1990; Myers 1989; Olsen 1991], aim at reducing the time and effort needed to implement user interfaces by introducing a separate software layer between the user and the code handling the functionality. The UIMS will take care of things like the drawing of dialog boxes and the tracking of the cursor as the user moves the mouse, leaving the code that needs to be written by the applications programmer to deal with higher-level abstractions like "request an answer to this question from the user." Not only will this reduce the amount of coding required for a graphical user interface, but it will also separate the user interface specification from the underlying functionality so that changes in one do not always require changes in the other. UIMS software may be the one technology that is closest to a practical breakthrough, and indeed some user interface builders are already in commercial use on some platforms. Potentially, user interface builders may allow the construction of some user interfaces by visual formalisms that are sufficiently task-oriented to be put together by end users without additional programming, the

---

2. See also Grudin [1991b, pp. 184–185] for a discussion of the history of the belief in speech technology as an effective solution to the usability problem.

3. Other terms covering more or less the same concept are "user interface development tools" (or "environments"), "user interface tool kits," "user interface builders," and "dialogue management systems."

way such end users currently construct table-based user interfaces in a spreadsheet [Johnson *et al.* 1993].

Once a user interface has been described· in a machine-readable language in a UIMS, it may be possible to perform various automatic checks of usability conformance on that specification [Bleser and Foley 1982; Reisner 1990]. For example, it can be checked that the syntax is the same throughout the interface. Attempts have also been made to analyze consistency quantitatively using a GOMS-like method [Tanaka *et al.* 1990] to count the proportion of words that are different in the formal descriptions of interactions with the two systems. This latter method seems to achieve fairly good results, but of course it depends not only on the correctness of a formal description of the interface but also on the correctness of a formal description of how the user would interact with the interface.

Given that user interface standards and guidelines are as hard to apply as discussed in Chapter 8, research is also under way to automatically evaluate a design's compliance with a standard [Löwgren and Nordqvist 1992]. Such advisory systems may provide some assistance in checking those aspects of a user interface that can easily be formally specified, but there are still many aspects of usability that do not lend themselves to such representation and automated analysis.

Several attempts have been made at implementing expert systems to choose the optimal interaction techniques automatically and maybe even design the entire interface [Bleser and Sibert 1990; Blumenthal 1990; de Baar *et al.* 1992; Kim and Foley 1990; Mackinlay 1988]. Slightly less ambitious projects aim at automatically translating a dialogue specification from a textual form to a graphical user interface, using various prespecified rules for how to represent each dialogue technique [Vander Zanden and Myers 1990; Wiecha and Boies 1990]. This latter type of system may be especially helpful for developers wanting to port a design across several platforms, each having their own user interface standard for the visual appearance of, say, radio buttons. In principle, the user interface designer only needs to specify the rules for the translation of dialogue techniques to a given interface style once, and future designs can then be generated automatically. There is some hope that such rule-based style translation systems may become practical within the near future, but the usability of the resulting design will still depend heavily on the appropriateness of the design specification that is fed into the rules. The more advanced systems that aim at designing the entire interface are much less likely to succeed except for small, well-defined domains such as generating daily weather maps for videotex systems.

Considerable efforts are being expended on the construction of intelligent help systems, possibly based on the peanut butter theory of usability, which states that covering something with a sufficiently thick layer will mask its original flavor. However, as stated in Section 5.10, help systems do not make an otherwise unusable system usable, since the use of the help system is an additional burden imposed on the user. Even worse, current intelligent help systems do not seem to help the user all that much and have not been tested under field use conditions. The premise of intelligent help is sound, in that help systems could be made more helpful if they could recognize what the user was trying to do and provide advice based on a model of what the user already knew. However, realistic systems to perform such a feat are many years in the future. Also, some usability specialists argue that users prefer systems that are not "intelligent" but just do as they are told [Shneiderman 1993].

I am more optimistic about the possibilities for using computers automatically to generate parts of sophisticated help interfaces that would be tedious and time-consuming (meaning: would not be done) if done manually, such as graphics that change according to the point being illustrated [Feiner and McKeown 1990, 1991; Seligmann and Feiner 1991] or animations showing how to perform direct manipulation interactions [Sukaviriya and Foley 1990].

10.3 CAUSE Tools: Computer-Aided Usability Engineering

I hope that the discussion of CAUSE tools can be upgraded to a chapter of its own in the next edition of this book, but for now, they only deserve a section in the chapter on possible future developments, since they are not widely used in practice yet. CAUSE stands for Computer-Aided USability Engineering, in the same way that CASE stands for Computer-Aided Software Engineering. Even though there are multiple tasks in the usability engineering lifecycle that could be performed more efficiently with computerized tools, there are almost no such tools commercially available at the moment. Many companies have developed a small assortment of CAUSE tools for their own, in-house use [Weiler *et al.* 1993], but these tools are not widely available, and they are not as sophisticated as one could have hoped for, because they have been developed on the side.

Some examples of CAUSE tools are

- Prototyping tools to rapidly construct a mock-up user interface for user testing.

- Tools for interactive construction of screen layouts, dialog boxes, icons, etc., by direct manipulation.

- Tools for interactive manipulation and easier use of formal notations, specifications, models, and task analysis techniques in order to lower the barriers to their use [Johnson and Johnson 1990].

- Hypermedia representation of user interface standards and guidelines, allowing designers to view animated examples of interaction techniques and to jump between related issues.

- Design rationale representations.

- Wizard of Oz support tools that allow the human simulating the advanced interface to construct replies more easily and that constrain those replies according to the rules of the experiment.

- Logging tools for use during a user test. Such tools typically allow an experimenter to record the time of various user actions or events and to annotate them with a prespecified set of codes as well as free-form comments. Often, the timestamps in the log are coordinated with the timing codes on a videotape of the experiment, thus allowing a playback tool to retrieve the taped record of the test, starting a minute or so before each event that needs to be studied in more detail.[4]

- Localization and translation support tools for international user interfaces.
- Keystroke and event loggers, either for use in user testing or for instrumentation of installed systems.
- Databases of user complaints and support line calls, as well as analysis tools to extract more general information from the database.

Many of these and other CAUSE tools exist in homemade versions in several companies, and some even exist as commercial products, but most of these early attempts have the problem of not being integrated, thus not allowing for complete support of the entire usability engineering lifecycle. Hoiem and Sullivan [1994] describe a system developed at Microsoft that is one of the few current examples of integrated CAUSE tools. A fully integrated CAUSE environment could allow a design rationale to link to video clips of user testing and to the hypertext of the usability guideline supporting the analysis of a certain test user problem. Furthermore, the localization support system would be linked to this information, allowing translators to avoid making the same mistake in producing the international versions.

10.4 Technology Transfer

About 4,000 years ago, Denmark was technologically primitive compared with southern Europe, which had started using bronze tools. The Danes kept using stone tools for almost 1,000 years after the first bronze tools had reached them through trade. Think about

---

4. It is recommended to start playback a short time interval *before* the event of interest to allow the person analyzing the event to better understand the context in which it occurred.

this when you complain that technology transfer is too slow in the computer field. In the late neolithic period, stonesmiths tried to keep up with fashion by producing flint daggers that looked (but probably did not feel) like imported bronze daggers. In a similar manner, character-based user interfaces were produced in the early 1990s to emulate the look of graphical user interfaces. It seems to be a basic fact of human nature that technological innovations are not immediately accepted by the majority of users. People prefer letting somebody else risk their skin with unproven novelties, and the installed base serves as a heavy stone of inertia to prevent even proven concepts from being used right away.

Several of the methods and tools described in this chapter hold considerable promise for improving user interfaces, even though they will not eliminate the need for systematic usability engineering efforts. Also, new methods and tools are being invented all the time.

Unfortunately, experience has shown a considerable time lag between the initial introductions of innovations and their broad-scale use. The computer industry may seem to be moving fast and changing constantly, but the computer systems experienced by the average user are in fact fairly conservative in nature. For example, the mouse was invented in 1964 [Engelbart 1988] and was not introduced on a widely sold personal computer until 20 years later. Even now, there are still many mouse-less computers in use by users who could benefit from having a mouse.[5]

In general, technology transfer proceeds through a process of innovation diffusion spreading from the center of innovation through a small group of early adopters, and the majority of users do not get the technology until much later. If $N(t)$ is the number of users of an innovation (such as a new usability engineering tool or method) at time t, the first zero point of the third derivative of the function $N(t)$ indicates the inflection point [Mahajan *et al.* 1990] where so-

---

5. There are of course also mouse-less computers in use in situations where a mouse would do no good. The idea is not that every innovation should necessarily take over everything.

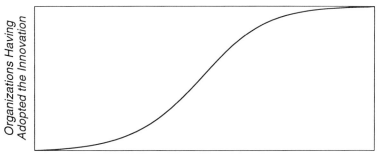

Time after Introduction of Innovation

Figure 23 *Typical Bass diffusion curve for the technology transfer of an innovation.*

called majority adopters start using the innovation and the diffusion starts moving fast. See [Kain and Nielsen 1991] for an example of the use of mathematical models of innovation diffusion from general marketing theory to characterize the spread of hypertext usage. In general, initial diffusion is very slow, since the curves look something like Figure 23 [Mahajan *et al.* 1990]. Only after the first inflection point of the curve do things start to move fast. Furthermore, there is normally a number of laggards who are on the trailing end of the curve after its second inflection point. The last holdouts of the laggards can resist adopting new technology for a *very* long time.

One way to speed up technology transfer is through the use of change agents: people who take on explicit responsibility for transferring technology and for pushing otherwise slow-moving organizations to change. In the usability engineering context, a change agent could be a project manager who decides to use a few simple usability methods on his or her project before corporate management has made an official commitment to usability. Once the results of this first, limited project are available, the change agent can push to have more projects adopt usability methods and for the use of more advanced usability methods.

Exercises

The following exercises provide some ideas for activities you can do to experiment with some of the methods discussed in this book. Of course, the best exercise is really gained from using the methods on a real development project, but maybe you would like something less daunting for a start.

The exercises are mostly intended to help readers who are using this book for self-study. If the book is being used as a textbook for a formal course, it will often be possible to arrange somewhat more elaborate exercises and laboratory projects.

Exercise 1: **Field Study**

Go to a large railroad station like Grand Central Station and stand next to the ticket vending machines. Observe how the machines are being used by three categories of users: regular commuters, who probably buy the same ticket every time, infrequent commuters, and tourists from other cities or abroad. How could the machine be made more efficient to use for the regular commuters? How could the machine be made easier to use for the tourists?

Alternatively, observe the stamp vending machine at a post office. You can also hang out by the photocopier for an hour and observe the range of jobs people bring in and their various levels of skill in operating the machine. How could the machine be made to support common jobs better? How could its design be changed to avoid any confusion or erroneous use you might observe, when casual users bring in complicated jobs?

Exercise 2: Interface Design

Choose some reasonable user interface hardware and system software as your design platform. For example, you could select a personal computer with which you are familiar. Later, you could try to design an interface for the same problem for a radically different platform such as a virtual reality system, a traditional alphanumeric mainframe terminal, or a telephone-based interface. In any case, it is important to clarify your constraints in advance.

For the given platform, using its standard user interface "look-and-feel," design a user interface for the programming of a VCR to tape a series of television shows. The interface should support immediate taping from a specified channel as well as taping of future shows, either only once or regularly every day or week. It should be possible to program the taping of several broadcasts, and it should be possible to cancel a scheduled taping. When designing the user interface, please remember to include any necessary error messages.

Modification: Assume that an online service was available to provide program listings for the various television channels for at least one week ahead. How would that change the interface compared to the situation where the system cannot use any knowledge of broadcasting schedules?

Exercise 3: Defining Measurable Usability Attributes

Consider the VCR user interface designed in the previous exercise. What usability attributes would be especially important for the success of such a product? Precisely define how you would measure the usability of this interface, and also provide estimates of reasonable goals for each attribute, specifying the minimally acceptable level, the planned level, and the best possible level (see Figure 7 on page 81).

As a supplementary exercise, you can measure the usability of your own VCR to get an idea of the current level of usability for each of the usability attributes.[1]

Exercise 4:   Less Is More

Choose some piece of software that you use regularly, such as a word processor, a spreadsheet, or a drawing package. Go through the reference manual and classify all the commands and features in one of the following categories:

• Use it frequently

• Use it occasionally

• Almost never use it, but have used it at least once

• Have never used it

Calculate how large a percentage of the manual could have been eliminated if the software had not included those features you have never used or those you almost never use that you could live without. Do you think there are other user groups that use some of these features frequently?

Exercise 5:   Iterative Design

Choose some computerized printout intended for the general public that contains a fair amount of somewhat complex information. Possible examples could include credit card statements, telephone bills, mortgage statements, and the annual report of an employee's income and other tax-related information. Enter the information from one such printout into a desktop publishing or graphics program on your computer, using the layout from the original statement. Define some sample questions that users could reasonably expect to get answered from the statement, and have one or two of your friends try to find the answers from a printout

---

1. The research literature can sometimes also be used as a source of benchmarks. For example, Hoffberg [1991] found that users needed 17.1 minutes to set the clock and program the taping of three shows when using a commercially available VCR and 8.4 minutes when using her prototype interface.

of your computerized version of the statement. Edit your version to compensate for the difficulties you observed your users having, and try again with some other friends. Repeat several times!

As a supplementary exercise, once you have arrived at a "perfect" design, try sending it to the people responsible for the original statement and see what happens.

Exercise 6: **Participatory Design**

Find a few children who are old enough to know the numbers and the clock but not old enough to read well. Design a VCR user interface they could use to program the taping of their favorite television shows. Assume that the input device will be a remote control with a numeric keypad and a few special keys and that the output device will be a color TV screen and some simple sound effects. Involve the kids in the design, using plenty of white paper, felt-tip markers, and sticky notes.

Exercise 7: **Low-Fidelity Prototyping**

Design an interface that would allow potential home-buyers to view houses on the market through their television set and a fiber optic connection to a remote video service. Users would dial into the service, which would allow them to specify various search criteria such as price and location, after which the system would show video segments of the available houses and allow the customer to set up an appointment to see a house for real.

Instead of implementing the system on a computer, design a prototype interface with paper, pens, and pictures cut from a newspaper or magazine. Perform some simple testing with a few friends to see how they would use the interface. Consider what aspects of the design remain underspecified because you are implementing a low-fidelity prototype, and how the differences between the full system and your prototype impact your user tests.

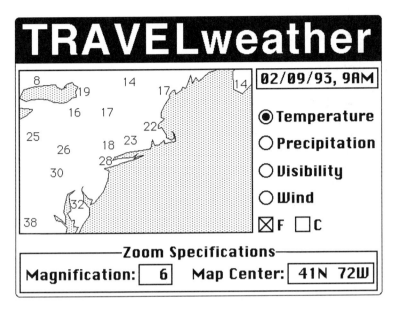

Figure 24 *Screen design for a hypothetical system to provide weather information and forecasts to travellers.*

Exercise 8: Heuristic Evaluation of a Paper Mock-Up

Figure 24 shows a design for a system to provide weather information to travelers. *TRAVELweather* (a non-existing system) can provide information about the weather at 3AM, 9AM, 3PM, and 9PM for the current day as well as the two next days, using reported readings for past weather and forecasts to predict future weather. The interface is designed for use on a graphical personal computer with a mouse, and will appear in a separate window on the screen.

The user operates the interface by typing the desired time into the box in the upper right part of the screen. If the user types a date other than today or the next two days, or if the user types a time other than the four times for which information is available, the system will show an alert dialog box with the following error message: "Weather Data Not Available." The only button in the error message box is an "OK" button. Clicking the OK button will make the dialog box go away and will reset the date and time specification to the previous value.

The user changes the map display by editing the boxes for zoom magnification and for the center of the map. The system ensures that only integer numbers can be typed in the map magnification box by simply beeping every time the user presses a non-number key in that box. If the user types anything in the map center box other than a valid set of coordinates (an integer from 0 to 90 followed by the letter N or S followed by an integer from 0 to 179 followed by the letter W or E), the system will show an alert dialog box with the following error message: "`Unknown Map Coordinates`." The only button in the error message box is an "OK" button. Clicking the OK button will make the dialog box go away and will reset the coordinates to their previous value.

With respect to all three input boxes, the user's changes take effect as soon as the user clicks the mouse outside a box after having edited it.

Perform a heuristic evaluation of this interface. Remember to evaluate the entire interface, including both the figure and the text describing what happens as a result of various user actions. The result of the heuristic evaluation should be a list of the usability problems in the interface with reference to some established usability principle violated by that aspect of the interface. It is not sufficient just to say that you do not like something; explain *why* you do not like it with reference to the heuristics in Chapter 5 or other usability results. Try to be as specific as possible and list each usability problem separately. For example, if there are three things wrong with a certain dialogue element, list all three with reference to the various usability principles that explain why that particular aspect of the interface element is a usability problem. There are two main reasons to note each problem separately: First, there is a risk of repeating some problematic aspect of the dialogue element, even if it were to be completely replaced with a new design, unless one is aware of all its problems. Second, it may not be possible to fix all usability problems in an interface element or to replace it with a new design, but it could still be possible to fix *some* of the problems.

See the hints in Table 13 on page 278 for a list of usability problems my colleagues and I found in this user interface. *Please do not look at the hints before you have written down your own list of usability problems.* Experience shows that it is easy to believe when reading a "solution" that you had thought of all the problems yourself, when in fact a written list may only contain a few of them.

For another exercise in heuristic evaluation of a paper mock-up, see [Molich and Nielsen 1990].

Exercise 9: Heuristic Evaluation of Implemented System

Analyze the stove in your kitchen. Is it perfectly clear which controls operate what parts of the stove and how you should set them to achieve various common tasks? If not, what established usability principles could explain the usability problems you found? If you happen to have a stove with uncommonly high usability, repeat the exercise with your washing machine or your neighbor's stove.

Exercise 10: Heuristic Evaluation with Multiple Evaluators

As seen in Figure 16 (page 156), heuristic evaluation really requires the use of multiple evaluators to be successful. Try to get three or four people (including you) to perform an evaluation of a small piece of software such as a shareware program or a utility package. Each evaluator should inspect the user interface independently of the other evaluators and should write down his or her list of usability problems on paper before discussing it with the others. After all the evaluators have concluded their evaluations, you should meet for a discussion session to arrive at an aggregate list of usability problems.

Exercise 11: User Testing

The most rewarding exercise in user testing is to test some software you designed yourself. If you do so, please remember the "shut-up" rule: You are not allowed to help the test user in any way or to comment on the way he or she uses your system, even when the user is making "obvious" errors. It will probably be very difficult for you to keep quiet, but it is essential that you do so. If you do not have software of your own available, a good second choice is some shareware product (typically available from computer networks, bulletin boards, or through user groups) that is still in its first release and thus has not yet been polished by user feedback.

For the given software, define one or two typical tasks that one can do with the software. Then get one or two test users who have not used the software before (you will get even more spectacular results if you pick test users who have not used *any* computer systems before) and ask them to perform the given task. If necessary, you can give the users general instructions about how to use the keyboard, the mouse, and such, but do not help them use the actual software that is being tested.

Exercise 12: **Individual Differences**

The next few times you go to the supermarket, measure the time the check-out clerk spends on ringing up your purchases. Divide by the number of items you bought, and you have that person's transaction time. What is the ratio between the fastest and slowest clerks? Compare with the numbers given in [Egan 1988] where a performance range of 2:1 is mentioned as typical for most noncomputer tasks.

Exercise 13: **International User Interfaces**

Figure 25 shows an example interface that was subjected to an admittedly poor translation into English. Try to guess the original meaning of the interface without looking at the hints. Would you buy a system with an interface translated like that?

Hints

Some hints are given for Exercises 8 and 13. Please do not look at the hints before you have worked out the exercise yourself. Once you know the information contained in the hints, it is impossible to erase your mind and go back and look at the interfaces with a fresh perspective.

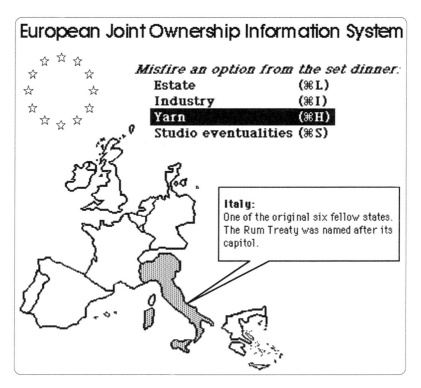

Figure 25 *Sample interface originally developed in Danish and then translated into English by the use of a dictionary. Some hints are given below (please do not look before you have tried working on the exercise yourself).*

The hints below list some of the terms in the figure together with the original Danish terms and more appropriate English translations.

Capitol should be Capital
Rum = Rom = Rome
Fellow = Medlem = Member
Studio eventualities = Studiemuligheder = Educational opportunities
Estate = Landbrug = Agriculture
Yarn = Historie = History
Set dinner = Menu = Menu
Misfire = Klik = Click
Joint Ownership = Fællesskab = Community

Table 13 *Hints for Exercise 8.*

The following is a list of the 31 usability problems found in the *TRAVELweather* interface when it was subjected to heuristic evaluation by four usability specialists. The comment in parentheses after each problem description refers to the heuristics in Chapter 5.

While I designed this interface, I noticed about ten usability problems which I deliberately left in so that there would be something for the readers to discover in the exercise. Later, when I evaluated the interface systematically myself, I was surprised to find as many as 20 usability problems, and a further 11 problems were found by three other evaluators. This only goes to show that usability is harder to achieve than even a usability specialist may think at first.

- The name of the system is displayed much too prominently. By making the name smaller, room could be provided for alternative dialogue elements, or the screen could be made less busy. (Simple and Natural Dialogue)

- The map should display the names of at least some larger cities and other locations of interest to allow users to better recognize these locations. One way of including additional names without cluttering up the map would be to pop up the names of cities close to the weather stations when the user slides the mouse over a weather reading. (Feedback)

- Even though weather does not respect political boundaries, it is hard to read a map without the display of state and country borders. The map shows the northeastern United States from New England over New York and New Jersey to Delaware (as well as a part of Canada). It would be even harder to read the map if the ocean and lakes had not been set off in a different pattern. (Speak the users' language)

- The pattern used to denote oceans and lakes does not make it sufficiently clear what parts of the map are land and what are water. Instead of the current pattern, use a wavy pattern (or blue on a color screen). (Feedback)

- Since Long Island is an island, it should be drawn as such and not as a peninsula (the long arm jutting out to the right at the 28° temperature), even if the resolution of the vector graphics map database makes it difficult to do so. Exaggeration may be needed in this case to match the way the users think about geography. (Speak the users' language)

- The user has no way of knowing that the box with a date and time can be edited since there is no label, prompt, or help text. (This issue is a mix of a feedback problem and a help and documentation problem)

Table 13 *Hints for Exercise 8 (continued).*

- The day/month/year date format may be misinterpreted by foreign tourists. One way of avoiding this problem is to represent months by their name instead of their number. (Prevent errors)

- The zeros in the date have slashes which is a computer-oriented way of writing zeros. Use a typeface with regular 0s. (Speak the users' language)

- The error message "Whether data not available" is not precise. Instead, the system should repeat the date and time as entered by the user and explain why they were not acceptable to the system. Different error messages should be used for dates and times that are not formatted correctly, dates and times that are before or after the time interval for which weather information is available, and times that are not one of the four hours for which information is available. (Good error messages)

- The error message "Weather data not available" is not constructive. The error message ought to inform the users about how to correct their input to make it acceptable to the system. For example, if the user's error was to specify 10AM as the time, the system could say that "Weather information is only available for 3AM, 9AM, 3PM, and 9PM." (Good error messages)

- Users should not be punished for making errors by having the system delete all their input. Instead, the erroneous user input should be retained to allow the user to edit it. Alternatively, to keep the fields on the main screen correct, repeat the erroneous input in the error dialog box and allow users to edit it there. (Good error messages/polite error handling)

- Having users enter a complete date and time specification is error prone, especially as only twelve times are acceptable to the system. Alternatively, the system could provide a pop-up menu with the twelve times. This redesign would also make it possible to simplify the reference to the current day and the next day by calling them "Today" and "Tomorrow." (Prevent errors)

- The term "Precipitation" may be hard to understand for foreign tourists (who are apparently envisioned as users, as can be seen from the nice feature of displaying temperatures in Fahrenheit or Celsius). Instead, consider using a label with simpler words like Rain/Snow. International usability might also be enhanced by adding icons like a thermometer for temperature and raindrops for precipitation. (Speak the users' language)

- Displays of temperatures in Fahrenheit and in Celsius are mutually exclusive, with exactly one of the two being active at any one time. Therefore, the choice of temperature scale should be made with radio buttons and not with checkboxes (which are used for options that are not mutually exclusive). (Consistency [with GUI standard])

Table 13 *Hints for Exercise 8 (continued).*

- The F/C selection is not an additional feature of the same nature as the Temperature/Precipitation/Visibility/Wind selection. Instead, the choice of temperature scale should be grouped with the selection of Temperature as the type of weather information displayed in the map. It can also be recommended to gray out the temperature scale selection when a non-temperature type of weather information is chosen. (Simple and natural dialogue)

- It may be easier for advanced users to understand weather patterns if they can see several types of weather data simultaneously. Thus, the displays of the four kinds of weather data should not be mutually exclusive (as indicated by the use of radio buttons) but should be toggle switches (check boxes), several of which can be on at any given time. To make the interface approachable for novice users, the default display should still only display a single kind of weather data. (Simple and natural dialogue)

- It is possible to enter a zoom magnification of zero, even though that value will lead to an undefined result. Also, users might enter extremely large magnification values, resulting in an unreadable map. The system should have a constructive error message for unreasonable magnification values. (Feedback)

- Beeping is a poor error message for the magnification box. It is probably acceptable as long as the user only types a few characters, but in case of repeated typing, a precise and constructive error message should be given, saying that only numbers can be entered as magnification factors. (Good error messages)

- Most people will not feel comfortable entering map locations as degrees longitude and latitude. Alternatively, it could be possible to allow users to specify the map center by clicking on the map or by searching for a city name or an airport code. If a search feature is included, it should be tolerant of spelling errors. (Speak the users' language)

- It is not clear from the specification to what extent the system will be used repeatedly by the same users (home or office use) or whether it will be used mainly by a flow of changing users (airport etc. use). If the same users can be expected to repeatedly use the system, they will probably also repeatedly ask for weather for the same areas. Support for this user need can be provided by having the system remember the last seven or so locations typed in the map center box and provide direct access to them through a pop-up menu. The next time the system was started, the map could also come up with the zoom specifications (magnification and center) set to the values from the last time the same user used the system. (Shortcuts)

Table 13 *Hints for Exercise 8 (continued).*

- The error message "Unknown map coordinates" is not precise. The error message should repeat the user's input and give different error messages, depending on whether the user has entered incorrectly formatted coordinates or coordinates that are out of bounds. (Good error messages)

- The system should be more forgiving in its acceptance of longitudes. For example, 190E should be interpreted as 170W. (Prevent errors)

- The system should be more forgiving in its acceptance of latitudes. For example, 0° (the Equator) should not need a letter to specify northern or southern hemisphere. Similarly, latitude 90N (the North Pole) and 90S (the South Pole) should not need specifications of a longitude. (Prevent errors)

- The system should display degree marks as part of its default entry in the map center box. In the example, the box could be populated with the text 41°N 72°W. The system should still accept user input without the degree marks, but the user's initial interpretation of the box will be easier if degree marks were used. (Speak the users' language)

- The way magnification factors is represented is obscure. What does it mean that the map has been magnified six times? Is a magnification of seven means more or less detailed than a magnification of six? A slider or a pair of zoom-in/zoom-out buttons might be easier to understand. (Simple and natural dialogue)

- The way the user navigates about the map is awkward. There are two navigational dimensions (north–south, east–west) that have been combined in a single text box, and a third (zoom in–out) that has been grouped with the other two even though it is different in nature. Alternatively, the map could have scroll bars to allow the user to move in the two geographical dimensions, and a zoom slider for zooming. (Simple and natural dialogue)

- Since a common user action will probably be to center the map around a desired location and zoom in on that location, a shortcut could be provided to combine both these actions when the user clicks on the map. (Shortcuts)

- Requiring the user to click outside the entry box before changes will take effect is error prone. It is likely that many users will forget this and will wonder why nothing happens after they changed the text. One possible way to reduce the likelihood of this error is to have an explicit "do it" button. Also, the user's changes should take effect if the user hits the enter or return keys. Redesigning the interface as suggested above to replace the text entry boxes with a combination of pop-up menus, scroll bars, zoom buttons, and a click shortcut would also solve the problem. (Prevent errors)

- It is not apparent from the screen how one quits the *TRAVELweather* system. For example, add a close box or a quit button. (Clearly marked exits)

- The system has no help feature. Hopefully, the interface will be redesigned so that most users can use it without help, but the system probably still has sufficient complexity to warrant a help screen. For example, the help screen could explain how the visibility data can be interpreted. (Help and documentation)

- Since one likely application of the system is to find the weather for a specific city over a period of time, consider adding a feature to get a full weather forecast for a given city in a single display rather than requiring the user to select multiple times and multiple data types. This display would probably have to be a separate window with a combination of a temperature and precipitation table and a written description of the expected weather conditions. (Shortcuts)

Table 13 Hints for Exercise 8 (continued).

Appendix B   *Bibliography*

The user interface field is very diverse, both in the kinds of work being done and in the background of its people. This is true both on the research–practice dimension and with respect to the disciplines involved, which certainly include computer science, psychology, human factors, anthropology, graphics design, and management, as well as several other fields. This diversity is reflected in the literature of the field, which is scattered over many different publications and societies. If you want to limit yourself to reading a single publication, I would definitely recommend the annual proceedings of the *CHI* conferences, but because of the broad nature of the field, such a limitation is not really advisable.

The main professional society in the user interface field is the Association for Computing Machinery's Special Interest Group on Computer–Human Interaction (ACM SIGCHI). For membership information, contact ACM, 1515 Broadway, New York, NY 10036, USA, or send email to `acmhelp@acm.org`. The membership benefits include the proceedings of the annual *CHI* conference (if you choose the so-called *C HI-Plus* membership option) and a subscription to the *SIGCHI Bulletin* newsletter.

This bibliography first lists some basic sources of information, including conferences, journals, books, and videotapes, and then gives bibliographic references to the works cited in this book.

B.1   Conference Proceedings

Because of the rapid developments in the field of user interfaces, many of the most important research results are reported in conference proceedings rather than in books or journals. The most important conferences in the field are the following:

- Association for Computing Machinery (ACM) Special Interest Group on Computer–Human Interaction (SIGCHI) *CHI* Conferences on Human Factors in Computing Systems: Boston 1983, San Francisco 1985, Boston 1986, Toronto 1987, Washington, DC 1988, Austin 1989, Seattle 1990, New Orleans 1991, Monterey 1992, Amsterdam, The Netherlands 1993, Boston 1994, Denver 1995, Vancouver 1996. Proceedings published by the ACM itself as special issues of the *SIGCHI Bulletin* until 1993 and as part of a special SIGCHI-Plus package from 1994. Furthermore, the proceedings from recent years have been copublished by Addison-Wesley and proceedings from early years were copublished by North-Holland. The *SIGCHI Bulletin* **17**:3 (January 1986) contained a combined keyword-in-context index to the proceedings of CHI'83 and '85 together with two "pre-CHI" conferences (Ann Arbor 1981 and Gaithersburg[1] 1982).

- Usability Professionals' Association's annual meeting: WordPerfect 1992, Microsoft 1993, Silicon Valley 1994. The proceedings from these meetings have so far not been published.

- International Federation for Information Processing (IFIP) *INTERACT* Conferences: London, U.K. 1984, Stuttgart, Germany 1987, Cambridge, U.K. 1990, Amsterdam, The Netherlands 1993,[2] Lillehammer, Norway 1995. Proceedings published by North-Holland.

- British Computer Society (BCS) Human–Computer Interaction (*HCI*) Conferences: East Anglia 1985, York 1986, Exeter 1987, Manchester 1988, Nottingham 1989,[3] Edinburgh 1991, York 1992,

---

1. Many people consider the 1982 Gaithersburg conference the birth of the user interface field as an organized discipline. It was not an "official" CHI conference, but it focused on user interface issues and brought together many of the pioneers in the field.

2. The 1993 INTERACT conference was replaced by the 1993 CHI conference in Amsterdam under the shared name "INTERCHI'93."

Loughborough 1993, Glasgow 1994, Surrey 1995, Liverpool 1996. Proceedings published by Cambridge University Press under the title *People and Computers*.

- *HCI-International* Conferences:[4] Hawaii 1987, Boston 1989, Stuttgart 1991, Orlando 1993, Tokyo 1995. Proceedings published by Elsevier Science Publishers.

- European Conferences on Cognitive Ergonomics (*ECCE*), organized by the European Association for Cognitive Ergonomics: Amsterdam 1982, Gmunden 1984, Paris 1986, Cambridge 1988, Urbino 1990, Hungary 1992. Proceedings from most of these conferences have been published by Academic Press.

Furthermore, the annual meetings of the Human Factors and Ergonomics Society have included special sessions on human–computer interaction for several years in addition to sessions on traditional human factors issues, and the ACM *SIGGRAPH* conferences and workshops also cover user interface issues to some extent. The ACM *SIGDOC* conferences cover issues in writing documentation, including online documentation. Recent conferences have included several papers on usability testing of manuals.

Major conferences in languages other than English include the German *Software Ergonomie* (organized by the German chapter of the ACM in cooperation with the Gesellschaft für Informatik), the Japanese *Human Interface Symposium* (organized by the Committee for Human Interface of the Japan Society of Instrument and Control Engineers), and the Swedish *STIMDI* (organized by the Interdisciplinary Interest Association for Human–Computer Interaction).

---

3. The HCI'90 conference was replaced by the IFIP INTERACT'90 conference in Cambridge, U.K.

4. Please do not confuse the *HCI'Intl.* conference series with the *HCI* conference series sponsored by the British Computer Society. These conferences have different sponsors and styles. The user interface field has many different conferences, many of which include the three words "computer," "human," and "interaction" in various permutations. As a further example, the Australian annual conference is called *OZCHI* and is sponsored by the CHISIG group of the Ergonomics Society of Australia.

In addition to these conferences on general user interface issues, there are several important conferences on more specialized issues. Again, these conferences are often the most important sources of information on developments in their respective subfields. The most important specialized conferences are as follows:

- ACM *CSCW* Conferences (Computer-Supported Cooperative Work): Austin 1986, Portland 1988, Los Angeles 1990, Toronto 1992, Chapel Hill 1994. This conference is held in even years, alternating with the European Conference on Computer-Supported Cooperative Work (*ECSCW*) in odd years (Gatwick 1989, Amsterdam 1991, Milano 1993).

- ACM *Hypertext* Conferences: Chapel Hill 1987, Pittsburgh 1989, Versailles (Paris) 1990, San Antonio 1991, Milano 1992, Seattle 1993, Edinburgh 1994. This conference is held in North America in odd years, and in Europe under the name European Conference on Hypertext (*ECHT*) in even years.

- ACM Symposium on User Interface Software and Technology: *UIST* (implementation issues, User Interface Management Systems, and such): Banff 1988, Williamsburg 1989, Snowbird 1990, Hilton Head 1991, Monterey 1992, Atlanta 1993.

Other events of interest include the workshops on *Empirical Studies of Programmers*, the Human Factors and Ergonomics Society's *Interface* conferences on consumer product design, the ACM *International Workshop on Intelligent User Interfaces*, the Computer Professionals for Social Responsibility's *Participatory Design Conference* (PDC), the IEEE *Visualization* conferences, and the *Work With Display Units* (WWDU) conferences on hardware ergonomics. Most of these meetings are held annually or biennially and are announced in the ACM *SIGCHI Bulletin*.

B.2   *Journals*

The most important journals in the field of human–computer interaction are the following:

- *ACM Transactions on Computer–Human Interaction* (TOCHI), published by the Association for Computing Machinery. This journal will probably be dominated by long in-depth papers reporting on major projects. Also, the computer science aspects of user interfaces may get more coverage than psychological and practical aspects.

- *Behaviour & Information Technology* (ISSN 0144-929X), published by Taylor & Francis. This journal is a good source for reports on empirical studies of various aspects of user interfaces. Issue 1&2 in 1994 was a special double issue on usability laboratories, providing detailed coverage of a range of laboratories and practical usability methods.

- *Human–Computer Interaction* (ISSN 0737-0024), published by Lawrence Erlbaum Associates. This journal is dominated by long, somewhat academic papers with a bias in favor of psychological studies.

- *Interacting with Computers* (ISSN 0953-5438), published by Butterworth-Heinemann in cooperation with the British Computer Society's specialist group on Human–Computer Interaction. This journal tends to have a fair number of conceptual papers and discussion pieces.

- *International Journal of Human–Computer Interaction* (ISSN 1044-7318), published by Ablex. This journal tends to have a broad perspective, with coverage of issues like occupational stress and organizational factors related to the use of computers.

- *International Journal of Human–Computer Studies* (ISSN 1071-5819), published by Academic Press. This journal is the oldest in the field (founded 1969) and was called *International Journal of Man–Machine Studies* (ISSN 1070-5819) until 1993. It publishes a mix of conceptual dialogue-analyses and empirical studies.

Furthermore, since 1994, the ACM has published a magazine sponsored by SIGCHI called *interactions* (ISSN 1072-5520). This publication seems to be the most important publication for practicing user interface designers and developers in industry.

The Human Factors and Ergonomics Society's *Human Factors* journal (ISSN 0018-7208) contains some papers on computer–human interaction in addition to papers on other types of human factors and is especially valuable for hardware ergonomics issues. The Human Factors and Ergonomics Society also publishes a magazine called *Ergonomics in Design: The Magazine of Human Factors Applications* (ISSN 1064-8046). This magazine includes coverage of industry-specific design issues for industries like aerospace, insurance, automobiles, medicine, and energy, as well as articles about broader applications. The *Information Design Journal* (ISSN 0142-5471) often has articles relevant to the design of screens, printouts, and documentation.

The Association for Computing Machinery's Special Interest Group on Computer–Human Interaction (ACM SIGCHI) publishes a quarterly magazine, *SIGCHI Bulletin*, which is an important source of information about current events in the field as it has a much shorter production cycle than the journals mentioned above. In fact, the *SIGCHI Bulletin* is probably the one publication to read on a regular basis for conference announcements and trip reports, updates on the standards committees, book reviews, and similar news. Furthermore, the Usability Professionals' Association (see page 165) publishes a newsletter called *Common Ground* four times per year with coverage of usability testing issues.

Finally, many other journals and magazines publish papers on aspects of user interface design, including:

- ACM SIGGRAPH *Computer Graphics* (User Interface Management Systems). Special issues: January 1983, April 1987.
- *ACM Transactions on Graphics* (graphical interfaces and interaction techniques). Special issues: April, July, and October 1986.
- *ACM Transactions on Information Systems* (interfaces for business professionals, cooperative work, etc.). This journal was previously called *ACM Transactions on Office Information Systems* but changed its name in 1989. Special issues: April 1987, October 1987, October 1988, January 1989, April 1991, October 1992, July 1993, October 1993.
- *BYTE* (good coverage of new user interfaces as they are implemented on personal computers). Special issues: April 1982, December 1983, July 1990, April 1992.
- *Communications of the ACM* (general articles as well as articles on software psychology and the human factors of the programming process). Special issues: April 1983, July 1986, November 1988,

December 1991, May 1992 (users with disabilities), April 1993 (next-generation user interfaces), June 1993 (participatory design), July 1993 (augmented reality).

- *Computer Supported Cooperative Work.*

- *Hypermedia* (user interfaces to hypertext and hypermedia systems).

- *IEEE Computer Graphics and Applications* (graphical interfaces). Special issues: November and December 1986. Also, July 1991 was a special issue on multimedia interfaces.

- *IEEE Software* (User Interface Management Systems and other software tools for user interfaces). Special issue: January 1989. Also, *IEEE Software* has a regular user interface column with two-page articles on "tools, techniques, and concepts to optimize user interfaces." These articles are often a very good source of information about practical usability methods.

- *IEEE Transactions on Professional Communication* (writing documentation). Special issues: December 1986, December 1989.

- *PRESENCE, the Journal on Teleoperators and Virtual Environments* (virtual reality).

- *User Modeling and User-Adapted Interaction.*

The graphics journals have reduced their emphasis on user interface issues in recent years as more dedicated user interface publications have appeared.

Finally, a kind of "online magazine" is provided by the discussions on the Internet newsgroup `comp.human-factors`. As with many other netnews groups, `comp.human-factors` has a lower signal-to-noise ration than edited publications. Some postings are regular "flame wars" between adherents of different user interface styles, but there are also many interesting announcements posted, and the newsgroup also provides an efficient way of quickly communicating with a large number of people who are working on user interface issues. For example, I posted a single message asking for volunteers to review the manuscript of this book and received 62 replies within a few days. Other newsgroups of interest include `bit.software.international` (international use), `sci.vir-`

`tual-worlds` (virtual reality), and `alt.hypertext` as well as groups for many GUI programming tools.

B.3   Introductions and Textbooks

Booth, P. (1989). *An Introduction to Human–Computer Interaction.* Lawrence Erlbaum Associates, Hove, U.K. ISBN 0-86377-123-8.

Provides good coverage of many usability issues while possibly remaining a little bit too abstract for some readers. This book is especially strong on interface theory and includes good annotated lists of references to the research literature. It has some coverage of the design process but very little material on user testing. See the review in the *International Journal of Human–Computer Interaction* **3**, 1 (1991), 113–114.

Heckel, P. (1991). *The Elements of Friendly Software Design, 2nd edition.* Sybex, San Francisco. ISBN 0-89588-768-1.

Extensive treatment of interfaces as a communication medium with many parallels and lessons from other media such as film, theater, architecture, painting, etc. Concentrates on the qualities of the end product and has very little coverage of the design process and test methods.

Hix, D., and Hartson, H.R. (1993). *Developing User Interfaces: Ensuring Usability Through Product & Process.* Wiley, New York, NY. ISBN 0-471-57813-4.

Good coverage of many aspects of the usability engineering lifecycle, with special emphasis on how to specify user interfaces (including the authors' "UAN" user action notation language). See the review in the *International Journal of Man–Machine Studies* **39**, 6 (December 1993), 1052–1053.

Lindgaard, G. (1994). *Usability Testing and System Evaluation: A Guide for Designing Useful Computer Systems.* Chapman & Hall, London, U.K. ISBN 0-412-46100-5.

Basic textbook on user testing with extensive coverage of "classic" issues in experiment design. The book also covers additional methods and has a good chapter on interviews and surveys. Each chapter includes an extensive list of questions for the student as well as exercises (with solutions to both provided in the back of the book).

Mayhew, D. J. (1992). *Principles and Guidelines in Software User Interface Design.* Prentice Hall, Englewood Cliffs, NJ. ISBN 0-13-721929-6.

More of a collection of interface advice than a textbook in the traditional sense, but still good to learn from. Good, extensive collection of guidelines for the design of various dialogue types, including menus, form fill-in, question-answer, command languages, function keys, and direct manipulation. Only a single chapter on the design process and almost nothing on test methods. See the review in the ACM *SIGCHI Bulletin* **25**, 2 (April 1993), 51–53.

Rubinstein, R., and Hersh, H. (1984). *The Human Factor: Designing Computer Systems for People.* Digital Press, Burlington, MA. ISBN 0-932376-44-4.

A nice introduction to the field with many good guidelines. Fair coverage of user testing. See the review in *Datamation* (1 May 1985), 161–162.

Shneiderman, B. (1992). *Designing the User Interface: Strategies for Effective Human–Computer Interaction, 2nd edition.* Addison-Wesley, Reading, MA. ISBN 0-201-57286-9.

One of the most popular textbooks for this topic. Includes extensive surveys of the user interface literature with special emphasis on presenting empirical results. The book is especially strong on dialogue techniques and screen design but has comparatively little coverage of the user test methods needed to generate empirical results or to test new interfaces. See my review of the first edition in the *ACM SIGCHI Bulletin* **18**, 3 (January 1987), 85–86. The second edition has been brought up to date and is a considerable improvement over the first. See the review of the second edition in the Human Factors Society Computer Systems Technical Group *Bulletin* **19**, 2 (December 1992), 11.

B.4 Handbook

Helander, M. (Ed.) (1988). *Handbook of Human–Computer Interaction.* Elsevier Science Publishers, Amsterdam, The Netherlands. ISBN 0-444-70536-8 (hardcover), 0-444-88673-7 (softcover).

Unfortunately, this book is very expensive, but it does contain a thorough coverage of the field on 1168 pages with many chapters written by some of the best-known specialists in the various subfields. See my review in the *ACM SIGCHI Bulletin* **21**, 3 (January 1990), 107–108. A softcover edition published in 1990 is considerably cheaper but still expensive.

B.5 Reprint Collections

Many of the most important papers in human–computer interaction may be hard to find, but the following reprint collections offer a good place to start:

Baecker, R. S. (Ed.) (1992). *Readings in Groupware and Computer-Supported Cooperative Work: Assisting Human–Human Collaboration.* Morgan Kaufmann Publishers, Los Altos, CA. ISBN 1-55860-241-0.

Extensive set of research papers in the CSCW area.

Baecker, R., and Buxton, W. A. S. (Eds.) (1987). *Readings in Human–Computer Interaction: A Multidisciplinary Approach.* Morgan Kaufmann Publishers, Los Altos, CA. ISBN 0-934613-24-9. (First edition.)

Baecker, R. M., Grudin, J., Buxton, W., and Greenberg, S. (Eds.) (1994). *Readings in Human–Computer Interaction: Toward The Year 2000.* Morgan Kaufmann Publishers, San Francisco, CA. ISBN 1-55860-246-1. (Second edition.)

A collection of many of the most important papers in the field supplemented with extensive and insightful comments and overviews. This collection could actually serve well as a textbook or an introduction to the field, provided the reader has some experience in independent study. The first edition was especially notable for containing many of the classic papers in the field that are otherwise hard to get hold of, and in a very unusual turn of the publishing business, the publisher has decided to keep the first edition in print in parallel with the second edition. See the review of the first edition in the *ACM SIGCHI Bulletin* **21**, 1 (July 1989), 118–119.

Curtis, B. (Ed.) (1985). *Tutorial: Human Factors in Software Development, 2nd edition.* IEEE Computer Society Press, Los Alamitos, CA. ISBN 0-8186-0577-4.

A collection of papers addressing the important special case where computer programmers are considered as being users of programming systems.

Greif, I. (Ed.) (1988). *Computer-Supported Cooperative Work: A Book of Readings.* Morgan Kaufmann Publishers, Los Altos, CA. ISBN 0-934613-57-5.

The most important pioneering papers in the "groupware" field of several users interacting using several computers. See the review in the *ACM SIGCHI Bulletin* **21**, 2 (October 1989), 125–128.

Marca, D., and Bock, G. (Eds.) (1992). *Groupware: Software for Computer-Supported Cooperative Work.* IEEE Computer Society Press, Los Alamitos, CA. ISBN 0-8186-2637-2.

A collection of CSCW papers with a slightly more technological emphasis than the others.

Preece, J., and Keller, L. (Eds.) (1990). *Human–Computer Interaction.* Prentice Hall, Hertfordshire, U.K. ISBN 0-13-444910-X.

A collection of papers from an Open University course that contains more European papers than the other collections. This set of readings reprints many of the most important classics in the field in a well-designed package (all the papers have been re-typeset with a consistent typography). It is probably the most accessible of the current reprint collections.

Sage, A. P. (Ed.) (1987). *System Design for Human Interaction.* IEEE Press, New York, NY. ISBN 0-87942-218-1.

These papers are mostly taken from the field of control room design and process control and have a slightly different flavor than the human–computer interaction mainstream literature.

Venturino, M. (Ed.) (1990). *Selected Readings in Human Factors.* The Human Factors and Ergonomics Society, Santa Monica, CA. ISBN 0-945289-00-6.

This book mostly contains traditional human factors papers, and therefore has fairly little overlap with the other collections listed here. The papers reprinted here have titles like "Review and analysis of color coding research for visual displays," "Properties of workload assessment techniques," and "Information capacity of discrete motor responses." See the review in the *Human Factors Society Bulletin* **34**, 7 (July 1991), 13.

B.6   Important Monographs and Collections of Original Papers

These are books I have read and enjoyed myself. In fact, there are several other good books on user interface issues, and more are being published every year as the field grows in importance. See the annual British *HCI BookViews* survey (discussed on page 304) for ratings of a wider selection of books.

Advances in Human–Computer Interaction. Ablex Publishing Corp., Norwood, NJ. Published annually. Vols. 1–4 edited by H. R. Hartson and D. Hix. Edited by J. Nielsen since Vol. 5.

The *Advances* is a kind of yearbook of the user interface field with review articles that summarize recent developments in selected areas. Not all areas are covered every year, but a collection of a few volumes provides broad coverage of where the field is going.

Bias, R. G., and Mayhew, D. J. (Eds.) (1994). *Cost-Justifying Usability.* Academic Press, Boston, MA. ISBN 0-12-095810-4.

A book discussing the business case for usability work, including coverage of different kinds of companies (vendors, internal development, contractors), case studies, and difficult matters such as accounting for intangible benefits.

Bolt, R. A. (1984). *The Human Interface: Where People and Computers Meet.* Lifetime Learning Publications and Van Nostrand Reinhold, New York, NY. ISBN 0-534-03380-6.

A description of much of the work at the MIT Media Lab on developing totally new possibilities for user interfaces, including wall-sized displays and using eyetracking as an input-medium.

Brand, S. (1987). *The Media Lab: Inventing the Future at MIT.* Viking Penguin, New York, NY. ISBN 0-670-81442-3.

A popular survey of research at the MIT Media Lab. Includes otherwise hard-to-find coverage of the *NewsPeek* personalized newspaper project, the *Vivarium* project, and several other projects in advanced interfaces for education and communication. See the review in *AI Magazine* Spring 1990, 99–100.

Card, S. K., Moran, T. P., and Newell, A. (1983). *The Psychology of Human–Computer Interaction.* Lawrence Erlbaum Associates, Hillsdale, NJ. ISBN 0-89859-243-7.

Probably the most famous and most cited book in the field. Introduced the GOMS (goals, operators, methods, and selection rules) analytical model of computer users. See the reviews in *Contemporary Psychology* **29**, 2 (1984), 119–120 and the *ACM SIGCHI Bulletin* **15**, 4 (April 1984), 26.

Carroll, J. M. (Ed.) (1987). *Interfacing Thought: Cognitive Aspects of Human–Computer Interaction*. The MIT Press, Cambridge, MA. ISBN 0-262-03125-6.

Many good papers on the cognitive issues that form the underlying science basis for much of HCI. See the review in the *ACM SIGCHI Bulletin* **20**, 2 (October 1988), 88–91.

Carroll, J. M. (1990). *The Nurnberg Funnel: Designing Minimalist Instruction for Practical Computer Skill*. The MIT Press, Cambridge, MA. ISBN 0-262-03163-9.

The minimalist approach to the design of documentation. See the review in *IEEE Transactions on Professional Communication* **33**, 4 (December 1990), 182–187, and the author's reply in *IEEE Transactions on Professional Communication* **34**, 1 (March 1991), 58. The ACM SIGDOC *Asterisk Journal of Computer Documentation* **16**, 1 (January 1992) was a special issue devoted to commentaries on this book.

Carroll, J. M. (Ed.) (1991). *Designing Interaction: Psychology at the Human–Computer Interface*. Cambridge University Press, Cambridge, U.K. ISBN 0-521-40056-2 (hardcover), 0-521-40921-7 (softcover).

Many papers on the theory of design practice (based on the 1989 Kittle House Inn workshop), including coverage of the artifact theory championed by Carroll, viewing concrete interface designs as the principal embodiments of usability theory. See the review in the *International Journal of Man–Machine Studies* **37**, 6 (December 1992), 812–821.

Duffy, T.M., Mehlenacher, B., and Palmer, J.E. (1992). *Online Help: Design and Evaluation*. Ablex, Norwood, NJ. ISBN 0-89391-848-2.

Reviews design principles for online help and provides an evaluation form with eight categories to be used in assessing the usability of a help system. Data is given from evaluations of 28 commercially available help systems.

Dumas, J. S., and Redish, J. C. (1993). *A Practical Guide to Usability Testing*. Ablex, Norwood, NJ. ISBN 0-89391-990-X (cloth), 0-89391-991-8 (paper).

Detailed advice on user testing from people who have experience from a large number of different studies. The book includes sample questionnaires and test forms. One weakness of this book is its emphasis on "deluxe usability engineering" methods requiring a usability laboratory and several collaborating usability specialists. See the review in the Usabilty Professionals Association's *Common Ground* newsletter **3**, 2 (June 1993), 5.

Grandjean, E. (1987). *Ergonomics in Computerized Offices*. Taylor & Francis, London, U.K. ISBN 0-85066-350-4.

A book on traditional hardware ergonomics (furniture, lighting, etc.) by one of the best-known scientists in the field.

Hopgood, F. R. A., Duce, D. A., Fielding, E. V. C., Robinson, K., and Williams, A. S. (Eds.) (1986). *Methodology of Window Management*. Springer-Verlag, Berlin, Germany. ISBN 3-540-16116-3.

A collection of papers discussing user interface and implementation issues of windows as well as the history of window systems.

Horton, W. K. (1990). *Designing and Writing Online Documentation: Help Files to Hypertext*. Wiley, New York, NY. ISBN 0-471-50772-5.

Survey of issues in the design of all kinds of online documentation, including error messages and help systems. Mostly about traditional linear text, though with some coverage of hypertext and the use of media other than text (e.g., sound and animation). See the reviews in the *ACM SIGCHI Bulletin* **23**, 3 (July 1991), 71–73, and *IEEE Transactions on Professional Communication* **33**, 4 (December 1990), 178–181.

Karat, J. (1991). *Taking Software Design Seriously: Practical Techniques for Human–Computer Interaction Design*. Academic Press, Boston, MA. ISBN 0-12-397710-X.

Chapters on many different interface design methods, including case studies from practitioners in industry, fairly general conceptualizations of the entire design process, and detailed research on techniques for individual steps in the design process.

Klemmer, E. R. (Ed.). (1989). *Ergonomics: Harness the Power of Human Factors in Your Business*. Ablex, Norwood, NJ. ISBN 0-89391-559-0.

Several case studies showing how large companies have organized and managed their human factors efforts. This book is one of the few sources to cover usability management issues in any great depth. See the review in the

Human Factors and Ergonomics Society Consumer Products Technical Group's *CP News* **16**, 1 (March 1991), 5–6.

Laurel, B. (Ed.) (1990). *The Art of Human–Computer Interface Design.* Addison-Wesley, Reading, MA. ISBN 0-201-51797-3.

Chapters by many avant-garde interface designers, including several associated with Apple Computer's Advanced Technology Human Interface Group.

Marcus, A. (1992). *Graphic Design for Electronic Documents and User Interfaces.* Addison-Wesley, Reading, MA. ISBN 0-201-54364-8.

The book covers many topics in graphic design and has an extensive annotated bibliography about graphic design. It also contains a comparative survey of the visual interface elements of six currently popular graphical user interfaces. See my review in *Science of Computer Programming* **18**, 2 (April 1992), 218–221.

Monk, A., Wright, P., Haber, J., and Davenport, L. (1993). *Improving Your Human–Computer Interface: A Practical Technique.* Prentice Hall International, Hemel Hempstead, U.K. ISBN 0-13-010034-X.

Brief guide to user testing using the so-called *cooperative evaluation* approach.

Mullet, K., and Sarro, D. K. (1994). *Designing Visual Interfaces: Communication Oriented Techniques.* Prentice Hall, Englewood Cliffs, NJ. ISBN 0-13-303389-9.

One of the very few books on graphic design that actually explain the principles needed to design good graphical user interfaces.

Nielsen, J. (Ed.) (1989). *Coordinating User Interfaces for Consistency.* Academic Press, Boston, MA. ISBN 0-12-518400-X.

The theory and practice of consistent user interfaces, including chapters describing the approaches taken by several major computer vendors. See the review in *IEEE Computer* **23**, 11 (November 1990), 131.

Nielsen, J. (Ed.) (1990). *Designing User Interfaces for International Use.* Elsevier Science Publishers, Amsterdam, The Netherlands. ISBN 0-444-88428-9.

Since many computer companies have more than half of their sales abroad, it has become important to study the issues related to international usability. Also, customers in various countries have become more critical of nonlocalized software than they were in the past. See the reviews in *Hypermedia* **3**, 1 (1991), 81–84, and *Ergonomics* **34**, 10 (October 1991), 1335–1336.

Nielsen, J. (1990). *Hypertext and Hypermedia*. Academic Press, Boston, MA. ISBN 0-12-518410-7 (hardcover), 0-12-518411-5 (paperback). Japanese translation ISBN 4-8337-8583-8.

Survey of hypertext systems, applications, history, and user interface issues. Includes an extensive annotated and indexed bibliography. See the reviews in *Computing Reviews* (review **9102-0048**, February 1991); *Electronic Publishing: Origination, Dissemination and Design* 3, 4 (November 1990), 235–236; *Hypermedia* 2, 3 (1990), 266–268; and *ACM SIGIR Forum* 21, 1 (Spring 1991), 24–25.

Nielsen, J., and Mack, R. L. (Eds.) (1994). *Usability Inspection Methods*. John Wiley & Sons, New York, NY, ISBN 0-471-01877-5.

Detailed advice on how to perform usability inspections, using methods like heuristic evaluation, cognitive walkthroughs, and pluralistic walkthroughs, with chapters by the inventors of these methods. Also contains chapters comparing the methods and presenting research results on the relative costs and benefits of the different methods under various circumstances.

Norman, D. A. (1988). *The Psychology of Everyday Things*. Basic Books, New York, NY. ISBN 0-465-06709-3.

Very entertaining book about the "user interfaces" to everyday things like door handles, consumer electronics, etc. Observing the human factors of non-computer systems like alarm clocks at conference hotels gives the computer professional an interesting chance to reflect on the ordinary user's experience. See the review in *Artificial Intelligence* 41, 1 (November 1989), 111–114. The softcover edition was renamed *The Design of Everyday Things* (ISBN 0-385-26774-6) since part of the management audience didn't like the "psychology" bit, but the softcover edition is otherwise identical to the hardcover edition.

Norman, D. A., and Draper, S. W. (Eds.) (1986). *User Centered System Design: New Perspectives on Human–Computer Interaction*. Lawrence Erlbaum Associates, Hillsdale, NJ. ISBN 0-89859-781-1.

The chapters in this book are written by many of the leading scientists in the field and address important conceptual issues in the design of user interfaces. See the review in the *ACM SIGCHI Bulletin* 18, 1 (July 1986), 67–68.

Olsen, D. R. (1991). *User Interface Management Systems: Models and Algorithms*. Morgan Kaufmann Publishers, San Mateo, CA. ISBN 1-55860-220-8.

Comprehensive survey of UIMS issues from the perspective of a programmer wanting to implement such a system. Less aimed at programmers interested in using an existing UIMS or choosing between the available offerings.

Tognazzini, B. (1992). *Tog on Interface*. Addison-Wesley, Reading, MA. ISBN 0-201-60842-1.

While he was at Apple, the author of this book was probably only person in the world with a job title of "interface evangelist." He has several years of experience trying to get third-party developers to conform to corporate standards and improve their interfaces and usability procedures. Much of the advice in this book is especially applicable to smaller software companies developing for personal computers with graphical user interfaces, but some pragmatic development recommendations should be helpful to others also. See my review in the *ACM SIGCHI Bulletin* **25**, 2 (April 1993), 54–55.

Tufte, E. R. (1990). *Envisioning Information*. Graphics Press, Cheshire, CT. No ISBN given in the book.

Beautifully illustrated book with examples of rich visualization design, emphasizing how graphic design can be used to communicate complex data. Unfortunately, the book is mostly about static images and does not discuss the potential of animation and similar modern computer media. It is written from an intuitive perspective, stressing what looked good to the author rather than relying on scientific evidence. See the reviews in the ACM *SIGDOC Journal of Computer Documentation* **15**, 3 (November 1991), 3–11, and *Journal of Classification* **8**, 2 (1991).

Vaske, J. J., and Grantham, C. E. (1990). *Socializing the Human–Computer Environment*. Ablex, Norwood, NJ. ISBN 0-89391-471-1.

On the use of methods from social psychology and anthropology in the user interface field.

Winograd, T., and Flores, F. (1987). *Understanding Computers and Cognition: A New Foundation for Design*. Addison-Wesley, Reading, MA. ISBN 0-201-11297-3.

A famous book that is unfortunately somewhat boring to read. The first 140 pages pontificate on philosophical issues in language understanding and artificial intelligence, but the last 40 pages contain advice on design that is also useful for designers of more common user interfaces. See the review in *IEEE Computer* **22**, 1 (January 1989), 156.

B.7 Guidelines

Many textbooks, such as [Mayhew 1992] (see page 291) contain extensive user interface design guidelines. In-house guidelines and standards are also an important part of the usability engineering process in many development organizations (see also Chapter 8). The following are some general guideline documents.

Brown, C. M. L. (1988). *Human–Computer Interface Design Guidelines*. Ablex, Norwood, NJ. ISBN 0-89391-332-4.

A nice collection with several examples of dos and don'ts. The guidelines are not sufficiently cross-referenced, leading to problems for people who just look one issue up in the index without being aware of related guidelines listed under other headings. For example, there is no cross-reference from the discussion of response times to the discussion of progress indicators which may be used in cases where the response time just cannot be made sufficiently good. See the review in the Human Factors and Ergonomics Society's *Computer Systems Technical Group Bulletin* **18**, 1 (April 1991), 12.

DIN (1988). *VDU Work Stations: Principles of Ergonomic Dialogue Design*. German Industrial Standard **DIN 66234 Part 8**.

The world's first national standard for user interfaces. It is actually more in the nature of broad principles and guidelines than very precise specifications. Note that the version in the German language (*Bildschirmarbeitsplätze: Grundsätze ergonomischer Dialoggestaltung*) is the official standard.

Felker, D. B., Pickering, F., Charrow, V. R., Holland, V. M., and Redish, J. C. (1981). *Guidelines for Document Designers*. Report from American Institutes for Research, 1055 Thomas Jefferson Street NW, Washington, DC 20007, USA.

Good collection of guidelines for writing manuals. Includes plenty of references to the research done on this topic. The guidelines are mostly for writing traditional, printed manuals but some also apply to online documentation.

Marshall, C., Nelson, C., and Gardiner, M. M. (1987). Design guidelines. In Gardiner, M. M., and Christie, B. (Eds.), *Applying Cognitive Psychology to User-Interface Design*. John Wiley & Sons, Chichester, U.K. 221–278.

An unusually principled approach to guidelines: Each of the 162 interface guidelines in this chapter are related to general principles from cognitive psychology that are explained in other chapters of the book.

Smith, S. L., and Mosier, J. N. (1986). *Design Guidelines for Designing User Interface Software*. Technical Report **MTR-10090**, The MITRE Corporation, Bedford, MA 01730, USA.

Probably the most extensive collection of guidelines for the different aspects of the user interface. Because of U.S. Government sponsorship, this publication is freely available and has been used as the basis for several hypertexts. People with sufficient network access can download the ASCII text of the report by FTP from the host `ftp.cis.ohio-state.edu` (IP address 128.146.8.52) as `pub/hci/guidelines`.

Style Guides

Apple Computer (1992). *Macintosh Human Interface Guidelines*. Addison-Wesley, Reading, MA. ISBN 0-201-62216-5.

This book is the second edition of the guidelines. It is about three times larger than the first edition which was entitled *Human Interface Guidelines: The Apple Desktop Interface*. Updates to the guidelines are available from Apple as "Human Interface Notes." These notes can be downloaded by people with FTP network access from the server named `ftp.apple.com`, IP address 130.43.2.3, on the Internet (probably in the directory `/dts/mac/docs/stacks/hinstack`).

Go Corporation (1992). *PenPoint User Interface Design Reference*. Addison-Wesley, Reading, MA. ISBN 0-201-60858-8.

A pencentric interface for pen computer interfaces based on handwriting recognition.

IBM (1993). *Object-Oriented Interface Design: IBM Common User Access Guidelines*. IBM Document **SC34-4399**. Que Publishing, Carmel, IN. ISBN 1-56529-170-0.

Microsoft Corporation (1992). *The Windows Interface: An Application Design Guide*. Microsoft Press, Redmond, WA. ISBN 1-55615-384-8.

For international issues see the following book: Microsoft Corporation (1993). *The GUI Guide : International Terminology for the Windows Interface*. Microsoft Press, Redmond, WA. ISBN 1-55615-538-7.

NeXT Corporation (1992). *NeXTSTEP User Interface Guidelines Release 3. Addison-Wesley Publishing*. ISBN 0-201-63250-0.

Open Software Foundation (1992). *OSF/Motif™ Style Guide Release 1.2*. Prentice Hall, Englewood Cliffs, NJ. ISBN 0-13-643123-2.

For further information, including design rationale, detailed examples, guidelines, and implementation details, see also Kobara, S. (1991). *Visual Design with OSF/Motif.* Addison-Wesley, Reading, MA. ISBN 0-201-56320-7.

Sun Microsystems (1990). *OPEN LOOK™ Graphical User Interface Application Style Guidelines.* Addison-Wesley, Reading, MA. ISBN 0-201-52364-7.

B.8   Videotapes

Since modern user interfaces are highly dynamic, they often cannot be adequately described in traditional papers. Therefore many interfaces are best described by the videotaped demonstrations that have become a major feature at the conferences on computer–human interaction. A convenient source for collections of videotapes is the ACM *SIGGRAPH Video Review.* Each issue contains a one-hour collection of videotapes. The first issue was "published" in 1980 and by now, several issues are made available each year. Especially recommended from a user interface point of view are the tapes produced on the basis of the video shows at the annual CHI conference (also distributed as part of the SIGGRAPH series). The *SIGGRAPH Video Review* is available from:

SVR Order Department
c/o First Priority
PO Box 576
Itasca, IL 60143-0576
USA
Tel. (24 hr.) (800) 523-5503 or (708) 250-0807
Fax (708) 250-0038

Regarding the use of video in the user interface field, see also the special issue of the *ACM SIGCHI Bulletin* on "Video as a Research and Design Tool," **21**, 2 (October 1989).

OSF/Motif and Motif are trademarks of the Open Software Foundation, Inc.
OPEN LOOK is a trademark of AT&T.

The Human Factors and Ergonomics Society has produced a tape entitled *Human Factors Success Stories* with brief presentations on the application of human factors principles to everything from aircrafts to computers, toothbrushes, and automobiles. The videotape is available for rental or purchase in both American and European video formats from:

Human Factors and Ergonomics Society
P.O. Box 1369
Santa Monica, CA 90406
USA
Tel. (310) 394-1811
Fax (310) 394-2410

An annual series of videotaped user interface lectures is being produced by Ben Shneiderman at the University of Maryland under the title *User Interface Strategies*. Each year, a new set of leading user interface specialists participate and discuss their recent work, often showing interesting video segments of new interface ideas. See the review in *IEEE Computer* **26**,1 (January 1993), p. 134. These tapes are available in both U.S. and European formats (the latter being slightly more expensive). The *UIS'94* show had extensive coverage of usability engineering issues, including a segment showing the SunSoft usability laboratory. For more information, contact:

The University of Maryland
Instructional Television Systems
Engineering Classroom Building, Room 2104
College Park, MD 20742
USA
Tel. (301) 405-4913
Fax (301) 413-9639

B.9 Other Bibliographies

The British Computer Society's Human–Computer Interaction Specialist Group (The British HCI Group) publishes the *HCI Book-Views* edited by Miles Macleod. The 1991 edition listed 75 user interface books with suitability ratings for students, researchers, and industry. These three sets of ratings were calculated as the average scores reported by a fairly large number of readers and are supplemented with one- or two-line comments from some of the readers. For further information about this bibliography, contact The British HCI Group, University of Glasgow, Department of Computing Science, 17 Lilybank Gardens, Glasgow G12 8RZ, U.K. Email membsec@dcs.glasgow.ac.uk.

The ACM Press published a book entitled *Resources in Human–Computer Interaction* (ISBN 0-89791-373-6) in late 1990 with the collected listings of user interface related references from the *ACM Guide to Computing Literature* and the *ACM Computing Reviews* from 1983 to 1989.

Some special-topic bibliographies are

- *IEEE Transactions on Professional Communication* **33**, 4 (December 1990). A special review issue with information about recent books on documentation, manuals, and technical writing.
- Greenberg, S. (1991). An annotated bibliography of computer supported cooperative work. *ACM SIGCHI Bulletin* **23**, 3 (July), 29–62.
- Nielsen, J. (1990). Annotated bibliography of hypertext and hypermedia. In Nielsen, J. (1990), *Hypertext and Hypermedia*, Academic Press, Boston, MA. 199–252.
- Ramey, J. (1989). A selected bibliography: A beginner's guide to usability testing. *IEEE Transactions on Professional Communication* **32**, 4 (December), 310–316. Covers usability testing with special emphasis on the testing of documentation.
- Sabol, L., Rosen, C. M., and Koltay, Z. (1991). Health hazards of video display terminals: A representative, annotated bibliography. *Science & Technology Libraries* **12**, 2, 85–129. Health-related issues of hardware ergonomics.

A database of literature references in the user interface field up to 1980 was published in issues 8–11 of the IFIP *INTERACT* Newsletter, March–December 1983. This database was based on bibliographies from several reports, including Eason, K. D. (1981), *An annotated bibliography on user friendly systems*, HUSAT Memo 232, Loughborough University of Technology, U.K., and Jørgensen, A. H. (1980), *An exploratory survey of the literature on man–computer dialogue engineering*, Report No. 80/15, Computer Science Department, Copenhagen University, Denmark.

Bibliographic Databases

Gary Perlman [1991] is collecting a machine-readable database of user interface references at Ohio State University, including the *CHI* conferences and several other conferences, journals, and books. The database includes tables of content for several books and abstracts for many papers, thus having a potential for automated searches as explained below. The bibliography currently contains about 8,000 entries. People with sufficient computer network capabilities can download the database by FTP from the host `ftp.cis.ohio-state.edu` (IP address 128.146.8.52) in the `pub/hcibib` directory.

People who do not have FTP access but who do have access to electronic mail can get files from the database by sending email to a special server at the address `hcibib@cis.ohio-state.edu` . Your initial message should consist of a single line with the text :
`Send: index`

A computerized search facility allows people with Internet electronic mail access to perform keyword searches in the Perlman bibliography. Queries should be sent by email to
`hcibib@rumpus.colorado.edu`
and should consist of lines of the following form:
`query: keyword1 keyword2 keyword3`

Several queries can be submitted in a single message, but each should be on a line by itself. Each query can use as many keywords as necessary. An automated server using the latent semantic indexing (LSI) information retrieval method [Deerwester *et al.*

1990] will search the bibliography and will return a list of the best matches and their abstracts by email. The server also allows repeated searches using relevance feedback once a relevant abstract has been found.

The HILITES database (HCI Information and Literature Enquiry Service) is an even more extensive bibliography with more than 32,000 entries [Shackel *et al.* 1992]. It is available on a CD-ROM from Loughborough University in the U.K.

B.10 References

The rest of this bibliography is a simple alphabetical list of the references cited in this book.

A

Abernethy, C. N. (1988). Human–computer interface standards: Origins, organizations and comment. In Oborne, D. J. (Ed.), *International Review of Ergonomics* **2**, 31–54.

Abowd, G. D., and Dix, A. J. (1992). Giving undo attention. *Interacting with Computers* **4**, 3 (December), 317–342.

ACM SIGCHI (1992). *Curricula for Human–Computer Interaction*. Association for Computing Machinery, New York, NY (ACM Order No. 608920). Also available for anonymous FTP downloading in rich text format (RTF) from archive.cis.ohio-state.edu [128.146.8.52] in the directory /pub/hci/ CDG.

Alben, L., Faris, J., and Saddler, H. (1994). Making It Macintosh: Designing the message when the message is design. *ACM interactions* **1**, 1 (January), 10–20.

Allen, R. B. (1984). Working paper on ethical issues for research on the use of computer services and interfaces. *ACM SIGCHI Bulletin* **16**, 1 (July), 12–16.

American Psychological Association (1982). *Ethical Principles in the Conduct of Research with Human Participants*. American Psychological Association, Washington, DC.

Andersen, M. H., Nielsen, J., and Rasmussen, H. (1989). A similarity-based hypertext browser for reading the Unix network news. *Hypermedia* **1**, 3, 255–265.

Angiolillo, J. S., and Roberts, L. A. (1991). What makes a manual look easy to use? *Proc. Human Factors Society 35th Annual Meeting*, 222–224.

Anonymous. (1990). Interface evolution: A collective timeline. In Laurel, B. (Ed.), *The Art of Human–Computer Interface Design*. Addison-Wesley, Reading, MA. 483.

Armstrong, J. S., and Lusk, E. J. (1988). Return postage in mail surveys. *Public Opinion Quarterly* **51**, 233–248.

Aspray, W., and Beaver, D. (1986). Marketing the monster: Advertising computer technology. *Annals of the History of Computing* **8**, 2 (April), 127–143.

B

Bachman, R. D. (1989). A methodology for comparing the software interfaces of competitive products. *Proc. Human Factors Society 33rd Annual Meeting*, 1214–1217.

Baecker, R. M. (1989). A vision of education in user-centered system and interface design. *ACM SIGCHI Bulletin* **20**, 3 (January), 10–13.

Baecker, R. M., Small, I., and Mander, R. (1991). Bringing icons to life. In *Proc. ACM CHI'91 Conf.* (New Orleans, LA, 28 April–2 May), 1–6.

Bailey, G. (1993). Iterative methodology and designer training in human–computer interface design. *Proc. ACM INTERCHI'93 Conf.* (Amsterdam, The Netherlands, 24–29 April), 198–205.

Bailey, R. W. (1991). Converting research into reality. *Proc. Human Factors Society 35th Annual Meeting*, 345–349.

Bailey, W. A., Knox, S. T., and Lynch, E. F. (1988). Effects of interface design upon user productivity. *Proc. ACM CHI'88 Conf.* (Washington, DC, 15–19 May), 207–212.

Bainbridge, L. (1979). Verbal reports as evidence of the process operator's knowledge. *Intl. J. Man–Machine Studies* **11**, 411–436.

Banning, J. (1984). Beyond the application program: A different approach to integrated software. *BYTE* **9**, 1 (January), 251–262.

Barratt, M. (1991). A nice thing about Windows. *Information Design Journal* **6**, 3, 257.

Becker, J. D. (1984). Multilingual word processing. *Scientific American* **251**, 1 (July), 82–93.

Bellantone, C. E., and Lanzetta, T. M. (1991). 'Works as advertised:' Observations and benefits of prototyping. *Proc. Human Factors Society 35th Annual Meeting*, 324–327.

Bellotti, V. (1988). Implications of current design practice for the use of HCI techniques. In Jones, D. M., and Winder, R. (Eds.), *People and Computers IV*. Cambridge University Press, Cambridge, U.K., 13–34.

Benel, D. C. R., Ottens, D., Jr., and Horst, R. (1991). Use of an eyetracking system in the usability laboratory. *Proc. Human Factors Society 35th Annual Meeting*, 461–465.

Bentley, J. (1985). Programming pearls: A spelling checker. *Communications of the ACM* **28**, 5 (May), 456–462.

Berg, J. L., and Schumny, H. (Eds.) (1990). *An Analysis of the Information Technology Standardization Process*. Elsevier Science Publishers, Amsterdam, The Netherlands.

Bernstein, M. (1988). The bookmark and the compass: Orientation tools for hypertext users. *ACM SIGOIS Bulletin* **9**, 4 (October), 34–45.

Berry, D. C., and Broadbent, D. E. (1990). The role of instruction and verbalization in improving performance on complex search tasks. *Behaviour & Information Technology* **9**, 3 (May–June), 175–190.

Berry, R. E. (1988). Common User Access—A consistent and usable human–computer interface for the SAA environment. *IBM Systems Journal* **27**, 3, 281–300.

Bewley, W. L., Roberts, T. L, Schroit, D., and Verplank, W. L. (1983). Human factors testing in the design of Xerox's 8010 'Star' office workstation. *Proc. ACM CHI'83 Conf.* (Boston, MA, 12–15 December), 72–77.

Bias, R. (1991). Walkthroughs: Efficient collaborative testing. *IEEE Software* **8**, 5 (September), 94–95.

Bickel, M. A. (1987). Automatic correction to misspelled names: A fourth-generation language approach. *Communications of the ACM* **30**, 3 (March), 224–228.

Biocca, F. (1992). Virtual reality technology: A tutorial. *Journal of Communication* **42**, 4 (Autumn), 23–72.

Bisseret, A. (1983). Psychology for man computer cooperation in knowledge processing. *Proc. IFIP 9th World Computer Congress* (Paris, 19–23 September), 113–120.

Bleser, T., and Foley, J. (1982). Towards specifying and evaluating the human factors of user–computer interfaces. *Proc. ACM Conf. Human Factors in Computer Systems* (Gaithersburg, MD, 15–17 March), 309–314.

Bleser, T. W., and Sibert, J. (1990). Toto: A tool for selecting interaction rules. *Proc. ACM UIST'90 Third Annual Symposium on User Interface Software and Technology* (Snowbird, UT, 3–5 October), 135–142.

Bloom, C. P. (1987–88). Procedures for obtaining and testing user-selected terminologies. *Human–Computer Interaction* **3**, 2, 155–177.

Blumenthal, B. (1990). Strategies for automatically incorporating metaphoric attributes in interface designs. *Proc. ACM UIST'90 Third Annual Symposium on User Interface Software and Technology* (Snowbird, UT, 3–5 October), 66–75.

Boies, S. J., Gould, J. D., Levy, S., Richards, J. T., and Schoonard, J. (1985). The 1984 Olympic Message System: A case study in system design. *Research Report* **RC11138**, IBM T. J. Watson Research Center, Yorktown Heights, NY.

Booth, P. A. (1990). Identifying and interpreting design errors. *Intl. J. Human–Computer Interaction* **4**, 2, 307–332.

Borenstein, N. S. (1985). The design and evaluation of on-line help systems. *Technical Report* **CMU-CS-85-151**, Department of Computer Science, Carnegie-Mellon University, Pittsburgh, PA.

Bradford, J. H., Murray, W. D., and Carey, T. T. (1990). What kind of errors do Unix users make? *Proc. IFIP INTERACT'90 Third Intl. Conf. Human–Computer Interaction* (Cambridge, U.K., 27–31 August), 43–46.

Brigham, F. R. (1989). Statistical methods for testing the conformance of products to user performance standards. *Behaviour & Information Technology* **8**, 4, 279–283.

Brooke, J., Bevan, N., Brigham, F. R., Harker, S., and Youmans, D. (1990). Usability assurance and standardization—work in progress in ISO. *Proc. IFIP INTERACT'90 Third Intl. Conf. Human–Computer Interaction* (Cambridge, U.K., 27–31 August), 357–361.

Brooks, F. P. (1975). *The Mythical Man-Month*. Addison-Wesley, Reading, MA.

Brooks, F. P. (1987). No silver bullet: Essence and accidents of software engineering. *IEEE Computer* **20**, 4 (April), 10–19.

Brooks, R. (1993). The case for the specialized interface. *IEEE Software* **10**, 2 (March), 86–88.

Brothers, L., Hollan, J., Nielsen, J., Stornetta, S., Abney, S., Furnas, G., and Littman, M. (1992). Supporting informal communication via ephemeral interest groups. *Proc. ACM CSCW'92 Conf. Computer-Supported Cooperative Work* (Toronto, Canada, 1–4 November), 84–90.

Brown, C. M. L. (1988). *Human–Computer Interface Design Guidelines*. Ablex, Norwood, NJ.

Brugger, C. (1990). Advances in the international standardization of public information symbols. *Information Design Journal* **6**, 1, 79–88.

Byrne, J. G. (1989). Competitive evaluation in industry: Some comments. *Proc. Human Factors Society 33rd Annual Meeting*, 423–425.

C

Caesar, G. J. (51 B.C.). *De Bello Gallico*. Manuscript, Roman Empire. Also available in several translations, including *The Conquest of Gaul*, translated by Handford, S. A., Penguin Books, London, U.K., 1951.

Campbell, R. L. (1992). Will the real scenario please stand up? *ACM SIGCHI Bulletin* **24**, 2 (April), 6–8.

Canadian Standards Association (1992). *Canadian Alphanumeric Ordering Standard for Character Sets of CSA Standard CAN/CSA-Z243.4*. **Standard Z243.4.1**, Canadian Standards Association, Rexdale, Ontario, Canada.

Caplan, S. (1990). Using focus groups methodology for ergonomic design. *Ergonomics* **33**, 5, 527–533.

Card, S. K., and Henderson, D. A. (1987). Catalogues: A metaphor for computer application delivery. *Proc. IFIP INTERACT'87 Second Intl. Conf. Human–Computer Interaction* (Stuttgart, Germany, 1–4 September), 959–964.

Card, S. K., and Moran, T. P. (1988). User technology: From pointing to pondering. In Goldberg, A. (Ed.), *A History of Personal Workstations*. Addison-Wesley, Reading, MA. 489–526.

Card, S. K., English, W. K., and Burr, B. J. (1978). Evaluation of the mouse, rate-controlled isometric joystick, step keys, and text keys for text selection on a CRT. *Ergonomics* **21**, 601–613.

Card, S. K., Moran, T. P., and Newell, A. (1983). *The Psychology of Human–Computer Interaction*. Lawrence Erlbaum Associates, Hillsdale, NJ.

Card, S. K., Robertson, G. G., and Mackinlay, J. D. (1991). The information visualizer: An information workspace. *Proc. ACM CHI'91 Conf.* (New Orleans, LA, 28 April–2 May), 181–188.

Carey, T. (1989). Position paper: The basic HCI course for software engineers. *ACM SIGCHI Bulletin* **20**, 3 (January), 14–15.

Carroll, J. M. (1990a). *The Nurnberg Funnel: Designing Minimalist Instruction for Practical Computer Skill*. The MIT Press, Cambridge, MA.

Carroll, J. M. (1990b). Infinite detail and emulation in an ontologically minimized HCI. *Proc. ACM CHI'90 Conf.* (Seattle, WA, 1–5 April), 321–327.

Carroll, J. M., and Campbell, R. L. (1986). Softening up hard science: Reply to Newell and Card. *Human–Computer Interaction* **2**, 3, 227–249.

Carroll, J. M., and Carrithers, C. (1984). Training wheels in a user interface. *Communications of the ACM* **27**, 8 (August), 800–806.

Carroll, J. M., and Rosson, M. B. (1987). Paradox of the active user. In Carroll, J. M. (Ed.), *Interfacing Thought: Cognitive Aspects of Human–Computer Interaction*. The MIT Press, Cambridge, MA. 80–111.

Carroll, J. M., and Rosson, M. B. (1990). Human–computer interaction scenarios as a design representation. *Proc. IEEE HICSS-23, 23rd Hawaii Intl. Conf. System Sciences* (Hawaii, 2–6 January), **Vol. II**, 555–561.

Carroll, J. M., and Rosson, M. B. (1991). Deliberated evolution: Stalking the View Matcher in design space. *Human–Computer Interaction* **6**, 3 and 4, 281–318.

Carroll, J. M., and Rosson, M. B. (1992). Getting around the task-artifact cycle: How to make claims and design by scenario. *ACM Transactions on Information Systems* **10**, 2 (April), 181–212.

Carroll, J. M., and Thomas, J. C. (1988). Fun. *ACM SIGCHI Bulletin* **19**, 3 (January), 21–24.

Carroll, J. M., Mack, R. L., Lewis, C. H., Grischkowsky, N. L., and Robertson, S. R. (1985). Exploring exploring a word processor. *Human–Computer Interaction* **1**, 3, 283–307.

Carroll, J. M., Smith-Kerker, P. L., Ford, J. R., and Mazur-Rimetz, S. A. (1987–88). The minimal manual. *Human–Computer Interaction* **3**, 2, 123–153.

Carroll, J. M., Mack, R. L., and Kellogg, W. A. (1988). Interface metaphors and user interface design. In Helander, M. (Ed.), *Handbook of Human–Computer Interaction*. North-Holland, Amsterdam, The Netherlands. 67–85.

Carroll, J. M., Kellogg, W. A., and Rosson, M. B. (1991). The task-artifact cycle. In Carroll, J. M. (Ed.), *Designing Interaction: Psychology at the Human–Computer Interface*. Cambridge University Press, Cambridge, U.K. 74–102.

Catrambone, R., and Carroll, J. M. (1987). Learning a word processing system with guided exploration and training wheels. *Proc. ACM CHI+GI'87 Conf.* (Toronto, Canada, 5–9 April), 169–174.

Chapanis, A. (1991). The business case for human factors in informatics. In Shackel, B., and Richardson, S. (Eds.), *Human Factors for Informatics Usability*. Cambridge University Press, Cambridge, U.K. 21–37.

Chapanis, A., and Budurka, W. J. (1990). Specifying human–computer interface requirements. *Behaviour & Information Technology* **9**, 6, 479–492.

Chin, J. P., Diehl, V. A., and Norman, K. L. (1988). Development of an instrument measuring user satisfaction of the human–computer interface. *Proc. ACM CHI'88 Conf.* (Washington, DC, 15–19 May), 213–218.

Clarke, L. (1991). The use of scenarios by user interface designers. In Diaper, D., and Hammond, N. (Eds.), *People and Computers VI*, Cambridge University Press, Cambridge, U.K. 103–115.

Coleman, W. D., Williges, R. C., and Wixon, D. R. (1985). Collecting detailed user evaluations of software interfaces. *Proc. Human Factors Society 29th Annual Meeting*, 240–244.

Comstock, E. M., and Clemens, E. A. (1987). Perceptions of computer manuals: A view from the field. *Proc. Human Factors Society 31st Annual Meeting*, 139–143.

Conklin, J., and Begeman, M. L. (1988). gIBIS: A hypertext tool for exploratory policy discussion. *ACM Trans. Office Information Systems* **6**, 4 (October), 303–331.

Conklin, J. E., and Yakemovic, K. C. B. (1991). A process-oriented approach to design rationale. *Human–Computer Interaction* **6**, 3 and 4, 357–391.

Connally, C. S., and Tullis, T. S. (1986). Evaluating the user interface: Video-taping without a camera. *Proc. Human Factors Society 30th Annual Meeting*, 1029–1033.

Cool, C., Fish, R. S., Kraut, R. E., and Lowery, C. M. (1992). Iterative design of video communication systems. *Proc. ACM CSCW'92 Conf. Computer-Supported Cooperative Work* (Toronto, Canada, 1–4 November), 25–32.

Cordes, R. E. (1993). The relationship between post-task and continuous-vicarious ratings of difficulty. *Intl. J. Human–Computer Interaction* **5**, 2, 115–127.

Cordingley, E. (1989). Knowledge elicitation techniques for knowledge based systems. In Diaper, D. (Ed.), *Knowledge Elicitation: Principles, Techniques, and Applications.* Ellis Horwood, Chichester, U.K. 89–172.

Cotterman, W. W., and Kumar, K. (1989). User cube: A taxonomy of end users. *Communications of the ACM* **32**, 11 (November), 1313–1320.

Curtis, B. (1981). Substantiating programmer variability. *Proceedings of the IEEE* **69**, 7 (July), 846.

Czaja, S. J. (1988). Microcomputers and the elderly. In Helander, M. (Ed.), *Handbook of Human–Computer Interaction,* Elsevier Science Publishers, Amsterdam, The Netherlands. 581–598.

Czaja, S. J., Hammond, K., Blascovich, J. J., and Swede, H. (1989). Age related differences in learning to use a text-editing system. *Behaviour & Information Technology* **8**, 4, 309–319.

D

Dale, E., and O'Rourke, J. (1981). *The Living Word Vocabulary.* World Book-Childcraft International, Chicago, IL.

Dayton, T., Barr, B., Burke, P. A., Cohill, A. M., Day, M. C., Dray, S., Ehrlich, K., Fitzsimmons, L. A., Henneman, R. L., Hornstein, S. B., Karat, J., Kliger, J., Löwgren, J., Rensch, J., Sellers, M., and Smith, M. R. (1993). Skills needed by user-centered design practitioners in real software development environments: Report on the CH'92 workshop. *ACM SIGCHI Bulletin* **25**, 3 (July), 16–31.

de Baar, D., Foley, J., and Mullet, K. (1992). Coupling application design and user interface design. *Proc. ACM CHI'92 Conf.* (Monterey, CA, 3–7 May), 259–266.

de Souza, F., and Bevan, N. (1990). The use of guidelines in menu interface design. *Proc. IFIP INTERACT'90 Third Intl. Conf. Human–Computer Interaction* (Cambridge, U.K., 27–31 August), 435–440.

Deerwester, S., Dumais, S. T., Landauer, T. K., Furnas, G. W., and Harshman, R. A. (1990). Indexing by latent semantic analysis. *Journal of the Society for Information Science* **41**, 6, 391–407.

del Galdo, E. (1990). Internationalization and translation: Some guidelines for the design of human–computer interfaces. In Nielsen, J. (Ed.), *Designing User Interfaces for International Use.* Elsevier Science Publishers, Amsterdam, The Netherlands. 71–102.

Denning, S., Hoiem, D., Simpson, M., and Sullivan, K. (1990). The value of thinking-aloud protocols in industry: A case study at Microsoft Corporation. *Proc. Human Factors Society 34th Annual Meeting,* 1285–1289.

Desurvire, H. W., Kondziela, J. M., and Atwood, M. E. (1992). What is gained and lost when using evaluation methods other than empirical testing. In

Monk, A., Diaper, D., and Harrison, M. D. (Eds.), *People and Computers VII*, Cambridge University Press, Cambridge, U.K. 89–102.

Diaper, D. (Ed.) (1989a). *Task Analysis for Human–Computer Interaction*. Ellis Horwood, Chichester, U.K.

Diaper, D. (1989b). Task observation for human–computer interaction. In Diaper, D. (Ed.), *Task Analysis for Human–Computer Interaction*. Ellis Horwood, Chichester, U.K. 210–237.

Diaper, D., and Johnson, P. (1989). Task analysis for knowledge descriptions: Theory and application in training. In Long, J., and Whitefield, A. (Eds.), *Cognitive Ergonomics and Human–Computer Interaction*. Cambridge University Press, Cambridge, U.K. 191–224.

DIN (1988). *Bildschirmarbeitsplätze: Grundsätze ergonomischer Dialoggestaltung* ("VDU work stations: Principles of ergonomic dialogue design," in German), Deutsches Institut für Normung **DIN 66234, Teil 8**.

Doane, S. M., Pellegrino, J. W., and Klatzky, R. L. (1990). Expertise in a computer operating system: Conceptualization and performance. *Human–Computer Interaction* **5**, 2 and 3, 267–304.

Doane, S. M., McNamara, D. S., Kintsch, W., Polson, P. G., and Clawson, D. M. (1992). Prompt comprehension in UNIX command production. *Memory & Cognition* **20**, 4 (July), 327–343.

Dourish, P., and Bly, S. (1992). Portholes: Supporting awareness in a distributed work group. In *Proc. ACM CHI'92 Conf.* (Monterey, CA, 3–7 May), 541–547.

Doyle, J. R. (1990). Naive users and the Lotus interface: A field study. *Behaviour & Information Technology* **9**, 1, 81–89.

Draper, S. W. (1984). The nature of expertise in Unix. *Proc. IFIP INTERACT'84 First Intl. Conf. Human–Computer Interaction* (London, U.K., 4–7 September), 465–471.

Dreger, L., Grauman, A., Ho, T., Howlett, V., Lehmann, R., Malamud, M., Marceau, R., and Tobey, C. (1992). An object-oriented evolution of Windows: Information at your fingertips (videotape). *ACM SIGGRAPH Video Review* **78**.

Dubberly, H., and Mitsch, D. (1987). Knowledge Navigator (videotape). *ACM SIGGRAPH Video Review* **79** (anthology published 1992; tape made in 1987).

Duffy, T. M., Palmer, J. E., and Mehlenbacher, B. (1992). *Online Help: Design and Evaluation*. Ablex, Norwood, NJ.

Duis, D., and Johnson, J. (1990). Improving user-interface responsiveness despite performance limitations. *Proc. IEEE Computer Society Intl. Conference* (February, San Francisco, CA), 380–386.

Durham, I., Lamb, D. A., and Saxe, J. B. (1983). Spelling correction in user interfaces. *Communications of the ACM* **26**, 10 (October), 764–773.

Durrett, H. J. (Ed.) (1987). *Color and the Computer*. Academic Press, Boston, MA.

Durrett, H. J., and Trezona, J. (1982). How to use color displays effectively. *BYTE* **7**, 4 (April), 50–53.

Dye, R., Arnott, J. L., Newell, A. F., Carter, K. E. P., and Cruikshank, G. (1990). Simulating the speech operated user interfaces of the future: The case of listening typewriters. In Life, M. A., Narborough-Hall, C. S., and Hamilton, W. I. (Eds.), *Simulation and the User Interface*. Taylor & Francis, London, U.K. 159–168.

Dzida, W. (1989). The development of ergonomic standards. *ACM SIGCHI Bulletin* **20**, 3 (January), 35–43.

E

Eberts, R. E., and MacMillan, A. G. (1987). Longitudinal study of a distributed system. *Proc. Human Factors Society 28th Annual Meeting*, 704–708.

Edgerton, E. A., Draper, S. W., and Barton, S. B. (1993). Feature checklists in HCI: Some basic results. *Adjunct Proceedings ACM INTERCHI'93 Conf.* (24–29 April), 189–190.

Edmonds, E. (1991). *The Separable User Interface*. Academic Press, London, U.K.

Edwards, A. D. N. (1988). The design of auditory interfaces for visually disabled users. *Proc. ACM CHI'88 Conf.* (Washington, DC, 15–19 May), 83–88.

Efe, K. (1987). A proposed solution to the problem of levels in error-message generation. *Communications of the ACM* **30**, 11 (November), 948–955.

Egan, D. E. (1988). Individual differences in human–computer interaction. In Helander, M. (Ed.), *Handbook of Human–Computer Interaction*. North-Holland, Amsterdam, The Netherlands. 543–568.

Egan, D. E., Remde, J. R., Gomez, L. M., Landauer, T. K., Eberhardt, J., and Lochbaum, C. C. (1989). Formative design-evaluation of SuperBook. *ACM Transactions on Information Systems* **7**, 1 (January), 30–57.

Egan, T. (1991). Oregon literacy test shows many lag in basics. *The New York Times* (April 24), p. A23.

Egido, C., and Patterson, J. (1988). Pictures and category labels as navigational aids for catalog browsing. *Proc. ACM CHI'88 Conf.* (15–19 May, Washington, DC), 127–132.

Ehrenreich, S. L. (1985). Computer abbreviations: Evidence and synthesis. *Human Factors* **27**, 143–155.

Ehrlich, K., Butler, M. B., and Pernice, K. (1994). Getting the whole team into usability testing. *IEEE Software* **11**, 1 (January), 89–91.

Engelbart, D. (1988). The augmented knowledge workshop. In Goldberg, A. (Ed.), *A History of Personal Workstations*. Addison-Wesley, Reading, MA. 185–236.

Ericsson, K. A., and Simon, H. A. (1984). *Protocol Analysis: Verbal Reports as Data*. The MIT Press, Cambridge, MA.

F

Farkas, D. K. (1993). The role of balloon help. *ACM SIGDOC *The Journal of Computer Documentation* **17**, 2 (May), 3–19.

Farrand, A. B., and Wolfe, S. J. (1992). On-line help: Are we tossing the users a lifesaver or an anchor? *Digest of ACM CHI'92 Conf. Posters and Short Talks* (Monterey, CA, 5 May), 21.

Fath, J. L., and Bias, R. G. (1992). Taking the task out of task analysis. *Proc. Human Factors Society 36th Annual Meeting*, 379–383.

Feiner, S. K., and McKeown, K. R. (1990). Generating coordinated multimedia explanations. *Proc. IEEE Conf. on AI Applications* (Santa Barbara, CA, 5–9 March), 290–296.

Feiner, S. K., and McKeown, K. R. (1991). COMET: Generating coordinated multimedia explanations. *Proc. ACM CHI'91 Conf.* (New Orleans, LA, 28 April–2 May), 449–450.

Fisher, D. L., Yungkurth, E. J., and Moss, S. M. (1990). Optimal menu hierarchy design: Syntax and semantics. *Human Factors* **32**, 6 (June), 655–683.

Fisher, P., and Sless, D. (1990). Information design methods and productivity in the insurance industry. *Information Design Journal* **6**, 2, 103–129.

Flohr, U. (1994). Teutonizing the Newton. *BYTE* **19**, 3 (March), 26.

Fowler, C. J. H., and Murray, D. (1987). Gender and cognitive style differences at the human–computer interface. *Proc. IFIP INTERACT'87 Second Intl. Conf. Human–Computer Interaction* (Stuttgart, Germany, 1–4 September), 709–714.

Frese, M., Brodbeck, F., Heinbokel, T., Mooser, C., Schleiffenbaum, E., and Thiemann, P. (1991). Errors in training computer skills: On the positive function of errors. *Human–Computer Interaction* **6**, 1, 77–93.

Furnas, G. W. (1985). Experience with an adaptive indexing scheme. *Proc. ACM CHI'85 Conf.* (San Francisco, CA, 14–18 April), 131–135.

Furnas, G. W., Landauer, T. K., Gomez, L. M., and Dumais, S. T. (1987). The vocabulary problem in human–system communication. *Communications of the ACM* **30**, 11 (November), 964–971.

G

Gaines, B. R. (1984). From ergonomics to the fifth generation: 30 years of human–computer interaction studies. *Proc. IFIP INTERACT'84 First Intl. Conf. Human–Computer Interaction* (London, U.K., 4–7 September), 3–7.

Gaines, B. R., and Shaw, M. L. G. (1986a). From timesharing to the sixth generation: The development of human–computer interaction. Part I. *Intl. J. Man–Machine Studies* **24**, 1 (January), 1–27.

Gaines, B. R., and Shaw, M. L. G. (1986b). Foundations of dialog engineering: The development of human–computer interaction. Part II. *Intl. J. Man–Machine Studies* **24**, 2 (February), 101–123.

Gantt, M., and Nardi, B. A. (1992). Gardeners and gurus: Patterns of cooperation among CAD users. *Proc. ACM CHI'92 Conf.* (Monterey, CA, 3–7 May), 107–117.

Garber, S. R., and Grunes, M. B. (1992). The art of search: A study of art directors. *Proc. ACM CHI'92 Conf.* (Monterey, CA, 3–7 May), 157–163.

Gates, B. (1990). *Information at Your Fingertips* (videotape). Microsoft Corp., Redmond, WA.

Gaver, W. W. (1989). The SonicFinder: An interface that uses auditory icons. *Human–Computer Interaction* **4**, 1, 67–94.

Gaylin, K. B. (1986). How are windows used? Some notes on creating an empirically-based windowing benchmark task. *Proc. ACM CHI'86 Conf.* (Boston, MA, 13–17 April), 96–100.

Gilmore, D. J. (1991). Visibility: A dimensional analysis. In Diaper, D., and Hammond, N. (Eds.), *People and Computers VI*, Cambridge University Press, Cambridge, U.K. 317–329.

Goldberg, A. (Ed.) (1988). *A History of Personal Workstations.* Addison-Wesley, Reading, MA.

Goldman, A. E., and McDonald, S. S. (1987). *The Group Depth Interview: Principles and Practice.* Prentice Hall, Englewood Cliffs, NJ.

Gomez, L. M., Egan, D. E., and Bowers, C. (1986). Learning to use a text editor: Some learner characteristics that predict success. *Human–Computer Interaction* **2**, 1, 1–23.

Good, M. (1989). Developing the XUI style. In Nielsen, J. (Ed.), *Coordinating User Interfaces for Consistency*, Academic Press, Boston, MA. 57–73.

Good, M., Spine, T. M., Whiteside, J., and George, P. (1986). User-derived impact analysis as a tool for usability engineering. *Proc. ACM CHI'86 Conf.* (Boston, MA, 13–17 April), 241–246.

Gould, J. D., and Lewis, C. H. (1985). Designing for usability: Key principles and what designers think. *Communications of the ACM* **28**, 3 (March), 300–311.

Gould, J. D., Conti, J., and Hovanyecz, T. (1983). Composing letters with a simulated listening typewriter. *Communications of the ACM* **26**, 4 (April), 295–308.

Gould, J. D., Boies, S. J., Levy, S., Richards, J. T., and Schoonard, J. (1987). The 1984 Olympic Message System: A test of behavioral principles of system design. *Communications of the ACM* **30**, 9 (September), 758–769.

Gould, J. D., Boies, S. J., and Lewis, C. (1991). Making usable, useful, productivity-enhancing computer applications. *Communications of the ACM* **34**, 1 (January), 74–85.

Gray, B. G., Barfield, W., Haselkorn, M., Spyridakis, J., and Conquest, L. (1990). The design of a graphics-based traffic information system based on user requirements. *Proc. Human Factors Society 34th Annual Meeting*, 603–606.

Gray, W. D., John, B. E., and Atwood, M. E. (1992). The precis of project Ernestine, or, an overview of a validation of GOMS. *Proc. ACM CHI'92 Conf.* (Monterey, CA, 3–7 May), 307–312.

Green, A. J. K., and Barnard, P. J. (1990). Iconic interfacing: The role of icon distinctiveness and fixed or variable screen locations. *Proc. IFIP INTERACT'90 Third Intl. Conf. Human–Computer Interaction* (Cambridge, U.K., 27–31 August), 457–462.

Greenbaum, T. L. (1988). *The Practical Handbook and Guide to Focus Group Research.* D. C. Heath & Co., Lexington, MA.

Greenbaum, T. L. (1993). *The Handbook for Focus Group Research.* Lexington Books, New York, NY.

Greenberg, S. (1993). *The Computer User as Toolsmith: The Use, Reuse, and Organization of Computer-Based Tools.* Cambridge University Press, Cambridge, U.K.

Greenberg, S., and Whitten, I. H. (1985). Adaptive personalized interfaces—A question of viability. *Behaviour & Information Technology* **4**, 1 (January), 31–45.

Greenberg, S., and Whitten, I. H. (1988). How users repeat their actions on computers: Principles for design of history mechanisms. *Proc. ACM CHI'88 Conf.* (Washington, DC, 15–19 May), 171–178.

Greif, I. (1992). Designing group-enabled applications: A spreadsheet example. In Coleman, D. (Ed.), *Groupware'92*, Morgan Kaufmann Publishers, San Mateo, CA. 515–525.

Greif, S. (1991). Organisational issues and task analysis. In Shackel, B., and Richardson, S. (Eds.), *Human Factors for Informatics Usability.* Cambridge University Press, Cambridge, U.K. 247–266.

Griffith, D. (1990). Computer access for persons who are blind or visually impaired: Human factors issues. *Human Factors* **32**, 4 (August), 467–475.

Grudin, J. (1988). Why CSCW applications fail: Problems in the design and evaluation of organizational interfaces. *Proc. ACM CSCW'88 Conf. Computer-Supported Cooperative Work* (Portland, OR, 26–28 September), 85–93.

Grudin, J. (1989). The case against user interface consistency. *Communications of the ACM* **32**, 10 (October), 1164–1173.

Grudin, J. (1990a). The computer reaches out: The historical continuity of interface design. *Proc. ACM CHI'90 Conf.* (Seattle, WA, 1–5 April), 261–268.

Grudin, J. (1990b). Obstacles to user involvement in interface design in large product development organizations. *Proc. IFIP INTERACT'90 Third Intl. Conf. Human–Computer Interaction* (Cambridge, U.K., 27–31 August), 219–224.

Grudin, J. (1991a). Interactive systems: Bridging the gaps between developers and systems. *IEEE Computer* **24**, 4 (April), 59–69.

Grudin, J. (1991b). Systematic sources of suboptimal interface design in large product development organizations. *Human–Computer Interaction* **6**, 2, 147–196.

Grudin, J. (1992). Utility and usability: Research issues and development contexts. *Interacting with Computers* **4**, 2 (August), 209–217.

Grudin, J. (1993). Interface: An evolving concept. *Communications of the ACM* **36**, 4 (April), 110–119.

Grudin, J., and Barnard, P. (1985). When does an abbreviation become a word? and related questions. *Proc. ACM CHI'85 Conf.* (San Francisco, CA, 14–18 April), 121–125.

Grudin, J., Ehrlich, S. F., and Shriner, R. (1987). Positioning human factors in the user interface development chain. *Proc. ACM CHI+GI'87 Conf.* (Toronto, Canada, 5–9 April), 125–131.

H

Hackman, G. S., and Biers, D. W. (1992). Team usability testing: Are two heads better than one? *Proc. Human Factors Society 36th Annual Meeting*, 1205–1209.

Hakiel, S. R., and Easterby, R. S. (1987). Methods for the design and evaluation of icons for human–computer interfaces. *Proc. IEE 2nd Intl. Conf. Command, Control, Communications and Management Information Systems* (Bournemouth, U.K., 1–3 April), 48–51.

Halasz, F., and Moran, T. P. (1982). Analogy considered harmful. *Proc. ACM Conf. Human Factors in Computer Systems* (Gaithersburg, MD, 15–17 March), 383–386.

Halstead-Nussloch, R. (1989). The design of phone-based interfaces for consumers. *Proc. ACM CHI'89 Conf.* (Austin, TX, 30 April–4 May), 347–352.

Happ, A. J. (1994). Usability foresight: Strategic usability planning. *ACM SIGCHI Bulletin* **26**, 1 (January), 17–21.

Harris, D. H. (1984). Human factors success stories. *Proc. Human Factors Society 28th Annual Meeting*, 1–5.

Hartson, H. R., and Hix, D. (1989). Human–computer interface development: Concepts and systems for its management. *ACM Computing Surveys* **21**, 1 (March), 5–93.

Hartson, H. R., and Smith, E. C. (1991). Rapid prototyping in human–computer interface development. *Interacting with Computers* **3**, 1, 51–91.

Hartson, H. R., Siochi, A. C., and Hix, D. (1990). The UAN: A user-oriented representation for direct manipulation interface. *ACM Transactions on Information Systems* **8**, 3 (July), 181–203.

Henderson, D. A., and Card, S. K. (1986). Rooms: The use of multiple virtual workspaces to reduce space contention in a window-based graphical user interface. *ACM Transactions on Graphics* **5**, 3, 211–243.

Hewett, T. T., and Scott, S. (1987). The use of thinking-out-loud and protocol analysis in development of a process model of interactive database searching. *Proc. IFIP INTERACT'87 Second Intl. Conf. Human–Computer Interaction* (Stuttgart, Germany, 1–4 September), 51–56.

Hill, W. C., and Hollan, J. D. (1992). Edit wear and read wear. *Proc. ACM CHI'92 Conf.* (Monterey, CA, 3–7 May), 3–9.

Hix, D. (1990). Generations of user-interface management systems. *IEEE Software* **7**, 5 (September), 77–87.

Hix, D., and Schulman, R. S. (1991). Human–computer interface development tools: A methodology for their evaluation. *Communications of the ACM* **34**, 3 (March), 74–87.

Hodges, M. E., Davis, B. H., and Sasnett, R. M. (1989). Investigations in multimedia design documentation. In Barrett, E. (Ed.), *The Society of Text: Hypertext, Hypermedia, and the Social Construction of Information*. The MIT Press, Cambridge, MA. 79–89.

Hoffberg, L. I. (1991). Designing user interface guidelines for time-shift programming on a video cassette recorder (VCR). *Proc. Human Factors Society 35th Annual Meeting*, 501–504.

Hoiem, D. E., and Sullivan, K. D. (1994). Designing and using integrated data collection and analysis tools: Challenges and considerations. *Behaviour & Information Technology* **13**, 1&2 (January–April), 160–170.

Holdaway, K., and Bevan, N. (1989). User system interaction standards. *Computer Communications* **12**, 2 (April), 97–102.

Hollan, J., and Stornetta, S. (1992). Beyond being there. *Proc. ACM CHI'92 Conf.* (Monterey, CA, 3–7 May), 119–125.

Holleran, P. A. (1991). A methodological note on pitfalls in usability testing. *Behaviour & Information Technology* **10**, 5 (September–October 1991), 345–357.

Horton, W. K. (1990). *Designing and Writing Online Documentation: Help Files to Hypertext*. Wiley, New York, NY.

Houde, S. (1992). Iterative design of an interface for easy 3-D direct manipulation. *Proc. ACM CHI'92 Conf.* (Monterey, CA, 3–7 May), 135–142.

Houghton, R. C., Jr. (1984). Online help systems: A conspectus. *Communications of the ACM* **27**, 2 (February), 126–133.

House, C. H., and Price, R. L. (1991). The return map: Tracking product teams. *Harvard Business Review* (January–February), 92–100.

I

Ishii, H. (1990). Cross-cultural communication and computer-supported cooperative work. *Whole Earth Review*, No. 69 (Winter 1990), 48–52.

J

Jacob, R. J. K. (1991). The use of eye movements in human–computer interaction techniques: What you look at is what you get. *ACM Trans. Information Systems* **9**, 2 (April), 152–169.

Jeffries, R., Miller, J. R., Wharton, C., and Uyeda, K. M. (1991). User interface evaluation in the real world: A comparison of four techniques. *Proc. ACM CHI'91 Conf.* (New Orleans, LA, 28 April–2 May), 119–124.

John, B. E., Miller, P. L., Myers, B. A., Neuwirth, C. M., and Shafer, S. A. (1992). Human–computer interaction in the School of Computer Science. *Technical Report CMU-CS-92-193*, Computer Science Department, Carnegie Mellon University, Pittsburgh, PA. Available by anonymous FTP from `reports.adm.cs.cmu.edu` [128.2.218.42] as `/1992/CMU-CS-92-193.ps`

Johnson, C. W. (1991). Applying temporal logic to support the specification and prototyping of concurrent multi-user interfaces. In Diaper, D., and Hammond, N. (Eds.), *People and Computers VI*, Cambridge University Press, Cambridge, U.K. 145–156.

Johnson, J. A., Nardi, B. A., Zarmer, C. L., and Miller, J. R. (1993). ACE: Building interactive graphical applications. *Communications of the ACM* **36**, 4 (April), 41–55.

Johnson, H., and Johnson, P. (1990). Designers-identified requirements for tools to support task analysis. *Proc. IFIP INTERACT'90 Third Intl. Conf. Human–Computer Interaction* (Cambridge, U.K., 27–31 August), 259–264.

Johnson, P. (1992). *Human Computer Interaction: Psychology, Task Analysis and Software Engineering*. McGraw-Hill, London, U.K.

Johnson, W., Jellinek, H. D., Klotz, L., Rao, R., and Card, S. K. (1993). Bridging the paper and electronic worlds: The paper user interface. *Proc. ACM INTERCHI'93 Conf.* (Amsterdam, The Netherlands, 24–29 April), 507–512.

Jordan, D. S., Russell, D. M., Jensen, A.-M. S., and Rogers, R. A. (1989). Facilitating the development of representations in hypertext with IDE. *Proc. ACM Hypertext'89 Conf.* (Pittsburgh, PA, 5–8 November), 93–104.

Jørgensen, A. H. (1989). Using the thinking-aloud method in system development. In Salvendy, G., and Smith, M. J. (Eds.), *Designing and Using Human–Computer Interfaces and Knowledge Based Systems*. Elsevier Science Publishers, Amsterdam. 743–750.

Jørgensen, A. H., and Sauer, A. (1990). The personal touch: A study of users' customization practice. *Proc. IFIP INTERACT'90 Third Intl. Conf. Human–Computer Interaction* (Cambridge, U.K., 27–31 August), 549–554.

K

Kacmar, C. J., and Carey, J. M. (1991). Assessing the usability of icons in user interfaces. *Behaviour & Information Technology* **10**, 6, 443–457.

Kain, H., and Nielsen, J. (1991). Estimating the market diffusion curve for hypertext. *Impact Assessment Bulletin* **9**, 1–2 (Spring), 145–157.

Karat, C. (1990). Cost-benefit analysis of iterative usability testing. *Proc. IFIP INTERACT'90 Third Intl. Conf. Human–Computer Interaction* (Cambridge, U.K., 27–31 August), 351–356.

Karat, C., and Karat, J. (Eds.) (1992). Some dialogue on scenarios. *ACM SIGCHI Bulletin* **24**, 4 (October), 7–17.

Karat, C., Campbell, R., and Fiegel, T. (1992). Comparison of empirical testing and walkthrough methods in user interface evaluation. In *Proc. ACM CHI'92 Conf.* (Monterey, California, 3–7 May), 397–404.

Karat, J., and Bennett, J. L. (1990). Supporting effective and efficient design meetings. *Proc. IFIP INTERACT'90 Third Intl. Conf. on Human–Computer Interaction* (Cambridge, U.K., 27–31 August), 365–370.

Karat, J., and Bennett, J. L. (1991a). Using scenarios in design meetings—A case study example. In Karat, J. (Ed.), *Taking Software Design Seriously: Practical Techniques for Human–Computer Interaction Design*. Academic Press, Boston, MA. 63–94.

Karat, J., and Bennett, J. (1991b). Working within the design process— Supporting effective and efficient design. In Carroll, J. M. (Ed.), *Designing Interaction: Psychology at the Human Computer Interface*. Cambridge University Press, Boston, MA. 269–285.

Karis, D., and Zeigler, B. L. (1989). Evaluation of mobile telecommunication systems. *Proc. Human Factors Society 33rd Annual Meeting*, 205–209.

Karlin, J. E., and Klemmer, E. T. (1989). An interview. In Klemmer, E. T. (Ed.), *Ergonomics: Harness the Power of Human Factors in Your Business*. Ablex, Norwood, NJ. 197–201.

Kato, T. (1986). What 'question-asking protocols' can say about the user interface. *Intl. J. Man–Machine Studies* **25**, 6 (December), 659–673.

Kay, A., and Goldberg, A. (1977). Personal dynamic media. *IEEE Computer* **10**, 3 (March), 31–41.

Kay, R. H. (1989). A practical and theoretical approach to assessing computer attitudes: The computer attitude measure (CAM). *Journal on Research on Computing in Education*, 456–463.

Kearsley, G. (1988). *Online Help Systems: Design and Implementation*. Ablex, Norwood, NJ.

Kellogg, W. A. (1987). Conceptual consistency in the user interface: Effects on user performance. *Proc. IFIP INTERACT'87 Second Intl. Conf. Human–Computer Interaction* (Stuttgart, Germany, 1–4 September), 389–394.

Kellogg, W. A. (1989). The dimensions of consistency. In Nielsen, J. (Ed.), *Coordinating User Interfaces for Consistency*. Academic Press, Boston, MA. 9–20.

Kellogg, W. A. (1990). Qualitative artifact analysis. *Proc. IFIP INTERACT'90 Third Intl. Conf. Human–Computer Interaction* (Cambridge, U.K., 27–31 August), 193–198.

Kennedy, S. (1989). Using video in the BNR usability lab. *ACM SIGCHI Bulletin* **21**, 2 (October), 92–95.

Kensing, F., and Munk-Madsen, A. (1993). PD: Structure in the toolbox. *Communications of the ACM* **36**, 4 (April), 78–85.

Kim, W. C., and Foley, J. D. (1990). DON: User interface presentation design assistant. *Proc. ACM UIST'90 Third Annual Symposium on User Interface Software and Technology* (Snowbird, UT, 3–5 October), 10–20.

Kincaid, J. P., Thomas, M., Strain, K., Couret, I., and Bryden, K. (1990). Controlled English for international technical communication. *Proc. Human Factors Society 34th Annual Meeting*, 815–819.

Klare, G. R. (1984). Readability. In Pearson, P. D. (Ed.), *Handbook of Reading Research*. Longman, New York, NY. 681–744.

Kurlander, D., and Feiner, S. (1992). A history-based macro by example system. *Proc. ACM UIST'92 Symposium on User Interface Software and Technology* (Monterey, CA, 15–18 November), 99–106.

Kurtenbach, G., and Hulteen, E. A. (1990). Gestures in human–computer communication. In Laurel, B. (Ed.), *The Art of Human–Computer Interface Design*, Addison-Wesley, Reading, MA. 309–317.

L

LaLomia, M. J., and Sidowski, J. B. (1990). Measurements of computer satisfaction, literacy, and aptitudes: A review. *Intl. J. Human–Computer Interaction* **2**, 3, 231–253.

LaLomia, M. J., and Sidowski, J. B. (1991). Measurements of computer attitudes: A review. *Intl. J. Human–Computer Interaction* **3**, 2, 171–197.

Lamb, J. (1988). Computer crashes and stranded travellers—air traffic control in Britain. *New Scientist* (8 September), 65.

Landauer, T. K. (1988a). Relations between cognitive psychology and computer system design. In Carroll, J. M. (Ed.), *Interfacing Thought: Cognitive Aspects of Human–Computer Interaction*. MIT Press, Cambridge, MA. 1–25.

Landauer, T. K. (1988b). Research methods in human–computer interaction. In Helander, M. (Ed.), *Handbook of Human–Computer Interaction*. North-Holland, Amsterdam, The Netherlands. 905–928.

Landauer, T. K. (1994). *The Trouble with Computers: Usefulness, Usability and Productivity*. Book under preparation.

Landauer, T. K., and Nachbar, D. W. (1985). Selection from alphabetic and numeric menu trees using a touch screen: Breadth, depth and width. *Proc. ACM CHI'85 Conf.* (San Francisco, CA, 14–18 April), 73–78.

Lederer, A. L., and Prasad, J. (1992). Nine management guidelines for better cost estimating. *Communications of the ACM* **35**, 2 (February), 51–59.

Lee, A. (1992). User support: Considerations, features, and issues. In Hartson, H. R., and Hix, D. (Eds.), *Advances in Human–Computer Interaction* **Vol. 3**, Ablex, Norwood, NJ. 184–228.

Lee, J. A. N., McCarthy, J., and Licklider, J. C. R. (1992). Time-sharing at MIT. *IEEE Annals of the History of Computing* **14**, 1, 13–32.

Lee, M. P., Darling, M. W. M., Peacock, D., and Jeffreys, S. (1990). Simulating user interfaces with dBase III+. In Life, M. A., Narborough-Hall, C. S., and Hamilton, W. I. (Eds.), *Simulation and the User Interface*. Taylor & Francis, London, U.K. 181–195.

LeFevre, J.-A., and Dixon, P. (1986). Do written instructions need examples? *Cognition and Instruction* 3, 1, 1–30.

Lehmann, E. L., and D'Abrera, H. J. M. (1975). *Nonparametrics: Statistical Methods Based on Ranks*. Holden-Day Inc., San Francisco, CA.

Lewis, C. (1982). Using the 'thinking-aloud' method in cognitive interface design. *Research Report RC9265*, IBM T. J. Watson Research Center, Yorktown Heights, NY.

Lewis, C., Hair, D., and Schoenberg, V. (1989). Generalization, consistency, and control. *Proc. ACM CHI'89 Conf.* (Austin, TX, 30 April–4 May), 1–5.

Lewis, C., Polson, P., Wharton, C., and Rieman, J. (1990). Testing a walk-through methodology for theory-based design of walk-up-and-use interfaces. *Proc. ACM CHI'90 Conf.* (Seattle, WA, 1–5 April), 235–241.

Lewis, J. R. (1992). Psychometric evaluation of the post-study system usability questionnaire: The PSSUQ. *Proc. Human Factors Society 36th Annual Meeting*, 1259–1263.

Licklider, J. C. R. (1960). Man–computer symbiosis. *IRE Trans. Human Factors in Electronics* 1, 1 (March), 4–11.

Life, M. A., Narborough-Hall, C. S., and Hamilton, W. I. (Eds.) (1990). *Simulation and the User Interface*. Taylor & Francis, London, U.K.

Lindgaard, G. (1991). Impressions from HUSAT. *CHISIG Newsletter* (Computer–Human Interaction Special Interest Group of the Ergonomics Society of Australia) (August), 1–2.

Lindgaard, G., Chessari, J., and Ihsen, E. (1987). Icons in telecommunications: What makes pictorial information comprehensible to the user? *Australian Telecommunication Research* 21, 2, 17–29.

Lodding, K. N. (1983). Iconic interfacing. *IEEE Computer Graphics and Applications* 3, 2 (March–April), 11–20.

Loshe, G., Walker, N., Biolsi, K., and Rueter, H. (1991). Classifying graphical information. *Behaviour & Information Technology* 10, 5, 419–436.

Löwgren, J., and Nordqvist, T. (1992). Knowledge-based evaluation as design support for graphical user interfaces. *Proc. ACM CHI'92 Conf.* (Monterey, CA, 3–7 May), 181–188.

Lund, A. M. (1994). Ameritech's usability laboratory: From prototype to final design. *Behaviour & Information Technology* 13, 1&2 (January–April), 67–80.

Lunde, K. (1993). *Understanding Japanese Information Processing*. O'Reilly and Associates, Inc.

M

Mack, R. L., and Burdett, J. M. (1992). When novices elicit knowledge: Question-asking in designing, evaluating and learning to use software. In Hoffman, R. (Ed.), *The Psychology of Expertise: Cognitive Research and Empirical AI.* Springer-Verlag, New York, NY. 245–268.

Mack, R. L., and Nielsen, J. (1987). Software integration in the professional work environment: Observations on requirements, usage, and interface issues. *Research Report* **RC12677**, IBM T. J. Watson Research Center, Yorktown Heights, NY.

Mack, R. L., and Nielsen, J. (1993). Usability inspection methods. *ACM SIGCHI Bulletin* **25**, 1 (January), 28–33.

Mack, R. L., Lewis, C. H., and Carroll, J. M. (1983). Learning to use word processors: Problems and prospects. *ACM Trans. Office Information Systems* **1**, 3 (July), 254–271.

Mackay, W. E., and Tatar, D. G. (1989). Introduction to this special issue on video as a research and design tool. *ACM SIGCHI Bulletin* **21**, 2 (October), 48–50.

Mackinlay, J. (1988). Applying a theory of graphical presentation to the graphic design of user interfaces. *Proc. ACM UIST'88 First Symposium User Interface Software and Technology* (Banff, Canada, 17–19 October), 179–189.

MacLean, A., Young, R. M., and Moran, T. P. (1989). Design rationale: The argument behind the artifact. *Proc. ACM CHI'89 Conf.* (Austin, TX, 30 April–4 May), 247–252.

MacLean, A., Bellotti, V., Young, R. M., and Moran, T. P. (1991a). Reaching through analogy: A design rationale perspective. *Proc. ACM CHI'91 Conf.* (New Orleans, LA, 28 April–2 May), 167–172.

MacLean, A., Bellotti, V., and Moran, T. P. (1991b). Questions, options, and criteria: Elements of design space analysis. *Human–Computer Interaction* **6**, 3 and 4, 201–250.

Magyar, R. L. (1990). Assessing the icon appropriateness and icon discriminability with a paired-comparison testing procedure. *Proc. Human Factors Society 34th Annual Meeting*, 1204–1208.

Mahajan, V., Muller, E., and Srivastava, R. K. (1990). Determination of adopter categories by using innovation diffusion models. *Journal of Marketing Research* **27**, 1 (February), 37–50.

Mantei, M. M. (1989). An HCI continuing education curriculum for industry. *ACM SIGCHI Bulletin* **20**, 3 (January), 16–18.

Mantei, M. M. (1990). The Strauss mouse (videotape). *SIGGRAPH Video Review* **56**, Association for Computing Machinery, New York, NY.

Mantei, M. M., and Teorey, T. J. (1988). Cost/benefit analysis for incorporating human factors in the software lifecycle. *Communications of the ACM* **31**, 4 (April), 428–439.

Mantei, M. M., Hewett, T., Eason, K., and Preece, J. (1991). Report on the INTERACT'90 workshop on education in HCI: Transcending disciplinary and national boundaries. *Interacting with Computers* **3**, 2, 232–240.

Marchionini, G. (1989). Making the transition from print to electronic encyclopedia: Adaptation of mental models. *Intl. J. Man–Machine Studies* **30**, 6 (June), 591–618.

Marcus, A. (1992). *Graphic Design for Electronic Documents and User Interfaces*. Addison-Wesley, Reading, MA.

Margono, S., and Shneiderman, B. (1987). A study of file manipulation by novices using commands vs. direct manipulation. *Proc. ACM D.C. Chapter 6th Annual Technical Symposium* (Washington, DC, 11 June).

Marshall, C., Nelson, C., and Gardiner, M. M. (1987). Design guidelines. In Gardiner, M. M., and Christie, B. (Eds.), *Applying Cognitive Psychology to User-Interface Design*. John Wiley & Sons, Chichester, U.K. 221–278.

Maulsby, D., Greenberg, S., and Mander, R. (1993). Prototyping an intelligent agent through Wizard of Oz. *Proc. ACM INTERCHI'93 Conf.* (Amsterdam, The Netherlands, 24–29 April), 277–284.

Mayes, J. T., Draper, S. W., McGregor, A. M., and Oatley, K. (1988). Information flow in a user interface: The effect of experience and context on the recall of MacWrite screens. In Jones, D. M., and Winder, R. (Eds.), *People and Computers IV*. Cambridge University Press, Cambridge, U.K. 275–289.

Mayhew, D. J. (1992). *Principles and Guidelines in Software User Interface Design*. Prentice Hall, Englewood Cliffs, NJ.

McClelland, I. L., and Brigham, F. R. (1990). Marketing ergonomics—how should ergonomics be packaged? *Ergonomics* **33**, 5, 519–526.

McCrobie, D. (1989). Human factors design considerations for military trains. *Proc. Human Factors Society 33rd Annual Meeting*, 536–540.

McDonald, J. E., and Schvaneveldt, R. W. (1988). The application of user knowledge to interface design. In Guindon, R. (Ed.), *Cognitive Science and its Applications for Human–Computer Interaction*, Lawrence Erlbaum Associates, Hillsdale, NJ. 289–338.

McDonald, J. E., Molander, M. E., and Noel, R. W. (1988). Color-coding categories in menus. *Proc. ACM CHI'88 Conf.* (Washington, DC, 15–19 May), 101–106.

Mercurio, P. J., and Erickson, T. D. (1990). Interactive scientific visualization: An assessment of a virtual reality system. *Proc. INTERACT'90 Third IFIP Conference Human–Computer Interaction* (Cambridge, U.K., 27–31 August), 741–745.

Merwin, D. H., Dyre, B. P., Humphrey, D. G., Grimes, J., and Larish, J. F. (1990). The impact of icons and visual effects on learning computer databases. *Proc. Human Factors Society 34th Annual Meeting* (Orlando, FL, 8–12 October), 424–428.

Miller, R. B. (1968). Response time in man–computer conversational transactions. *Proc. AFIPS Spring Joint Computer Conference* **Vol. 33**, 267–277.

Mirel, B. (1991). Critical review of experimental research on the usability of hard copy documentation. *IEEE Trans. Professional Communication* **34**, 2 (June), 109–122.

Molich, R., and Nielsen, J. (1990). Improving a human–computer dialogue. *Communications of the ACM* **33**, 3 (March), 338–348.

Monk, A. (1986). Mode errors: A user-centered analysis and some preventative measures using keying-contingent sounds. *Intl. J. Man–Machine Studies* **24**, 4 (April), 313–327.

Monk, A. (1989). The personal browser: A tool for directed navigation in hypertext systems. *Interacting with Computers* **1**, 2 (August), 190–196.

Monmonier, M. (1991). *How to Lie with Maps*. The University of Chicago Press, Chicago, IL.

Moran, T. P., and Carroll, J. M. (Eds.) (1994). *Design Rationale*. Lawrence Erlbaum Associates, Hillsdale, NJ.

Mosier, J. N., and Smith, S. L. (1986). Application of guidelines for designing user interface software. *Behaviour & Information Technology* **5**, 1 (January–March), 39–46.

Mrazek, D., and Rafeld, M. (1992). Integrating human factors on a large scale: 'Product usability champions.' *Proc. ACM CHI'92 Conf.* (Monterey, CA, 3–7 May), 565–570.

Muller, M. J. (1991). PICTIVE—An exploration in participatory design. *Proc. ACM CHI'91 Conf.* (New Orleans, La, 28 April–2 May), 225–231.

Muller, M. J. (1992). Retrospective on a year of participatory design using the PICTIVE technique. *Proc. ACM CHI'92 Conf.* (Monterey, CA, 3–7 May), 455–462.

Mulligan, R. M., Altom, M. W., and Simkin, D. K. (1991). User interface design in the trenches: Some tips on shooting from the hips. *Proc. ACM CHI'91 Conf.* (New Orleans, LA, 28 April–2 May), 232–236.

Mulligan, R. M., Dieli, M., Nielsen, J., Poltrock, S., Rosenberg, D., and Rudman, S. E. (1992). Designing usable systems under real-world constraints: A practitioners forum. *Proc. ACM CHI'92 Conf.* (Monterey, CA, 3–7 May), 149–152.

Mullins, P. M., and Treu, S. (1991). Measurement of stress to gauge user satisfaction with features of the computer interface. *Behaviour & Information Technology* **10**, 4 (July–August), 325–343.

Myers, B. A. (1985). The importance of percent-done progress indicators for computer–human interfaces. *Proc. ACM CHI'85 Conf.* (San Francisco, CA, 14–18 April), 11–17.

Myers, B. A. (1989). User-interface tools: Introduction and survey. *IEEE Software* **6**, 1 (January), 15–23.

Myers, B. A., and Rosson, M. B. (1992). Survey on user interface programming. *Proc. ACM CHI'92 Conf.* (Monterey, CA, 3–7 May), 195–202.

Mynatt, E. D., and Edwards, W. K. (1992). Mapping GUIs to auditory interfaces. *Proc. ACM UIST'92 Symposium on User Interface Software and Technology* (Monterey, CA, 15–18 November), 61–70.

N

Nagel, D. C. (1988). Human error in aviation operations. In Weiner, E. L., and Nagel, D. C. (Eds.), *Human Factors in Aviation*. Academic Press, Boston, MA. 263–303.

Nardi, B. A., and Miller, J. R. (1991). Twinkling lights and nested loops: Distributed problem solving and spreadsheet development. *Intl. J. Man–Machine Studies* **34**, 2 (February), 161–184.

Neal, A. S., and Simons, R. M. (1983). Playback: A method for evaluating the usability of software and its documentation. *Proc. ACM CHI'83 Conf.* (Boston, MA, 12–15 December), 78–82.

Neal, A. S., and Simons, R. M. (1984). Playback: A method for evaluating the usability of software and its documentation. *IBM Systems Journal* **23**, 1, 82–96.

Neumann, P. G. (1991). Inside RISKS: Putting on your best interface. *Communications of the ACM* **34**, 3 (March), 138.

Newell, A. F. (1993). Interfaces for the ordinary and beyond. *IEEE Software* **10**, 5 (September), 76–78.

Nicol, A. (1990). Interfaces for learning: What do good teachers know that we don't? In Laurel, B. (Ed.), *The Art of Human–Computer Interface Design*. Addison-Wesley, Reading, MA. 113–122.

Nielsen, J. (1986). A virtual protocol model for computer–human interaction. *Intl. J. Man–Machine Studies* **24**, 3, 301–312.

Nielsen, J. (1987a). Using scenarios to develop user friendly videotex systems. *Proc. NordDATA'87 Joint Scandinavian Computer Conference* (Trondheim, Norway, 15–18 June), 133–138.

Nielsen, J. (1987b). A user interface case study of the Macintosh. In Salvendy, G. (Ed.), *Cognitive Engineering in the Design of Human–Computer Interaction and Expert Systems*, Elsevier Science Publishers, Amsterdam. 241–248.

Nielsen, J. (1987c). Classification of dialog techniques. *ACM SIGCHI Bulletin* **19**, 2 (October), 30–35.

Nielsen, J. (1989a). Prototyping user interfaces using an object-oriented hypertext programming system. *Proc. NordDATA'89 Joint Scandinavian Computer Conference* (Copenhagen, Denmark, 19–22 June), 485–490.

Nielsen, J. (1989b). Usability engineering at a discount. In Salvendy, G., and Smith, M. J. (Eds.), *Designing and Using Human–Computer Interfaces and Knowledge Based Systems*. Elsevier Science Publishers, Amsterdam, The Netherlands. 394–401.

Nielsen, J. (1989c). *Coordinating User Interfaces for Consistency.* Academic Press, Boston, MA.

Nielsen, J. (1989d). The matters that really matter for hypertext usability. *Proc. ACM Hypertext'89 Conf.* (Pittsburgh, PA, 5–8 November), 239–248.

Nielsen, J. (1989e). What do users really want? *Intl. J. Human–Computer Interaction* **1**, 2, 137–147.

Nielsen, J. (1990a). *Hypertext and Hypermedia.* Academic Press, Boston, MA.

Nielsen, J. (1990b). Big paybacks from 'discount' usability engineering. *IEEE Software* **7**, 3 (May), 107–108.

Nielsen, J. (1990c). A meta-model for interacting with computers. *Interacting with Computers* **2**, 2 (August), 147–160.

Nielsen, J. (1990d). Paper versus computer implementations as mockup scenarios for heuristic evaluation. *Proc. IFIP INTERACT'90 Third Intl. Conf. Human–Computer Interaction* (Cambridge, U.K., 27–31 August), 315–320.

Nielsen, J. (1990e). Traditional dialogue design applied to modern user interfaces. *Communications of the ACM* **33**, 10 (October), 109–118.

Nielsen, J. (1990f). *Designing User Interfaces for International Use.* Elsevier Science Publishers, Amsterdam, The Netherlands.

Nielsen, J. (1990g). Miniatures versus icons as a visual cache for videotex browsing. *Behaviour & Information Technology* **9**, 6 (Nov.–Dec.), 441–449.

Nielsen, J. (1990h). International user interfaces: An exercise. *ACM SIGCHI Bulletin* **21**, 4 (April), 50–51.

Nielsen, J. (1990i). The art of navigating through hypertext. *Communications of the ACM* **33**, 3 (March), 296–310.

Nielsen, J. (1992a). Evaluating the thinking aloud technique for use by computer scientists. In Hartson, H. R., and Hix, D. (Eds.), *Advances in Human–Computer Interaction* **Vol. 3**, Ablex, Norwood, NJ. 69–82.

Nielsen, J. (1992b). The usability engineering life cycle. *IEEE Computer* **25**, 3 (March), 12–22.

Nielsen, J. (1992c). Finding usability problems through heuristic evaluation. *Proc. ACM CHI'92 Conf.* (Monterey, CA, 3–7 May), 373–380.

Nielsen, J. (1993a). Noncommand user interfaces. *Communications of the ACM* **36**, 4 (April), 83–99.

Nielsen, J. (1993b). Iterative user interface design. *IEEE Computer* **26**, 11 (November), 32–41.

Nielsen, J. (1994a). Usability laboratories. *Behaviour & Information Technology* **13**, 1&2 (January–April), 3–8.

Nielsen, J. (1994b). Heuristic evaluation. In Nielsen, J., and Mack, R. L. (Eds.), *Usability Inspection Methods.* John Wiley & Sons, New York, NY. 25–62.

Nielsen, J. (1994c). Guerrilla HCI: Using discount usability engineering to penetrate the intimidation barrier. In Bias, R. G., and Mayhew, D. J. (Eds.), *Cost-Justifying Usability.* Academic Press, Boston, MA.

Nielsen, J. (1994d). Enhancing the explanatory power of usability heuristics. *Proc. ACM CHI'94 Conf.* (Boston, MA, April 24–28).

Nielsen, J., and Landauer, T. K. (1993). A mathematical model of the finding of usability problems. *Proc. ACM INTERCHI'93 Conf.* (Amsterdam, The Netherlands, 24–29 April), 206–213.

Nielsen, J., and Levy, J. (1994). Measuring usability—preference vs. performance. *Communications of the ACM* **37**, 4 (April).

Nielsen, J., and Lyngbæk, U. (1990). Two field studies of hypermedia usability. In McAleese, R., and Green, C. (Eds.), *Hypertext: State of the Art.* Ablex, Norwood, NJ. 64–72.

Nielsen, J., and Mack, R. L. (1994). *Usability Inspection Methods.* John Wiley & Sons, New York, NY.

Nielsen, J., and Molich, R. (1989). Teaching user interface design based on usability engineering. *ACM SIGCHI Bulletin* **21**, 1 (July), 45–48.

Nielsen, J., and Molich, R. (1990). Heuristic evaluation of user interfaces. *Proc. ACM CHI'90 Conf.* (Seattle, WA, 1–5 April), 249–256.

Nielsen, J., and Phillips, V. L. (1993). Estimating the relative usability of two interfaces: Heuristic, formal, and empirical methods compared. *Proc. ACM INTERCHI'93 Conf.* (Amsterdam, The Netherlands, 24–29 April), 214–221.

Nielsen, J., and Richards, J. T. (1989). The experience of learning and using Smalltalk. *IEEE Software* **6**, 3 (May), 73–77.

Nielsen, J., and Schaefer, L. (1993). Sound effects as an interface element for older users. *Behaviour & Information Technology* **12**, 4 (July–August), 208–215.

Nielsen, J., Mack, R. L., Bergendorff, K. H., and Grischkowsky, N. L. (1986). Integrated software in the professional work environment: Evidence from questionnaires and interviews. *Proc. ACM CHI'86 Conf.* (Boston, MA, 13–17 April), 162–167.

Nielsen, J., Frehr, I., and Nymand, H. O. (1991). The learnability of HyperCard as an object-oriented programming system. *Behaviour & Information Technology* **10**, 2 (March–April), 111–120.

Nielsen, J., Bush, R. M., Dayton, T., Mond, N. E., Muller, M. J., and Root, R. W. (1992). Teaching experienced developers to design graphical user interfaces. *Proc. ACM CHI'92 Conf.* (Monterey, CA, 3–7 May), 557–564.

Nielsen, J., Desurvire, H., Kerr, R., Rosenberg, D., Salomon, G., Molich, R., and Stewart, T. (1993). Comparative design review: An exercise in parallel design. *Proc. ACM INTERCHI'93 Conf.* (Amsterdam, The Netherlands, 24–29 April), 414–417.

Nielsen, J., Fernandes, T., Wagner, A., Wolf, R., and Ehrlich, K. (1994). Diversified parallel design: Contrasting design aproaches. *ACM CHI'94 Conference Companion* (Boston, MA, April 24–28).

Nolan, P. R. (1989). Designing screen icons: Ranking and matching studies. *Proc. Human Factors Society 33rd Annual Meeting*, 380–384.

Nolan, P. R. (1991). The design of keyboard templates. *Proc. Human Factors Society 35th Annual Meeting*, 486–490.

Norman, D. A. (1983). Design rules based on analyses of human error. *Communications of the ACM* **26**, 4 (April), 254–258.

Nussbaum, B., and Neff, R. (1991). I can't work this thing. *Business Week* (29 April), 58–66.

Nyce, J. M., and Kahn, P. (Eds.) (1991). *From Memex to Hypertext: Vannevar Bush and the Mind's Machine.* Academic Press, Boston, MA.

Nygren, E., Lind, M., Johnson, M., and Sandblad, B. (1992). The art of the obvious. *Proc. ACM CHI'92 Conf.* (Monterey, CA, 3–7 May), 235–239.

O

O'Donnell, P. J., Scobie, G., and Baxter, I. (1991). The use of focus groups as an evaluation technique in HCI. In Diaper, D., and Hammond, N. (Eds.), *People and Computers VI.* Cambridge University Press, Cambridge, U.K. 211–224.

Olsen, D. R. (1990). Propositional production systems for dialog description. *Proc. ACM CHI'90 Conf.* (Seattle, WA, 1–5 April), 57–63.

Olsen, D. R. (1991). *User Interface Management Systems: Models and Algorithms.* Morgan Kaufmann Publishers, San Mateo, CA.

Olsen, D. R. (1992). Bookmarks: An enhanced scroll bar. *ACM Trans. Graphics* **11**, 3 (July), 291–295.

Olsen, D. R., and Halversen, B. W. (1988). Interface usage measurements in a user interface management system. *Proc. ACM UIST'88 First Symposium User Interface Software and Technology* (Banff, Canada, 17–19 October), 102–108.

Olson, J. R., and Nilsen, E. (1987–88). Analysis of the cognition involved in spreadsheet software interaction. *Human–Computer Interaction* **3**, 4, 309–349.

Olson, J. R., and Olson, G. M. (1990). The growth of cognitive modeling in human–computer interaction since GOMS. *Human–Computer Interaction* **5**, 2 and 3, 221–265.

O'Malley, C. E., Draper, S. W., and Riley, M. S. (1984). Constructive interaction: A method for studying human–computer–human interaction. *Proc. IFIP INTERACT'84 First Intl. Conf. Human–Computer Interaction* (London, U.K., 4–7 September), 269–274.

P

Paap, K. R., and Roske-Hofstrand, R. J. (1988). Design of menus. In Helander, M. (Ed.), *Handbook of Human–Computer Interaction*. North-Holland, Amsterdam. 205–235.

Pausch, R. (1991). Virtual reality on five dollars a day. In *Proc. ACM CHI'91 Conf.* (New Orleans, LA, 28 April–2 May), 265–270.

Payne, S. J., and Green, T. R. G. (1986). Task-action grammars: A model of the mental representation of task languages. *Human–Computer Interaction* **2**, 2, 93–133.

Payne, S. J., and Green, T. R. G. (1989). The structure of command languages: An experiment on task-action grammar. *Intl. J. Man–Machine Studies* **30**, 2, 213–234.

Pedhazur, E. J., and Schmelkin, L. P. (1991). *Measurement, Design, and Analysis: An Integrated Approach*. Lawrence Erlbaum Associates, Hillsdale, NJ.

Perlman, G. (1988). Teaching user interface development to software engineers. *Proc. Human Factors Society 32nd Annual Meeting*, 391–394.

Perlman, G. (1989). Coordinating consistency of user interfaces, code, online help, and documentation with multilingual/multitarget software specification. In Nielsen, J. (Ed.), *Coordinating User Interfaces for Consistency*, Academic Press, Boston, MA. 35–55.

Perlman, G. (1990). Teaching user-interface development. *IEEE Software* **7**, 6 (November), 85–86.

Perlman, G. (1991). The HCI bibliography project, *ACM SIGCHI Bulletin* **23**, 3 (July), 15–20.

Perratore, E., Thompson, T., Udell, J., and Malloy, R. (1993). Fighting fatware. *BYTE* **18**, 4 (April), 98–108.

Perry, T. S., and Voelcker, J. (1989). Of mice and menus: Designing the user-friendly interface. *IEEE Spectrum* **29**, 9 (September), 46–51.

Peterson, J. L. (1980). Computer programs for detecting and correcting spelling errors. *Communications of the ACM* **23**, 12 (December), 676–687.

Polson, P. G. (1988). The consequences of consistent and inconsistent user interfaces. In Guindon, R. (Ed.), *Cognitive Science and its Applications for Human–Computer Interaction*, Lawrence Erlbaum Associates, Hillsdale, NJ. 59–108.

Polson, P. G., Muncher, E., and Engelbeck, G. (1986). A test of a common elements theory of transfer. *Proc. ACM CHI'86 Conf.* (Boston, MA, 13–17 April), 78–83.

Poltrock, S. E. (1994). Participant-observer studies of user interface design and development. In Rudisill, M., McKay, T., Lewis, C., and Polson, P. (Eds.), *Human–Computer Interface Design: Success Cases, Emerging Methods, and Real-World Context*, Morgan Kaufmann Publishers, San Francisco, CA.

Potosnak, K. M., Hayes, P. J., Rosson, M. B., Schneider, M. L., and Whiteside, J. A. (1986). Classifying users: A hard look at some controversial issues. *Proc. ACM CHI'86 Conf.* (Boston, MA, 13–17 April), 84–88.

Potter, S. S., Cook, R. I., Woods, D. D., and McDonald, J. S. (1990). The role of human factors guidelines in designing usable systems: A case study of operating room equipment. *Proc. Human Factors Society 34th Annual Meeting* (Orlando, FL, 8–12 October), 392–395.

Preece, J., and Keller, L. S. (1990). Why, what and how? Issues in the development of an HCI training course. *Proc. IFIP INTERACT'90 Third Intl. Conf. Human–Computer Interaction* (Cambridge, U.K., 27–31 August), 3–7.

Preece, J., and Keller, L. S. (1991). Teaching the practitioners: Developing a distance learning postgraduate HCI course. *Interacting with Computers* **3**, 1, 92–118.

R

Ramsey, H. R., and Grimes, J. D. (1983). Human factors in interactive computer dialog. In Williams, M. E. (Ed.), *Annual Review of Information Science and Technology* **18**, American Society for Information Science, 29–59.

Rappaport, A. S., and Halevi, S. (1991). The computerless computer company. *Harvard Business Review* **69**, 4 (July–August), 69–80.

Rasmussen, J. (1983). Skills, rules, and knowledge: Signals, signs, and symbols, and other distinctions in human performance models. *IEEE Trans. Systems, Man, and Cybernetics* **13**, 3 (May/June), 257–266.

Rauterberg, M. (1992). An empirical comparison of menu-selection (CUI) and desktop (GUI) computer programs carried out by beginners and experts. *Behaviour & Information Technology* **11**, 4 (July–August), 227–236.

Reason, J. (1990). *Human Error.* Cambridge University Press, Cambridge, U.K.

Reed, S. (1992). Who defines usability? You do! *PC/Computing* **5**, 12 (December), 220–232.

Reisner, P. (1981). Formal grammar and human factors design of an interactive graphics system. *IEEE Trans. Software Engineering* **SE-7**, 2, 229–240.

Reisner, P. (1990). What is inconsistency? *Proc. IFIP INTERACT'90 Third Intl. Conf. Human–Computer Interaction* (Cambridge, U.K., 27–31 August), 175–181.

Reitman, P. (1988). Streamlining your documentation using quick references. *IEEE Trans. Professional Communication* **31**, 2 (June), 75–83.

Rettig, M. (1991). Nobody reads documentation. *Communications of the ACM* **34**, 7 (July), 19–24.

Rheingold, H. (1985). *Tools for Thought: The People and Ideas Behind the Next Computer Revolution.* Simon and Schuster, New York, NY.

Rheingold, H. (1991). *Virtual Reality.* Summit Books, NY.

Rhyne, J. R., and Wolf, C. G. (1993). Recognition-based user interfaces. In Hartson, H. R., and Hix, D. (Eds.), *Advances in Human–Computer Interaction Vol. 4.* Ablex, Norwood, NJ. 191–250.

Rice, J. F. (1991). Display color coding: 10 rules of thumb. *IEEE Software* **8**, 1 (January), 86–88.

Rideout, T. (1991). Changing your methods from the inside. *IEEE Software* **8**, 3 (May), 99–100, 111.

Roach, J. W., and Nickson, M. (1983). Formal specifications for modeling and developing human/computer interfaces. *Proc. ACM CHI'83 Conf.* (Boston, MA, 12–15 December), 35–39.

Robertson, G. G., Card, S. K., and Mackinlay, J. D. (1993). Information visualization using 3D interactive animation. *Communications of the ACM* **36**, 4 (April), 57–71.

Rock, I., and Palmer, S. (1990). The legacy of gestalt psychology. *Scientific American* **263**, 6 (December), 84–90.

Rogers, Y. (1986). Evaluating the meaningfulness of icon sets to represent command operations. In Harrison, M. D., and Monk, A. F. (Eds.), *People and Computers: Designing for Usability.* Cambridge University Press, Cambridge, U.K. 586–603.

Rogers, Y. (1989). Icons at the interface: Their usefulness. *Interacting with Computers* **1**, 1 (April), 105–117.

Root, R. W., and Draper, S. (1983). Questionnaires as a software evaluation tool. *Proc. ACM CHI'83 Conf.* (Boston, MA, 12–15 December), 83–87.

Rosenberg, D. (1989). A cost benefit analysis for corporate user interface standards: What price to pay for a consistent 'look and feel'? In Nielsen, J. (Ed.), *Coordinating User Interfaces for Consistency.* Academic Press, Boston, MA. 21–34.

Rosenberg, J. K., and Moran, T. P. (1984). Generic commands. In *Proc. INTERACT'84 First IFIP Conf. Human–Computer Interaction* (London, U.K., 4–7 September), 245–249.

Rosson, M. B. (1984). Effects of experience on learning, using, and evaluating a text-editor. *Human Factors* **26**, 4 (August), 463–475.

Rowley, D. E., and Rhoades, D. G. (1992). The cognitive jogthrough: A fast-paced user interface evaluation procedure. *Proc. ACM CHI'92 Conf.* (Monterey, CA, 3–7 May), 389–395.

Russo, P., and Boor, S. (1993). How fluent is your interface? Designing for international users. *Proc. ACM INTERCHI'93 Conf.* (Amsterdam, The Netherlands, 24–29 April), 342–347.

S

Salasoo, A. (1990). Towards usable icon sets: A case study from telecommunications engineering. *Proc. Human Factors Society 34th Annual Meeting*, 203–207.

Sandewall, E. (1978). Programming in the interactive environment: The LISP experience. *ACM Computing Surveys* **10**, 1 (March), 35–71.

Sassone, P. G. (1987). Cost–benefit methodology for office systems. *ACM Trans. Office Information Systems* **5**, 3 (July), 273–289.

Schiele, F., and Green, T. (1990). HCI formalisms and cognitive psychology: The case of task–action grammar. In Harrison, M., and Thimbleby, H. (Eds.), *Formal Methods in Human–Computer Interaction*. Cambridge University Press, Cambridge, U.K. 9–62.

Schleifer, L. M. (1990). System response time and method of pay: Cardiovascular stress effects in computer-based tasks. *Ergonomics* **33**, 1495–1509.

Schmidt, K. (1988). Functional analysis instrument. In Schaefer, G., Hirschheim, R., Harper, M., Hansjee, R., Domke, M., and Bjørn-Andersen, N. (Eds.), *Functional Analysis of Office Requirements: A Multiperspective Approach*. Wiley, Chichester, U.K. 261–289.

Schrier, J. R. (1992). Reducing stress associated with participating in a usability test. *Proc. Human Factors Society 36th Annual Meeting*, 1210–1214.

Sculley, J. (1992). Interview. *Forbes ASAP Magazine* (December 7), 93–100.

Sein, M. K., and Bostrom, R. P. (1989). Individual differences and conceptual models in training novice users. *Human–Computer Interaction* **4**, 3, 197–229.

Seligmann, D. D., and Feiner, S. (1991). Automated generation of intent-based 3D illustrations. *Proc. ACM SIGGRAPH'91 Conf.* (Las Vegas, NV, 28 July–2 August), 123–132.

Sellen, A., and Nicol, A. (1990). Building user-centered online help. In Laurel, B. (Ed.), *The Art of Human–Computer Interface Design*, Addison-Wesley, Reading, MA. 143–153.

Sellen, A. J., Kurtenbach, G. P., and Buxton, W. A. S. (1990). The role of visual and kinesthetic feedback in the prevention of mode errors. *Proc. IFIP INTERACT'90 Third Intl. Conf. Human–Computer Interaction* (Cambridge, U.K., 27–31 August), 667–673.

Senay, H., and Stabler, E. P. (1987). Online help system usage: An empirical investigation. *Abridged Proceedings 2nd Intl. Conf. Human–Computer Interaction* (Honolulu, HI, 10–14 August), 244.

Senders, J. W., and Moray, N. P. (1991). *Human Error: Cause, Prediction, and Reduction*. Erlbaum, Hillsdale, NJ.

Shackel, B. (1971). Human factors in the P.L.A. meat handling automation scheme. A case study and some conclusions. *Intl. J. Prod. Res.* **9**, 1, 95–121.

Shackel, B. (1991). Usability—Context, framework, definition, design and evaluation. In Shackel, B., and Richardson, S. (Eds.), *Human Factors for Informatics Usability*. Cambridge University Press, Cambridge, U.K. 21–37.

Shackel, B., Alty, J. L., and Reid, P. (1992) HILITES—The information service for the world HCI community. *ACM SIGCHI Bulletin* **24**, 3 (July), 40–49.

Sheldon, K. M. (1991). ASCII goes global. *BYTE* **16**, 7 (July), 108–116.

Shneiderman, B. (1982). Designing computer system messages. *Communications of the ACM* **25**, 9 (September), 610–611.

Shneiderman, B. (1983). Direct manipulation: A step beyond programming languages. *IEEE Computer* **16**, 8 (August), 57–69.

Shneiderman, B. (1991). A taxonomy and rule base for the selection of interaction styles. In Shackel, B., and Richardson, S. (Eds.), *Human Factors for Informatics Usability.* Cambridge University Press, Cambridge, U.K. 325–342.

Shneiderman, B. (1993). Beyond intelligent machines: Just do it! *IEEE Software* **10**, 1 (January), 100–103.

Silverstein, L. D. (1987). Human factors for color display systems: Concepts, methods, and research. In Durrett, H. J. (Ed.), *Color and the Computer,* Academic Press, Boston, MA. 27–61.

Simonelli, N. M. (1989). Product design and human factors diversity: What you see is where you came from. In Klemmer, E. T. (Ed.), *Ergonomics: Harness the Power of Human Factors in Your Business.* Ablex, Norwood, NJ. 88–122.

Siochi, A. C., and Ehrich, R. W. (1991). Computer analysis of user interfaces based on repetition in transcripts of user sessions. *ACM Trans. Information Systems* **9**, 4 (October), 309–335.

Sless, D. (1991). Designing a new bill for Telecom Australia. *Information Design Journal* **6**, 3, 255–257.

Smith, S. L., and Mosier, J. N. (1986). *Design Guidelines for Designing User Interface Software.* Technical Report **MTR-10090**, The MITRE Corporation, Bedford, MA 01730, USA. See page 301 for information on downloading this report over the network.

Smith, W. (1988). Standardizing colors for computer screens. *Proc. Human Factors Society's 32nd Annual Meeting,* 1381–1385.

Søndergaard, G. (1987). *Oversigt over efternavne i Danmark* ("Survey of family names in Denmark"; in Danish), Nordic Institute, Odense University, Odense, Denmark.

Springer, C. J. (1987). Retrieval of information from complex alphanumeric displays: Screen formatting variables' effect on target identification time. In Salvendy, G. (Ed.), *Cognitive Engineering in the Design of Human–Computer Interaction and Expert Systems.* Elsevier Science Publishers, Amsterdam, The Netherlands. 375–382.

Sprung, R. C. (1990). Two faces of America: Polyglot and tongue-tied. In Nielsen, J. (Ed.), *Designing User Interfaces for International Use.* Elsevier Science Publishers, Amsterdam. 71–102.

Stammers, R. B., and Hoffman, J. (1991). Transfer between icon sets and ratings of icon concreteness and appropriateness. *Proc. Human Factors Society 35th Annual Meeting,* 354–258.

Steuer, J. (1992). Defining virtual reality: Dimensions determining telepresence. *Journal of Communication* **42**, 4 (Autumn), 73–93.

Stewart, T. (1990). SIOIS—Standard interfaces or interface standards. *Proc. IFIP INTERACT'90 Third Intl. Conf. Human–Computer Interaction* (Cambridge, U.K., 27–31 August), xxix–xxxiv.

Stotts, P. D., and Furuta, R. (1989). Petri-net-based hypertext: Document structure with browsing semantics. *ACM Transactions on Information Systems* **7**, 1 (January), 3–29.

Streeter, L. A., Ackroff, J. M., and Taylor, G. A. (1983). On abbreviating command names. *The Bell System Technical Journal* **62**, 1807–1828.

Strong, G. W. (1989). Introductory course in human computer interaction. *ACM SIGCHI Bulletin* **20**, 3 (January), 19–21.

Sukaviriya, P., and Foley, J. D. (1990). Coupling a UI framework with automatic generation of context-sensitive animated help. *Proc. ACM UIST'90 Third Annual Symposium on User Interface Software and Technology* (Snowbird, UT, 3–5 October), 21–30.

Sukaviriya, P., and Moran, L. (1990). User interface for Asia. In Nielsen, J. (Ed.), *Designing User Interfaces for International Use*. Elsevier Science Publishers, Amsterdam. 71–102.

Sutherland, I. E. (1963). Sketchpad: A man–machine graphical communication system. *Proc. AFIPS Spring Joint Computer Conference*, 329–346.

T

Tanaka, T., Eberts, R. E., and Salvendy, G. (1990). Derivation and validation of a quantitative method for the analysis of consistency for interface design. *Proc. Human Factors Society 34th Annual Meeting*, 329–333.

Teasley, B., Leventhal, L., Blumenthal, B., Instone, K., and Stone, D. (1994). Cultural diversity in user interface design: Are intuitions enough? *ACM SIGCHI Bulletin* **26**, 1 (January), 36–40.

Teitelman, W. (1972). Do what I mean: The programmer's assistant. *Computers and Automation* **21** (April), 8–11.

Teitelman, W. (1986). Ten years of window systems: A retrospective view. In Hopgood, F. R. A., Duce, D. A., Fielding, E. V. C., Robinson, K., and Williams, A. S. (Eds.), *Methodology of Window Management*. Springer-Verlag, Berlin, Germany. 35–46.

Telles, M. (1990). Updating an older interface. *Proc. ACM CHI'90 Conf.* (Seattle, WA, 1–5 April), 243–247.

Tesler, L. (1981). The Smalltalk environment. *BYTE* **6**, 8 (August), 90–147.

Tesler, L. G. (1991). Networked computing in the 1990s. *Scientific American* **265**, 3 (September), 86–93.

Tetzlaff, L., and Schwartz, D. R. (1991). The use of guidelines in interface design. *Proc. ACM CHI'91 Conf.* (New Orleans, LA, 28 April–2 May), 329–333.

Thomas, J. C., and Stuart, R. (1992). Virtual reality and human factors. *Proc. Human Factors Society 36th Annual Meeting*, 207–210.

Thompson, D. A., McEvers, D. C., and Olson, C. H. (1986). Case study in data entry system design. *Proc. Human Factors Society 30th Annual Meeting*, 744–748.

Thovtrup, H., and Nielsen, J. (1991). Assessing the usability of a user interface standard. *Proc. ACM CHI'91 Conf.* (New Orleans, LA, 28 April–2 May), 335–341.

Tognazzini, B. (1989). Achieving consistency for the Macintosh. In Nielsen, J. (Ed.), *Coordinating User Interfaces for Consistency,* Academic Press, Boston, MA. 57–73.

Tognazzini, B. (1990). User testing on the cheap. *Apple Direct* **2**, 6 (March), 21–27. Also available as Chapter 14 of Tognazzini, B. (1992), *Tog on Interface,* Addison-Wesley, Reading, MA.

Tombaugh, J., Lickorish, A., and Wright, P. (1987). Multi-window displays for readers of lengthy texts. *Intl. J. Man–Machine Studies* **26**, 5 (May), 597–615.

Tousséa-Oulaï, A., and Ura, S. (1991). Information technology transfer: Problems facing African developing nations. *Intl. J. Human–Computer Interaction* **3**, 1, 79–93.

Travis, D. (1991). *Effective Color Displays: Theory and Practice.* Academic Press, London, U.K.

Tucker, P., and Jones, D. M. (1991). Voice as interface: An overview. *Intl. J. Human–Computer Interaction* **3**, 2, 145–170.

Tullis, T. S. (1985). Designing a menu-based interface to an operating system. *Proc. ACM CHI'85 Conf.* (San Francisco, CA, 14–18 April), 79–84.

V

van der Veer, G. C., and White, T. N. (1990). University education on human–computer interaction—The Dutch situation. *Proc. IFIP INTERACT'90 Third Intl. Conf. Human–Computer Interaction* (Cambridge, U.K., 27–31 August), 9–13.

van Nes, F. L., and van Itegem, J. P. M. (1990). Hidden functionality: How an advanced car radio is really used. In *IPO Annual Progress Report* **25**, Institute for Perception Research, Eindhoven, The Netherlands. 101–112.

Vander Zanden, B., and Myers, B. A. (1990). Automatic, look-and-feel independent dialog creation for graphical user interfaces. *Proc. ACM CHI'90 Conf.* (Seattle, WA, 1–5 April), 27–34.

Vertelney, L. (1989). Using video to prototype user interfaces. *ACM SIGCHI Bulletin* **21**, 2 (October), 57–61.

Vincente, K. J., and Williges, R. C. (1988). Accommodating individual differences in searching a hierarchical file system. *Intl. J. Man–Machine Studies* **29**, 6, 647–668.

Virzi, R. A. (1989). What can you learn from a low-fidelity prototype? *Proc. Human Factors Society 33rd Annual Meeting* (Denver, CO, 16–20 October), 224–228.

Virzi, R. A. (1991). A preference evaluation of three dialing plans for a residential, phone-based information service. *Proc. Human Factors Society 35th Annual Meeting* (San Francisco, CA, 2–6 September).

Voltaire, F. M. A. (1764). *Dictionnaire Philosophique.* English translation published in 1765 as *Philosophical Dictionary.*

von Hippel, E. (1988). *The Sources of Innovation.* Oxford University Press, New York, NY.

W

Walker, J. H. (1987). Issues and strategies for online documentation. *IEEE Trans. Professional Communication* **30**, 4 (December), 235-248.

Want, R., Hopper, A., Falcão, V., and Gibbons, J. (1992). The active badge location system. *ACM Transactions on Information Systems* **10**, 1 (January), 91–102.

Wasserman, A. S. (1989). Redesigning Xerox: A design strategy based on operability. In Klemmer, E. T. (Ed.), *Ergonomics: Harness the Power of Human Factors in Your Business,* Ablex, Norwood, NJ. 7–44.

Wastell, D. (1990). Mental effort and task performance: Towards a psychophysiology of human computer interaction. *Proc. IFIP INTERACT'90 Third Intl. Conf. Human–Computer Interaction* (Cambridge, U.K., 27–31 August), 107–112.

Weiler, P., Cordes, R., Hammontree, M., Hoiem, D., and Thompson, M. (1993). Software for the usability lab: A sampling of current tools. *Proc. ACM INTERCHI'93 Conf.* (Amsterdam, The Netherlands, 24–29 April), 57–60.

Wellner, P. D. (1989). Statemaster: A UIMS based on statecharts for prototyping and target implementation. *Proc. ACM CHI'89 Conf.* (Austin, TX, 30 April–4 May), 177–182.

Wharton, C., Bradford, J., Jeffries, R., and Franzke, M. (1992). Applying cognitive walkthroughs to more complex user interfaces: Experiences, issues, and recommendations. *Proc. ACM CHI'92 Conf.* (Monterey, CA, 3–7 May), 381–388.

Whitefield, A., Wilson, F., and Dowell, J. (1991). A framework for human factors evaluation. *Behaviour & Information Technology* **10**, 1 (January–February), 65–79.

Whiteside, J., and Wixon, D. (1987). The dialectic of usability engineering. *Proc. IFIP INTERACT'87 Conf.* (Stuttgart, Germany, 1–4 September), 17–20.

Whiteside, J., Jones, S., Levy, P. S., and Wixon, D. (1985). User performance with command, menu, and iconic interfaces. *Proc. ACM CHI'85 Conf.* (San Francisco, CA, 14–18 April), 185–191.

Whiteside, J., Bennett, J., and Holtzblatt, K. (1988). Usability engineering: Our experience and evolution. In Helander, M. (Ed.), *Handbook of Human–Computer Interaction*, North-Holland, Amsterdam. 791–817.

Wichansky, A. M., Abernethy, C. N., Antonelli, D. C., Kotsonis, M. E., and Mitchell, P. P. (1988). Selling ease of use: Human factors partnerships with marketing. *Proc. Human Factors Society 32nd Annual Meeting*, 598–602.

Wiecha, C., and Boies, S. J. (1990). Generating user interfaces: Principles and use of ITS style rules. *Proc. ACM UIST'90 Third Annual Symposium on User Interface Software and Technology* (Snowbird, UT, 3–5 October), 21–30.

Wiecha, C. and Henrion, M. (1987). Linking multiple program views using a visual cache. *Proc. IFIP INTERACT'87 Second Intl. Conf. Human–Computer Interaction* (Stuttgart, Germany, 1–4 September), 689–694.

Wiecha, C., Bennett, W., Boies, S., and Gould, J. (1989). Tools for generating consistent user interfaces. In Nielsen, J. (Ed.), *Coordinating User Interfaces for Consistency*, Academic Press, Boston, MA. 107–130.

Wiggins, B. (1991). DTI Usability Now! programme. Talk presented at the British Computer Society's *HCI'91* conference (Edinburgh, U.K., 20–23 August).

Winograd, T. (1990). What can we teach about human–computer interaction. *Proc. ACM CHI'90 Conf.* (Seattle, WA, 1–5 April), 443–449.

Wixon, D., and Jones, S. (1994). Usability for fun and profit: A case study of the re-design of the VAX RALLY. In Rudisill, M., McKay, T., Lewis, C., and Polson, P. (Eds.), *Human–Computer Interface Design: Success Cases, Emerging Methods, and Real-World Context*, Morgan Kaufmann Publishers, San Francisco, CA.

Wixon, D., Jones, S., Tse, L., and Casaday, G. (1994). Inspections and design reviews: Framework, history, and reflection. In Nielsen, J., and Mack, R. L. (Eds.), *Usability Inspection Methods*. John Wiley & Sons, New York, NY.

Wolf, R. (1989). Consistency as process. In Nielsen, J. (Ed.), *Coordinating User Interfaces for Consistency*, Academic Press, Boston, MA. 89–92.

Wozny, L. A. (1989). The application of metaphor, analogy, and conceptual models in computer systems. *Interacting with Computers* **1**, 3, 273–283.

Wright, P. (1983). Manual dexterity: A user-oriented approach to creating computer documentation. *Proc. ACM CHI'83 Conf.* (Boston, MA, 12–15 December), 11–18.

Wright, P. (1991). Designing and evaluating documentation for I.T. users. In Shackel, B., and Richardson, S. (Eds.), *Human Factors for Informatics Usability*. Cambridge University Press, Cambridge, U.K. 343–358.

Wright, P. C., and Monk, A. F. (1991). A cost-effective evaluation method for use by designers. *Intl. J. Man–Machine Studies* **35**, 6 (December), 891–912.

Wright, R. B., and Converse, S. A. (1992). Method bias and concurrent verbal protocol in software usability testing. *Proc. Human Factors Society 36th Annual Meeting*, 1220–1224.

Y

Yang, Y. (1990). Interface usability engineering under practical constraints: A case study in the design of undo support. *Proc. IFIP INTERACT'90 Third Intl. Conf. Human–Computer Interaction* (Cambridge, U.K., 27–31 August), 549–554.

Yang, Y. (1992). Motivation, practice, and guidelines for 'undoing.' *Interacting with Computers* **4**, 1 (April), 23–40.

Young, D., Lansdale, M. W., and Bass, C. A. (1990). Using HyperTalk as a specification tool and a simulation vehicle in the development of a personal data base system. In Life, M. A., Narborough-Hall, C. S., and Hamilton, W. I. (Eds.), *Simulation and the User Interface*. Taylor & Francis, London, U.K. 169–180.

Z

Ziegler, J. E., Hoppe, H. U., and Fähnrich, K. P. (1986). Learning and transfer for text and graphics editing with a direct manipulation interface. *Proc. ACM CHI'86 Conf.* (Boston, MA, 13–17 April), 72–77.

Zwaga, H. J. (1989). Comprehensibility estimates of public information symbols: Their validity and use. *Proc. Human Factors Society 33rd Annual Meeting*, 979–983.

Author Index

Subject Index

Numerics

1-2-3 (spreadsheet) 216
2000, year 260

A

Abbreviations 13, 54, 139, 250
Abductive interfaces 61
Ablex 287
Absenteeism 111
Abstractions 261
Abstracts, machine-readable 305
Academic Press 287
Accelerators 41, 55, 139
Acceptability 24, 25
ACM 283, 284, 285, 287
   Communications of the 288
   Computing Reviews 304
   German chapter 285
   Guide to Computing Literature 304
   Interactions 287
   SIGCHI, *see* SIGCHI
   SIGDOC, *see* SIGDOC
   SIGGRAPH, *see* SIGGRAPH
   Transactions on Computer–Human
      Interaction 286
   Transactions on Graphics 288
   Transactions on Information Systems 288
   Transactions on Office Information
      Systems 288
   User interface magazine 287
Acronyms 23

Active badges 65
Actors 101
Adaptive indexing 126
Adaptive interfaces 66, 289
Added value 8
Adopters 266
Adrenaline 34
Advertising 50, 97
Aesthetics 39
Africa 238
Age 46, 176
Aircraft 3, 7
Aliases 126, 140
alt.hypertext 290
American English 123
Amikake 241
Analogy 114, 239
Analytic methods 256
Anchors 220
Angry fruit salad 119
Animation 62, 92, 136, 235, 263
ANSI 231
Anthropology 299
Anthropomorphism 23
Apple 105, 235
Apple Computer 297, 301
Appliances 50
Application generators 98
Applications 63
Approachability 34
Arbitrary icons 240
Art exhibits 235